Advance Praise for *God-Given or Bust*

"Cheryl Chumley, in *God-Given or Bust*, has not only shown why God matters in America, and how faith is tied to freedom, but also how the idea of 'God-given' rights and liberties, as envisioned by Founding Fathers, actually works and pragmatically plays for both individual and country. This is a powerful book that moves the concept of 'God-given' off paper and into real life."

—**Mike Pompeo**,
Former Secretary of State

"The neo-Marxist attack from within is the most existential threat America has ever faced. And the only way to save this country before it's truly too late is to return to God. This indispensable book provides a vivid, inspiring roadmap to getting our national spiritual house in order and restoring America's exceptionalism, greatness, and goodness via its original faith-based principles."

—**Monica Crowley, PhD**, News Analyst, Host of "The Monica Crowley Podcast," and Former Assistant Secretary of the Treasury

"The best offense against the frightening specter of totalitarianism is fact-based truth. In her book *God-Given or Bust*, Cheryl Chumley has amassed a huge trough of information that presents the reader with the 'how' behind the progressive socialist quest. Chapter Nine on how George Soros money has corrupted the information industry is a shocker."

—**Bill O'Reilly**, Host of *No Spin News* and Former Host of the Top-Rated *The O'Reilly Factor* on Fox News; *New York Times* Bestselling Author and Syndicated Columnist

"Once again, Cheryl Chumley cuts right through the political lies and division and goes straight to the rotten heart of the problem: America increasingly embraces socialism and Marxism, a hatred of Western civilization, cultural depravity, and moral relevance, simply because we've turned our backs on God and His Biblical truths. Read this book. It is a *critical reminder* that fundamental American rights and freedoms are not reliant on government or on ourselves, but are God-given. To turn our backs on God is to participate in our own demise."

—**Shea Bradley-Farrell, PhD**, President, Counterpoint Institute; Author, *Last Warning to the West: Hungary's Triumph Over Communism and the Woke Agenda*

GOD-GIVEN OR BUST

GOD-GIVEN OR BUST

DEFEATING MARXISM *and* SAVING AMERICA *with* BIBLICAL TRUTHS

CHERYL K. CHUMLEY

BOMBARDIER
BOOKS

Published by Bombardier Books
An Imprint of Post Hill Press
ISBN: 979-8-88845-524-1
ISBN (eBook): 979-8-88845-525-8

God-Given or Bust:
Defeating Marxism and Saving America with Biblical Truths
© 2025 by Cheryl K. Chumley
All Rights Reserved

Cover Design by Cody Corcoran

This is a work of nonfiction. All people, locations, events, and situations are portrayed to the best of the author's memory.

BOMBARDIER
BOOKS

Post Hill
PRESS

Post Hill Press
New York • Nashville
posthillpress.com

Published in the United States of America
1 2 3 4 5 6 7 8 9 10

For the glory of Jesus and to all Americans who cherish true liberty.

CONTENTS

Foreword xi
Author's Note xvii

Chapter 1   American Exceptionalism's
               "God-Given" Is Under Attack 1

Chapter 2   Anthony Fauci Is Not God and
               Scientists Frequently Lie 21

Chapter 3   The Evil One Has the Family Unit in
               His Crosshairs 47

Chapter 4   It's Really Looking Like an Oligarchy
               Out There 69

Chapter 5   The Chip War, and the Growing
               National Security Threat from Rising
               Secularism 95

Chapter 6   Protecting Pedophiles, Prosecuting
               Presidents, and Politics of Pure Evil 121

Chapter 7   The False Prophet Called Bill Gates 143

Chapter 8   Living in Great Reset Times 173

Chapter 9   Marxists in the Media and the Devilish
               Designs of the Brainwashers 205

Chapter 10 God-Given or Bust: The Clock Is
             Ticking, America 235

Acknowledgments 261

FOREWORD

BY PASTOR JACK HIBBS

What could possibly go wrong?

These words in any context would, at the very least, generate immediate concern. Such a naive and cavalier question is more like a statement that is preceded by an individual or group who believes the thrill of experiencing something "new," no matter the cost, far outweighs the risks and injuries that are most likely to arise.

"Damn the torpedoes...full speed ahead" is the belief system of many in our day. I am, of course, talking about today's Western culture and its headlong romance with socialism and Marxist ideology. This imagined theoretical worldview could have only happened in a vacuum where world history and American history were not only deliberately denied to the general populace but specifically so to the students of the American educational system.

There is an intentional war raging by the powers that be to bring about a complete and total reshaping of the American mind by a well-organized and full-blown assault to end our constitutional republic. What is being peddled in our nation today, dare I say the world, is a doctrine of thinking that has been so long in its germination that it has finally found fertile soil therein to grow right here in the good ole United States.

For some one hundred years now, the long road to indoctrinating the American culture has clearly taken root. You might ask, "How could this have happened?" Well, it's no mystery to solve nor a game of whodunit. The collective, steadfast, and committed Marxists have not only been patient but have also been devoted disciples to the tenets of the *Communist Manifesto*, and they have not been shy about preaching their message of humanism. Humanism in the sense that communism is a man-made construct that replaces God with a lesser god, that being man. This reality would have been hard to entertain in years prior, but now, the delusion of believing in a godless worldview has been replaced with man seeking to create a new god in the image of him or herself.

Marxism and socialism share this one powerful motivation—they hate competition. For them, the existence of the one true God is absolutely unacceptable. Thus, their religion deifies man and his quest to elevate himself into all areas of power with the desire to control. These seeds of humanism have now sprouted and are yielding the end product of godlessness—a mass collective ignorance of the true history of both the impact and influence of the Judeo-Christian worldview benefits and accurate American history. The results of this are a matter of historical fact.

A biblically based American culture is what birthed the most remarkable, never-before-seen exceptionalism, which resulted in such meteoric levels of religious freedom, wealth, liberty, technology, and power, unlike any other people, group, or nation in the history of man. Harvard graduate, attorney, and American Founding Father John Adams wrote, "Facts are stubborn things." However, in our day, facts have been redefined into lies. And lies, well, they have become the new facts, the new truths, the 'your truths' and 'my truths'—just ask the fact-checkers.

Thankfully, and in sharp contrast to such illogic, there is a voice on the horizon, albeit as one crying in the wilderness, and that is the voice of Cheryl Chumley. In this vivid and excellent work, investigative reporter, journalist, US military veteran, and friend Cheryl pulls the mask off the deceptive and invasive tactics of the most powerful lies that have put our nation in a state of twilight. Falsehoods and beliefs that, if not vehemently confronted and defeated, will render the United States of America all but a historical reference in the annals of time. The hour is very critical for us as a nation and as freedom-loving people. This is true not only for you and me but also for our children and our children's children.

The deception is rampant and all around us, hidden in plain sight. Perhaps another way to say it is how Jesus Christ said it, as recorded in the Bible, "The kingdom of heaven is like a man who sowed good seed in his field; but while men slept, his enemy came and sowed tares among the wheat and went his way. But when the grain had sprouted and produced a crop, then the tares also appeared." (Matthew 13: 24–26, NKJV) Did you catch those four haunting words "but while men slept"? What a terrifying indictment that best describes our culture.

Jesus's words could be the diagnosis of the United States today. A similar message is offered by another meaningful quote, often attributed to Edmund Burke, a member of Parliament, in 1774, though the true source is unknown: "The only thing necessary for the triumph of evil is for good men to do nothing." So painfully reminiscent of Jesus's words, "but while men slept." Little did we know that while we were hard at work pursuing our careers, getting married, raising kids, attending church or synagogue, and being involved in community service—"while men slept"—the enemy entered within our walls. So pervasive and terminal are these socialistic beliefs that, in a short time, any people, group, or nation that adopts such an ideology soon finds themselves either with their necks under the heel of a rising despot (there is always a dictator, lord, or despot in the wings of any socialist agenda), or they are reduced to abject poverty for the betterment of the collective.

Today's Marxist crusaders and their likeminded political jihadists have deceived themselves into thinking that they have actually come up with a better idea for human governance, which is a testimony to their self-inflicted ignorance. Such theorists and their way of thinking seek to trump all other historical attempts to establish a man-made, godless, egocentric society that defies logic. But that doesn't keep them from believing in the lie.

In *God-Given or Bust: Defeating Marxism and Saving America with Biblical Truths*, Cheryl sends us all a wake-up call and outlines exactly what we need to do to defend our country, our God-given freedoms, and our blood-bought liberties.

For those of us who have read the Bible and have subsequently experienced its transformational power to change the way we think and live, there is great hope—a never-ending hope in Christ. But until that day comes when we see Him face-to-face, let us be faithful to fight the good fight of faith out loud, in the public square, in the halls of power, and across this nation—from sea to shining sea.

—**Jack Hibbs**
Senior Pastor of Calvary Chapel Chino Hills
President of The Real Life Network

AUTHOR'S NOTE

To the youth of America:

You've been told a bunch of lies.

For the majority of your lives, you've been told the following: The government has your back. The government's job is to level the playing field to make it easier for everyone to succeed. The government cares about the poor, the hungry, and the despondent. The government exists to fight for the interests of these classes of society. And the government, ultimately and overwhelmingly, is a force for good.

For the majority of your public education experiences, you've been treated to the following notions: All the world's ailments are due to America's colonizing, occupying, selfish, and domineering ways. The Founding Fathers were racists, and therefore, the founding documents, inherently racist; and therefore, the founding ideals must be dismantled and replaced. Capitalism produces an unjust class society of 1-percenters ruling the 99 percent. Free markets are enslaving. And socialism is the only fair and ethical economic system.

For the majority of your formative, maturing years, you've been fed a steady diet of bloody, beastly, brutal pornographic images in entertainment and media to the point where normal human senses have become dulled, and anything but the most shockingly graphic produces yawns. You've been fed to the point where the abnormal, immoral, and deviant have become much more than curiosities but rather desired and demanded, then ultimately, quietly expected. And you've been fed to the point where it's even seen that the level of blood, brutality, and beastly and pornographic imagery is indicative of the talent and bravery of the creator, with the more the shock factor, the more esteemed the creator of the shock—so that, for instance, "real"-looking blood in a video game is more prized than the strategies of the game itself, and that "real"-looking sex scenes in a movie are more appreciated than the plot itself.

You've been brainwashed into these beliefs: Sex is as normal as eating and drinking and sleeping and breathing. It's a function of animals, and humans are simply a higher evolution of animals. It's just another physical act, and perhaps even need, that does not require considerations of "when, where, and with whom." And it certainly, laughably, does not require any exchange of vows or marital commitments, let alone formal promises of monogamy.

For the majority of your time on Earth, you've been conditioned to believe that one truth is as good as another truth, and, in fact, the more truths in any given situation, the merrier—that is to say that an absolute truth does not exist; truth is in the eye of the beholder; God, if God even exists, is concerned only with love and not law; He represents love without boundaries; and love is without standards and expectations and restrictions. Love is love is love, as they say.

If it feels good, do it.

If it's not harming others, go for it.

If nobody objects—well then, what's the objection?

These are lies. And more than that, these are dangerous lies. These are the types of lies that lead to the crumbling of a country because they remove the much-needed moral clarities and boundaries that actually keep society and society's citizens free.

Freedom for the individual does not mean freedom to live absent accountability, consequence, repercussion, or in some instances, punishment. That's the biggest lie of all, and it's a lie that leads to tyranny, chaos, confusion, and collapse.

And this is the precipice upon which America now stands.

The turning away depends on the ability of America's youth to see the peril, acknowledge the peril, and commit to fight the peril. The peril, in a single concise phrase, is this: Godless society.

The founders warned that America's limited government would not last without a moral and virtuous citizenry—that the growing of government powers would occur in direct correlation with the decaying of morals and values. Look around. We're here. America's final days have dawned. One more lost generation, and all in America is lost. One more generational shift toward secularized society, and the Marxists will have won; the socialists, progressives, globalists, communists, and collectivists will have won.

The war is to preserve God-given liberties.

But you can't have God-given liberties if God is removed.

Either you're with God, or you're not. For America, for the fate of American liberties and exceptionalism and individualism, it's God-given or bust—it's the final time of choosing.

This is why God matters for individual liberty....

This is how God keeps us all free....

CHAPTER 1

AMERICAN EXCEPTIONALISM'S "GOD-GIVEN" IS UNDER ATTACK

Try and picture America in ten years. Close your eyes, take a deep breath, and imagine how this nation will look: what the state of its freedoms will be, whether the Constitution will matter—at all, and whether our borders will have become so invaded and invalidated as to render words like "sovereignty" and "citizen" completely meaningless.

See it? See it.

It's coming. The demise of America is coming on strong, moving from concept to reality, morphing from warning to real life, sliding from the pages of remote historical books teaching abstract, normative stages leading to the crumbling of republics, then—*smack!*—playing out right onto the streets of today's society, through the halls of modern politics and places of governance, into present-day public-school classrooms, and within the walls of economic power and financial planning. The demise is real. See it, then see this: we have moved past the time where elections fix things.

We have moved into a time where only divine intervention can save us.

The fact that a large percentage of the nation's people would read that statement and laugh, and another large percentage would get angry, disgusted, dismissive, and either attack or shoulder-shrug in response, further underscores its deep truth—that only divine intervention can save us. Why's that? It's the trap of circles and cycles. The more secular America grows, the more our problems become unsolvable by the normal means, which is to say, by the secular means. But since secularism brings blindness toward the things of the spiritual world—since secularism, by definition, is devoid of religion and spiritual faith—the more impossible it then becomes to turn to the one source that can solve the problems: God. Godless people don't generally look to God for salvation. But godless societies don't generally remain free for long. This is the cycle of which America now finds herself; this is the circle of destruction Americans are now walking.

Something must snap.

As America's belief in God goes, so, too, does the concept of American exceptionalism and the idea that individual liberties are inherent and bestowed by the Creator, and that government cannot—rightfully, morally, or even constitutionally—seize those freedoms except by consent of the individuals. It's simple. The choice is clear-cut. Either America falls, or America sets God at the helm. There is no straddling of sides any longer.

The wolves are panting at the door.

In April 2023, the Brookings Institution ran a commentary that argued "American exceptionalism" needed a radical overhaul because too many people were being left behind, and therefore, the United States should adopt the Sustainable Development Goals (SDGs) outlined in the *2030 Agenda* from the United Nations.[1]

They are redefining American exceptionalism to fit a mold they want. The wolves are cleverly circling the foundations.

America's greatness is rooted in individualism, based on God-given liberties, and to shift this guiding governing principle to put others first and the self second is to shift toward collectivism. That the argument for the shift comes under cover of a moral good—a quest for, say, equality and justice for all—only makes the shift even more dangerous. It opens the door for pure brainwashing that practically guarantees a permanent societal change. It's one thing when the wolf comes, teeth bared, lips snarling; it's another when it comes dressed as a kindly altruistic force for good—encouraging, enticing, shaming others to join the goodness. But the United Nations is not America, nor should America ever become the United Nations.

From the UN Sustainable Development Group webpage on "Principle Two" of the SDGs:

> Leave no one behind (LNOB) is the central, transformative promise of the 2030 Agenda for Sustainable Development and its Sustainable Development Goals (SDGs). It represents the unequivocal commitment of all UN Member States to eradicate poverty in all its forms,

---

[1] Sarah E. Mendelson, "The US is leaving millions behind: American exceptionalism needs to change by 2030," Brookings, April 10, 2023, https://www.brookings.edu/articles/the-us-is-leaving-millions-behind-american-exceptionalism-needs-to-change-by-2030/.

end discrimination and exclusion, and reduce the inequalities and vulnerabilities that leave people behind and undermine the potential of individuals and of humanity as a whole.[2]

That sounds wonderful.

It's an enticing, titillating message—that every man, woman, and child around the world be granted the keys to success, prosperity, ease, comfort, and well, let's just say it, nirvana. No more suffering. No more struggle. No more war. No more division.

But it's a lie.

The lie is that government can accomplish these goals, simply by the regulation, redistribution, and reallocation of resources. The lie is that humanity itself is equipped with the necessary tools to bring about an end to poverty, an end to discrimination, an end to inequality, and an end to unjust exclusivity.

Moreover, it's a lie pushed by the forces of evil.

After all, if life on Earth is heaven, then why the need for a real heaven? In the end, a government promise of perfection is a rebellion against God because it's a refusal to acknowledge the sinful nature of humanity, and therefore a prideful embrace of the idea that a heavenly savior isn't necessary.

It's not that humans shouldn't try for perfection; it's not that people shouldn't work toward eradicating poverty, ensuring all have enough to eat, and fighting for justice, law and order, equality, and the rest.

It's that these campaigns should first and foremost come from the place of individual effort and charity, with government

---

[2] United Nations Sustainable Development Group, "Universal Values, Principle Two: Leave No One Behind," UNSDG.un.org, accessed February 8, 2024, https://unsdg.un.org/2030-agenda/universal-values/leave-no-one-behind.

playing solely a supporting role for the individual—that is, with government serving to clear the way to best equip and enable the individual to fulfill the needs of others. Lower taxes, for instance, means more money in the hands of individuals who can, in turn, provide the services and resources for those with lesser abilities and greater needs. Then we don't need food stamps. Then we won't need welfare. Then we're putting God first.

In a nation like America where liberties and rights come from a heavenly Creator, the government needs to get out of the way to allow the individual to develop, foster, grow, and expand the gifts God gave each at birth, so the individual can build personal esteem; so the individual can increase personal resources; so the individual can find personal satisfaction and success; so the individual can provide for the self, family, and loved ones; and so the individual can ultimately share with those who have need.

That's the target. That's the ideal.

In Matthew 25:14–30 (NASB1995), Jesus speaks about three servants whose master had given them money—talents— as he was departing for a journey. "To one he gave five talents, to another, two, and to another, one, each according to his own ability," the passage reads. The parable recounts how the first and second went and traded with their five and two talents, respectively, both doubling their pools. The third, however, dug a hole, put in his one talent, covered it, and hid it. Eventually, the master returned and asked his servants for an accounting of their talents. When the first and second servants told of their trades that doubled their resources, the master responded with praise. Specifically, he told each:

> Well done, good and faithful slave. You were
> faithful with a few things, I will put you in
> charge of many things; enter into the joy of
> your master.

Then the third servant gave account for his talent, and told his master, "I knew you to be a hard man, reaping where you did not sow, and gathering where you scattered no seed. And I was afraid and, went away and hid your talent in the ground. See, you have what is yours." The master was angered by his servant's words and responded with a scolding—and more. He said:

> You wicked, lazy slave, you knew that I reap
> where I did not sow and gathered where I
> scattered no seed. Then you ought to have
> put my money in the bank, and on my arrival
> I would have received my money back with
> interest. Therefore take away the talent from
> him, and give it to the one who has ten talents.

Moreover, the master banished his servant from his home:

> Throw out the worthless slave into the outer
> darkness; in that place there will be weeping
> and gnashing of teeth.

Bible scholars offer a range of meanings and takeaways from this "Parable of the Talents," as it's called.

But first: A talent was the term for a considerable amount of money, with a value that was determined either by weight or by wage and a modern-day equivalency that's difficult to pinpoint. Some say one talent of gold would be worth more than $2 million today;[3] others put the modern value somewhere between $1,000 and $30,000;[4] and still others say a talent is the amount of money it would take an average worker twenty years to earn.[5]

Regardless, the parable is not so much about money as it is about value and where priorities are placed.

- From Crosswalk.com: "More importantly, it is talking about stewardship, responsibility, and preparedness. When you look at this parable, it really is one of self-examination."[6]

- From Christianity.com: "The master of this parable is clearly meant to represent Jesus. The servants are Christ-followers. Similar to the parable, Jesus has also given responsibility to his followers, and similar to the parable, he, the master, has promised to one day return. This parable is often interpreted as a lesson about the importance of wisely using one's God-given talents and resources and not squandering them out of fear or complacency. It emphasizes the idea that those who are faithful and responsible in using what they've been

3 Mark Giszczak, "Two Ways to Calculate the Value of a Talent," Catholic Bible Student, January 2022, https://catholicbiblestudent.com/2022/01/two-ways-to-calculate-the-value-of-a-talent.html.

4 Mary Fairchild, "How Heavy Was a Talent in the Bible?" Learn Religions, October 15, 2019, https://www.learnreligions.com/what-is-a-talent-700699#:~:text=Some%20calculate%20the%20talent%20in,%241%2C000%20to%20%202430%2C000%20dollars%20today.

5 Ibid.

6 Clarence L. Haynes Jr., "What Does the Parable of the Talents Mean for Us Today?" Crosswalk.com, August 17, 2020, https://www.crosswalk.com/faith/bible-study/4-top-takeaways-from-the-parable-of-the-talents.html.

given will be rewarded, while those who are negligent or fearful will face consequences."[7]

- From Bible.org: First, the website discusses a reference to the biblical account of Pharaoh and his persecution of the Israelites, who were slaves to Egypt. On one occasion, Pharaoh refused to provide the Jews with the necessary materials to make bricks, but at the same time, ordered them to make bricks. Pharaoh, in that respect, was truly a hard master—which is how the third servant in the Parable of the Talents described his master. Second, Bible.org goes on to write, "But the master [in the Parable of the Talents] did provide the means for his slave to make a profit. He entrusted him with money, money suited to his abilities. It was not the master's problem; it was the slave's problem. Is this not the way that our Lord's adversaries looked at Him? They justified their rejection of Jesus by claiming that He was the problem. Indeed, they accused Him of being a wicked sinner, more worthy of death than Barabbas," the murderer who was excused from execution at the pressing of those who hated Jesus.[8]

So, what does all this have to do with American exceptionalism and the need for God-given individualism to be kept alive and well if this country is to keep from its destruction?

Only everything.

The Parable of the Talents is to individualism what the UN SDGs and its "leave no one behind" mantra are to collectivism.

---

[7] Joel Ryan, "What Is the Parable of the Talents? Bible Story and Meaning," Christianity.com, October 11, 2023, https://www.christianity.com/wiki/jesus-christ/what-is-the-parable-of-the-talents.html.

[8] Bob Deffinbaugh, "The Parable of the Talents," Bible.org, August 4, 2005, https://bible.org/seriespage/27-parable-talents-matthew-2514-30-luke-1912-28.

One viewpoint says individuals are accountable for their actions to a higher authority; the other that individuals are not. One says that individuals are responsible for working for their wealth and resources; the other that it's government's role to provide. One says that material differences among humans are due, at least in part, to the differing levels of effort made by individuals to achieve material goods; the other that inequality of all kinds is unfair and that government must take steps to offset any inequalities. One says that hard work pays off; the other that work is only profitable in terms of what it provides the government to distribute and redistribute.

One says "God-given." The other says "government-granted."

Thing is, Jesus wasn't a socialist. Jesus wanted his followers, from a place of love, to give from their own pockets to others in need, not simply stand around with stupid signs carrying messages that demand the political class give to those in need by dipping into tax dollars. So goes the proper direction of a country built on God-given individualism, rather than government-granted rights and privileges.

That's the difference.

That's the difference power-hungry politicians—alongside the globalist bureaucrats who detest American liberty—don't want noticed. From Brookings:

> In 2015, the global community adopted the 2030 Agenda and the Sustainable Development Goals (SDGs) with the watchwords "leave no one behind." It is a framework that recognizes development happens everywhere—not just in the Global South or in "developing" countries. Yet experts, policymakers, and the media still

stubbornly categorize countries as "developed" or "developing." The United States, of course, is part of this "developed" category.... Midway to 2030, it is time to not only retire the label of the U.S. as developed but to deploy disaggregated data by race, gender, and where possible, locality—city-level data—and align with SDG targets and indicators to forge more just and healthy communities. In fact, when we have such data, the findings make clear why the SDGs apply to the U.S. and not just the Global South. If that does not happen, numerous communities and millions of Americans will continue to be left behind well beyond 2030.[9]

This is classic liberal-speak.

It's a narrative that professes compassion over some sad-and-sorry cause, case, or condition, and then, before the eyes can dry and the tears be swept away by tissues, it's a narrative that also offers a solution, almost always government-based, and almost always taxpayer-funded—all while conveniently side-stepping the oh-so-small matter that it's the government that created the sad-and-sorry cause, case, and condition in the first place. Government's great at that: creating crises, then swooping in with solutions that either exacerbate the existing crisis or generate new ones. War on poverty, anyone? Sure, for a few years, the 1960s-era poverty levels of such professed compassion

[9] Sarah E. Mendelson, "The US is leaving millions behind: American exceptionalism needs to change by 2030," Brookings, April 10, 2023, https://www.brookings.edu/articles/the-us-is-leaving-millions-behind-american-exceptionalism-needs-to-change-by-2030/.

and concern to President Lyndon B. Johnson dropped. They dropped by double digits, in fact.[10] Then the money ran out and poverty levels surged once again. Meanwhile, taxpayers over the span of fifty years poured about $22 trillion into fighting this lost war.[11] That's how socialism generally progresses; tax dollars for entitlements only go so far, for so long, and then—failure.

Smart people learn it's a destructive and unsustainable model. Even the *New York Times* finally copped to the ridiculousness of handing out gobs of government-backed freebies to the poor with the expectation that the giveaways would move them into higher economic and educational classes. In a 1998 news piece on poverty-stricken Owsley County, Kentucky, writer Michael Janofsky found that the funds that had been funneled from tax coffers for years into this one community ultimately yielded little success in terms of lifting residents from their financial distresses.

As the Foundation for Economic Education wrote:

> Janofsky visited Owsley County, Kentucky, and found a poverty rate of over 46 percent, with over half the adults illiterate and half unemployed.... For years, the government [had] been trying to treat the despair with welfare programs: two-thirds of the inhabitants receive[d] federal assistance, including food stamps, AFDC [Aid to Families with Dependent Children], and

10 Ron Haskins, "The War on Poverty: What Went Wrong?" Brookings, November 19, 2013, https://www.brookings.edu/articles/the-war-on-poverty-what-went-wrong/.
11 Rachel Sheffield and Robert Rector, "The War on Poverty After 50 Years," The Heritage Foundation, September 15, 2014, https://www.heritage.org/poverty-and-inequality/report/the-war-poverty-after-50-years.

SSI [Supplemental Security Income] disability payments. This, it now appears, is part of the area's problems. "The war on poverty was the worst thing that ever happened to Appalachia," Janofsky quotes one resident as saying. "It gave people a way to get by without having to do any work."[12]

Work, under leftist influence, has been turned into a despicable act.

The modern leftist narrative promotes victimhood above all—an angry victimhood that breeds entitlement attitudes that somewhere along the list of demands, and whether by lack of resources or by changing political tunes, turn into unfulfilled demands. Viva la protest! Let the streets be filled with the discontents.

America should be in the business of building up the individual, not sucking out the soul, poisoning the mind, and blackening the heart of the individual.

The first approach flows from a viewpoint of God-given, where it's taken as granted that an individual, endowed by his or her Creator, is supposed to provide for self and family, based on personal interests, passions, talents, skills, and so forth. The second approach is pure Marxism, aimed at degrading all that's godly, all that's good, and all that's individualist. If Americans aren't filled with a passion for some sort of worthwhile pursuit—whether that be an artistic or creative endeavor that drives them

---

12 FEE, "Why the War on Poverty Failed: Handouts Provide the Wrong Incentives," The Foundation for Economic Education, January 1, 1999, https://fee.org/articles/why-the-war-on-poverty-failed/?gclid=EAIaIQobChM ImcWx3MKKggMVgklHAR2g4w67EAAYAyAAEgKcC_D_BwE.

to achieve and produce, or simply a job that pays the bills—then what results is a cracked door toward victimhood. The power-hungry and exploiters of the world can swarm and swoop in with their messages of social injustices, and they can put into play their class separation tactics. They can mobilize their angry masses to take to the streets, take to the businesses, take to the residences of all those who have more and scream foul—to throw bricks and set things on fire, even. And the power-hungry and exploiters have so perfected their class division narratives that they make it seem as if they're doing the morally righteous work of the Lord, and so, too, are their violent minions, because they're correcting societal wrongs that need to be corrected.

The counter to this evil—to this soul-sucking, Marxist, collectivist evil—is God. More specifically, the counter to this Marxist evil is teaching, reminding, rewarding, and insisting upon the manifestation of biblical truths regarding work, individual talents, life missions, and, to sum it up simply, the God-given. This is how it works:

> From 1 Corinthians 12:4–14—the gifts of the Spirit: "Now there are varieties of gifts, but the same Spirit. And there are varieties of ministries, and the same Lord. There are varieties of effects, but the same God who works all things in all persons. But to each one is given the manifestation of the Spirit for the common good. For to one is given the word of wisdom through the Spirit, and to another the word of knowledge according to the same Spirit; to another faith by the same Spirit, and to another gifts of healing by the one Spirit, and to another the effecting

of miracles, and to another prophecy, and to another the distinguishing of spirits, to another various kinds of tongues, and to another the interpretation of tongues. But one and the same Spirit works all these things, distributing to each one individually just as He wills. For even as the body is one and yet has many members, and all the members of the body, though they are many, are one body, so also is Christ. For by one Spirit we were all baptized into one body, whether Jews or Greeks, whether slaves or free, and we were all made to drink of one Spirit. For the body is not one member, but many."

(1 Cor. 12:4-14, NASB1995)

Spiritual gifts only work for believers, though. It's not that God deems some of his creations worthy of gifts and some not so worthy; He endows all with talents and equips all with the tools that are necessary to carry out the missions he fashioned for each during creation. But non-believers don't buy into this promise, and that means they don't know or understand fully their worth in God. And an individual who does not understand that he or she was created with a special purpose by God and for God, and therefore is possessed of certain skills, talents, and gifts to accomplish this special purpose, is an individual who is adrift, vulnerable to the pressings of the world, and at risk of the influences of the power-hungry and exploiters who want to use such individuals for their own selfish purposes.

Watch a horde of Black Lives Matter and antifa thugs smash into store windows and pilfer from the shelves and recognize that these are people who probably don't believe in God and who definitely don't know they've been created by God for wonderful purposes. They don't grasp their God-given talents.

As such, they have no regard for a nation built on God-given liberties. They are the exploited masses used by the elitist classes for anti-American, anti-constitutional, anti-liberty, and anti-individualist designs.

This is the work set before believers—to tell the unbelievers who they are in Christ. It's about not only the salvation of their souls but also the salvation of America and American exceptionalism.

> Again, from 1 Corinthians 12, repeating verse 14 then moving to verse 26: "For the body is not one member, but many. If the foot says, 'Because I am not a hand, I am not a part of the body,' it is not for this reason any the less a part of the body. And if the ear says, 'Because I am not an eye, I am not a part of the body,' it is not for this reason any the less a part of the body. If the whole body were an eye, where would the hearing be? If the whole were hearing, where would the sense of smell be? But now God has placed the members, each one of them, in the body, just as He desired. If they were all one member, where would the body be? But now there are many members, but one body. And the eye cannot say to the hand, 'I have no need for you'; or again, the head to the feet, 'I have no need of you.'…And if one member suffers, all the members suffer with it; if one member is

honored, all the members rejoice with it. Now
you are Christ's body, and individually members
of it."

(1 Cor. 12:14–21, 1 Cor. 12:26–27, NASB1995)

All are important. All matter. All have purpose and mission.
All contribute to society. All are individuals—individualists—
making up the body of Christ. Moreover, ignorance of those
truths does not just change the truths, either for the believer or
the non-believer. It is not for that reason that the truth changes.

Another application for the cause of American exceptionalism? If it's true that if one member suffers then all members
suffer, then it's crucially important for the stronger members to
take care of the weaker members, not only because it's God's
will—as a good Christian duty—but because it keeps the
weaker members from falling into a victimhood attitude and
subsequently, serving as food for the exploiters.

Look at the differences between a nation of people who take
their rights and liberties from God, who recognize their value as
individuals in God and from God—and those who don't know
God, don't know their worth in God's eyes, and who therefore
depend on government, politicians, and other citizens to determine the level of success in their lives:

- Those who understand God's in charge, not government, aren't swayed into using billions of tax dollars
  to fight fabricated climate change perils—because they
  understand God's in charge of weather, not humans.
- Those who cherish the idea of God-given liberties know
  that taking tax dollars to forgive the student loans of col-
  lege-age adults is not only economically abhorrent—a

form of socialism—but also morally bankrupt because it creates an entitlement mindset in an entire generation of emerging American leaders.

- Those who live by a creed of God-given see the wokeism in the corporate world as, yes, fiscally irresponsible but, worse, spiritually depressing because it teaches, through the free market, that certain classes of society are prone to failure and it's the job of other classes—other better classes, other superior classes—to provide for these inferior classes.

- Those who demand a culture of God-given rights and liberties see the deep state attacks that have gone forth in recent years, and that continue to go forth, against political enemies of the reigning Democrats as rooted in pride, arrogance, hubris, and hate. They see these attacks as evidence of a government that thinks it exists to be served by the people. They see them as an extension of a system that lets laws be determined at whim and order upheld at will, with the final say on what constitutes lawful and what defines order left, soon enough, to the minds and devices of select, chosen elites.

- Those who insist on a society of God-given freedoms know that any attempt to stifle free speech, free expression, free assembly, freedom to travel, and freedom to carry and possess firearms—they know the attempts come from a fleshly desire to control. They know that the more society is moved to believe it's the government who holds the rightful authority to control these freedoms, the less free society becomes. They know that the less free and more tyrannical and chaotic society becomes, the more radical the idea of God-given liberty seems—and that it's this destructive cycle the exploiters and power-hungry desire to bring into existence.

- Those who recognize that their rights and liberties come from God don't have a problem with telling wicked school board members—those who promote the sexual grooming of young children with inappropriate library books, inappropriate drag queen shows, and inappropriate courses, classes, and teachings—that they're wrong, that they ought to be fired, and that they're fueling the exploitation of the youngest and most innocent. They don't have a problem with telling these people that no, they're not tolerant and inclusive, but rather evil—because they know God gave them children as a blessing, to raise in the proper way; that teachers and school officials are, at root, public servants; and that parents' rights trump unions' agendas.

- Those who are unafraid and unabashed with their embrace of God-given liberties know that government has zero right to slap masks on their faces, inject experimental shots into their arms, strip their abilities to go to work and their children's abilities to go to school, shut down their churches, shut off their access to public transportation, and tell them to shut up, stay home, and wait for the stimulus check—and, for goodness' sake, stay off social media if the narrative doesn't advance the government message du jour. Those who are unafraid and unabashed with their embrace of the God-given know that Anthony Fauci may have a degree in science and know more about viruses; Bill Gates may have a background in computers and know more about programming; and the staff of the Food and Drug

Administration, the Centers for Disease Control and Prevention, and the Department of Health and Human Services may have the experience, the education, and the skill sets that deal with health and medicine and may know more about diseases, ailments, illnesses, and the like—but none of them know freedom like the average American.

And here, in America, freedom should never be squashed for safety and security, especially when there are no guarantees of safety and security.

God-given: It's an attitude. It's a source of strength. It's a line in the sand that should never be erased.

CHAPTER 2

ANTHONY FAUCI IS NOT GOD AND SCIENTISTS FREQUENTLY LIE

B y now, almost everybody in America has heard of Anthony Fauci—and not because of his kindly demeanor and calm manner of speaking. He was the drunk-with-power doctor who used his platform as Covid-19 czar to seize individual liberties and clamp down controls on an entire population. Why? Because he was enamored with his own intelligence, obsessed with his own wills and desires, driven by a moral righteousness that relied on his own ego for sustenance, and unconstrained by any concerns for accountability. He was an atheist who was handed the reins of government. And that's a disaster no matter how you slice it.

Between 1984 and 2022, he served as director of the National Institute of Allergy and Infectious Diseases (NIAID).[13] He came to the world of science bureaucracy in 1968, when he joined the NIAID as a clinical associate.[14] After a couple of moves through the NIAID ranks, he was appointed its director by none other than Ronald Reagan, then stayed in that role through six more presidents.[15]

Fauci—the son of Catholic parents, whose father owned his own pharmacy in Brooklyn, New York—attended Regis High School in Manhattan followed by the College of the Holy Cross in Worcester, Massachusetts.[16] He was educated in the way of the Jesuits, an order within the Catholic Church, along with the Augustinians, Dominicans, Franciscans, and Benedictines. Jesuits, short for the Society of Jesus, are known for their progressive values and their mission to serve not only the spiritual needs of humanity, but also the physical, educational, charitable, and psychological needs—the whole of the person.[17]

That's a quick backgrounder. But it's Fauci's religious beliefs that are most interesting.

---

[13]   National Institute of Allergy and Infectious Diseases, "Anthony S. Fauci, M.D.," NIAID website, undated, https://www.patheos.com/blogs/jacoblupfer/2016/07/do-jesuit-schools-turn-students-into-atheists/.

[14]   American Masters, "Anthony Fauci biography and career timeline," PBS.org, February 15, 2023, https://www.pbs.org/wnet/americanmasters/anthony-fauci-biography-and-career-timeline/26116/.

[15]   CNN Health, "Dr. Anthony Fauci's career under 7 US presidents," CNN, November 22, 2022, https://www.cnn.com/2020/04/02/health/gallery/anthony-fauci/index.html.

[16]   American Masters, "Anthony Fauci biography and career timeline," PBS.org, February 15, 2023, https://www.pbs.org/wnet/americanmasters/anthony-fauci-biography-and-career-timeline/26116/.

[17]   Editorial Staff, "Differences between Jesuits and Roman Catholics," Difference. guru, October 10, 2023, https://difference.guru/difference-between-jesuits-and-roman-catholics/.

What started as a root of religious upbringing, and ostensibly the belief in God that goes along with that kind of schooling, eventually became Fauci later self-identifying as a "humanist"—which is to say, in basically all respects, an atheist. Then, rather remarkably, years after professing a faith of humanism, which again is to say atheism, he was actually recognized by the Holy Cross for his—get this—personification of Jesuit principles. Think about that for a moment.

He was an atheist who received kudos by a religious institution for advancing non-religion.

So, on one hand, there's this: "The Jesuits are an apostolic religious community called the Society of Jesus. They are grounded in love for Christ and animated by the spiritual vision of their founder, St. Ignatius of Loyola, to help others and seek God in all things. As members of a worldwide society within the Catholic Church, the Jesuits are committed to the service of faith and the promotion of justice," Georgetown University wrote on its "The Jesuit Mission: Seeking God in All Things" webpage.[18]

On the other hand, there's this: "Dr. Anthony Fauci Named Humanist of the Year"—a headline in Charisma News from 2021.[19]

And then on the heels of all that, came this: "Holy Cross to Name Science Complex for Dr. Anthony Fauci '62"—a

[18] Georgetown University, "The Jesuit Mission: Seeking God in All Things," Georgetown University, July 31, 2023, https://www.georgetown.edu/news/the-jesuit-mission-seeking-god-in-all-things/#:~:text=The%20Society%20of%20Jesus%20%E2%80%93%20or,and%20universities%20around%20the%20world.

[19] Nadia Joy Schult, "Dr. Anthony Fauci Named Humanist of the Year," Charisma News, July 2, 2021, https://charismanews.com/news/us/cn-morning-rundown-dr-anthony-fauci-named-humanist-of-the-year/.

headline from *Holy Cross Magazine* from April 2022. In that story, Holy Cross's president, Vincent D. Rougeau, was quoted as saying, "Dr. Fauci vividly personifies the distinctive characteristics of a Holy Cross education, and we know his life and work are already inspiring the next generation of empathetic service leaders."[20]

Fauci may be more so a believer in the power of his mind than a believer in the sovereignty of God. But he still gets kudos for his service being rooted in faith. Astonishing.

"Do Jesuit schools turn students into atheists?" one writer asked in a Patheos.com headline in July 2016.[21]

No. Maybe. Yes.

That's a debate for another day. But here's why it all matters: Fauci was the face of tyrannical lockdowns during the Covid-19 years. He was given wide latitude in politics and media to recommend so-called best medical practices for an entire nation of people—best medical practices that flipped and flopped, twisted and turned, shifted and swayed, mutated and moved, changed, and flipped then flopped again on a near-daily basis. He said he was science, and that those who questioned his advisements were actually questioning science.[22] He said he didn't dictate policy, only science—but then warned of all the death, doom,

---

20 College of the Holy Cross, "Holy Cross to Name Science Complex for Dr. Anthony Fauci '62," College of the Holy Cross, April 4, 2022, https://news.holycross.edu/blog/2022/04/04/holy-cross-to-name-science-complex-for-dr-anthony-fauci-62/?utm_source=twitter&utm_medium=socialmedia&utm_campaign=2021socialmedia&fbclid=IwAR1x6sgHKTsJ208vqXTPIuI8wCO-HNySauz5eEoa3buAou316eCScZkI2yE.

21 Jacob Lupfer, "Do Jesuit schools turn students into atheists?" Patheos.com, July 23, 2016, https://www.patheos.com/blogs/jacoblupfer/2016/07/do-jesuit-schools-turn-students-into-atheists/.

22 Peter Sullivan, "Fauci: Attacks on me are really also 'attacks on science,'" The Hill, June 9, 2021, https://thehill.com/policy/healthcare/557602-fauci-attacks-on-me-are-really-also-attacks-on-science/.

and gloom that would come to those who didn't obey his supposed science-backed policy recommendations.

He epitomizes the need for America to keep God-given liberties at the helm and government subservient to the people. It's said politics is downwind of the culture—and that's true. But then so is the notion that medical bureaucrats are the product of their personal morality. America could have used more of Psalm 91 and less of "I am zee law!" bureaucratic class.

> From Psalm 91: "He who dwells in the shelter of the Most High will abide in the shadow of the Almighty. I will say to the Lord, 'My refuge and my fortress, my God in whom I trust!' For it is He who delivers you from the snare of the trapper and from the deadly pestilence. He will cover you with His pinions, and under His wings you may seek refuge; His faithfulness is a shield and bulwark. You will not be afraid of the terror by night, or of the arrow that flies by day; of the pestilence that stalks in darkness, or of the destruction that lays waste at noon. A thousand may fall at your side and ten thousand at your right hand, but it shall not approach you. You will only look on with your eyes and see the recompense of the wicked. For you have made the Lord, my refuge, even the Most High, your dwelling place. No evil will befall you, nor will any plague come near your tent."
>
> (Psalm 91:1–10, NASB1995)

This is not to say that belief in God will automatically shield the believer from sickness, virus, plague, and pestilence. That's an immature spirituality that leads to disappointment and false teachings, like prosperity gospels—the idea that God, à la magic genie, rewards his faithful with material blessings, and conversely, that material wealth is indicative of the favor of God. But Psalm 91 is to say that faith in God will lead to a peace that surpasses all understanding so that when sickness, virus, plague, and pestilence do come, the believer is anchored in that faith, able to resist the tempests brought by secular fear and changing human conditions, and fully equipped by the Spirit to discern truths from myths.

The fact that the government's response to Covid-19 was led by secular science utterly devoid of the godly truths put forth in Psalm 91, and other biblical passages, and broadcasted by secular scientists with little regard for God, gave free passage for fear to guide the decision-making process and for arrogance to drive the dictates.

Think of Fauci's character traits and how he steered America through the Covid-19 years. He was certain of himself. He was positive about his predictions. He was blinded by his own intelligence, blind to the fact that not everybody was equally enamored with his intelligence, and more than that, unconcerned about the freedoms he stomped.

Worse, his hubris was coupled with a willingness to deceive.

His moral compass was self, followed by self-protection.

He was given the opportunity to be the calm voice of reason and science during a time of national panic. But rather than serve the public in a manner befitting a humble servant, as a meek advisor with awareness of the limits of his own knowledge and a recognition for the rights of others—for the American individual—to analyze, research, and choose the correct course of action for self and family, he dug in deep and insisted he was right. Then even when he was wrong, he wiggled and cast blame on others. Covid-19 was not the time for pride in self. It was a crucial time for godly leadership.

Fauci didn't mind lying, spinning, and obfuscating to protect his own prestige. And one of the worst lies Fauci told—because it rendered him largely untouchable—was the one where he said he had nothing to do with policy, politics, or the pushing of policy or politics: He was purely science, purely a medical adviser. He never shut anything down. He never closed schools, businesses, and churches. And he had nothing to do with any of those policy decisions.

That's about as far from truth as left is from right.

He may not have explicitly ordered shutdowns; he couldn't—he didn't hold that power. But he was the whisperer in the ears of those who did claim those powers. And by sly slips of the tongue and clever turns of phrases, he managed to get the political class to carry out his wishes and wills, which almost always countered the interests of the individual and almost always conflicted with basic civil liberties. An article about Fauci, in April 2020, from Politico stated:

> Dr. Anthony Fauci, director of the National Institute of Allergy and Infectious Diseases, suggested Thursday [April 2, 2020] that the federal government should impose a nationwide stay-at-home order to help prevent the spread of the coronavirus in the United States. Asked whether all states have to be "on the same page" in terms of issuing those directives, Fauci

told CNN, "I don't understand why that's not happening," and acknowledged the Trump administration's hesitance to encroach upon local authorities. "As you said, you know, the tension between 'federal mandate' versus 'states rights' to do what they want is something that I don't want to get into," Fauci said. "But if you look at what's going on in this country, I just don't understand why we're not doing that. We really should be."[23]

Message sent, message received. In Fauci's best medical opinion, states should shut down—they "really should."

He didn't order shutdowns. But he put it out there that he agreed with shutdowns, then stood back and let the media talking heads, pundits, and politicians carry forth that message.

"Fauci open to a 14-day national shutdown to stem coronavirus," the Associated Press reported in March 2020. The story went on to explain how Fauci thought Americans should do as much as "we possibly could" to stop the surge of Covid-19, even if it seemed as if politicians and medical professionals were "overreacting." And then he said this: "I think Americans should be prepared that they are going to have to hunker down significantly more than we as a country are doing.… Everybody has got to get involved in distancing themselves socially. Everything is on the table. Right now, myself personally, I wouldn't go to a

---

restaurant.... I don't want to be in a situation where I'm going to be all of a sudden self-isolating for 14 days."[24]

Again: He didn't order shutdowns. But he came pretty close. Headlines, in fact, interpreted his words to mean a shutdown was warranted—an interpretation that would be cited over and over and over as sacrosanct because, after all, Fauci was the expert. Who were—fill-in-the-blank—to argue otherwise?

So no, nope, no again, Fauci never ordered shutdowns. He never had to dirty his reputation that way. But he used his considerable influence to drive others to do the ordering for him and in a way that allowed him to duck responsibility, feign innocence, and sidestep accountability for his role in the nation's lockdowns, shutdowns, and ridiculously random restrictions. Even post-Covid-19, he continued this charade of innocence. Fauci, in a 2023 article from the *New York Times*, stated:

> I certainly think things could have been differently—and better—on both sides. I mean, anybody who thinks that what we or anybody else did was perfect is not looking at reality. Nothing was done perfectly. But what I can say is that, at least to my perception, the emphasis strictly on the science and public health—that is what public-health people should do. I'm not an economist. The Centers for Disease Control and Prevention is not an economic organization. The surgeon general

---

24   Associated Press, "Fauci open to a 14-day national shutdown to stem coronavirus," AP in *Los Angeles Times*, March 15, 2020, https://www.latimes.com/world-nation/story/2020-03-15/fauci-open-to-a-14-day-national-shutdown-to-stem-virus.

is not an economist. So we looked at it from a purely public-health standpoint. It was for other people to make broader assessments—people whose positions include but aren't exclusively about public health. Those people have to make the decisions about the balance between the potential negative consequences of something versus the benefits of something.

Certainly there could have been a better understanding of why people were emphasizing the economy. But when people say, "Fauci shut down the economy"—it wasn't Fauci. The C.D.C. was the organization that made those recommendations. I happened to be perceived as the personification of the recommendations. But show me a school that I shut down and show me a factory that I shut down. Never. I never did. I gave a public-health recommendation that echoed the C.D.C.'s recommendation, and people made a decision based on that. But I never criticized the people who had to make the decisions one way or the other.[25]

Really?

Thing is, that's not true.

Politico discussed Fauci in April 2020 with this headline: "Fauci: Kids could get 'infected' if Florida reopens schools." The

<hr>

[25] David Wallace-Wells, "Dr. Fauci Looks Back: 'Something Clearly Went Wrong,'" *New York Times*, April 24, 2023, https://www.nytimes.com/interactive/2023/04/24/magazine/dr-fauci-pandemic.html.

headline came at a time when Florida governor Ron DeSantis, a Republican, was considering a May reopening of schools in his state. Fauci was asked his opinion of the matter. He said this: "If you have a situation where you don't have a real good control over an outbreak and you allow children together, they will likely get infected."[26]

Sounds like a criticism. There are more.

NBC News published an article in September 2020 with the headline: "Fauci says it's 'very concerning' that Florida is reopening bars and restaurants at full capacity." The headline came from Fauci's response to DeSantis announcing the intent to lift all restrictions on eating and drinking establishments in Florida. NBC went on to cite Fauci as saying on ABC's *Good Morning America*, "Well that is very concerning to me, I mean, we have always said that, myself and Dr. Deborah Birx, who is the coordinator of the task force, that that is something we really need to be careful about because when you're dealing with community spread, and you have the kind of congregate setting where people get together, particularly without masks, you're really asking for trouble. Now's the time actually to double down a bit, and I don't mean close."[27]

What does that even mean? Double down—but don't close. Be careful—but reopening is careless. It's "concerning"—it's "asking for trouble." Are those the words of a true scientist? He was a master at obfuscating.

---

26 Matt Dixon, "Fauci: Kids could get 'infected' if Florida reopens schools," Politico, April 10, 2020, https://www.politico.com/states/florida/story/2020/04/10/fauci-kids-could-get-infected-if-florida-reopens-schools-1274822.

27 David K. Li, "Fauci says it's 'very concerning' that Florida is re-opening bars and restaurants at full capacity," ABC News, September 28, 2020, https://www.nbcnews.com/news/us-news/fauci-says-it-s-very-concerning-florida-re-opening-bars-n1241236.

Then there were his outright lies.

In an email dated February 5, 2020, brought to light by a Freedom of Information Act request, Fauci responded to a question from then Health and Human Services secretary Sylvia Burwell about the protection a face mask might provide during travel with this: "Masks are really for infected people to prevent them from spreading infection to people who are not infected rather than protecting uninfected people from acquiring infection. The typical mask you buy in the drug store is not really effective in keeping out [the] virus, which is small enough to pass through material. It might, however, provide some slight benefit in keep[ing] out gross droplets if someone coughs or sneezes on you. I do not recommend that you wear a mask."[28]

A month later, on March 8, 2020, during a televised interview with Dr. Jon LaPook on CBS's *60 Minutes*, Fauci again disdained the idea of face masks for virus protection, saying, "People should not be walking around with masks," and, "There's no reason for people to be walking around with a mask."[29]

But by the time January 2021 rolled around, Fauci was advocating the complete opposite. In fact, he was even suggesting double-masking, calling it a "common sense" bit of science.[30]

When asked on NBC's *Today* if two face masks could protect better than one, Fauci replied, "It likely does," then went

---

[28] Darragh Roche, "Fauci Said Masks 'Not Really Effective in Keeping Out Virus,' Email Reveals," *Newsweek*, June 2, 2021, https://www.newsweek.com/fauci-said-masks-not-really-effective-keeping-out-virus-email-reveals-1596703.

[29] YouTube video, Anthony Fauci with Dr. Jon LaPook, "March 2020: Dr. Anthony Fauci talks with Dr. Jon LaPook about Covid-19," CBS "60 Minutes" via YouTube, March 8, 2020, https://www.youtube.com/watch?v=PRa6t_e7dgI.

[30] Darragh Roche, "Fauci Said Masks 'Not Really Effective in Keeping Out Virus,' Email Reveals," *Newsweek*, June 2, 2021, https://www.newsweek.com/fauci-said-masks-not-really-effective-keeping-out-virus-email-reveals-1596703.

on to explain, disingenuously, at best: "So if you have a physical covering with one layer, you put another layer on, it just makes common sense that it likely would be more effective."[31]

That's called dancing with the truth. And the real shame is that Fauci demanded the entire nation dance with him—and oh, so many complied.

How did this happen?

Entire books could be written about Fauci's three years of conflicting, sketchy, duck-and-dodgy, unclear, obfuscating, deceptive, lying, purposefully ambiguous recommendations, bits of guidance, and dictates-cloaked-as-doctorly-advice—all of which were designed, by him, to elevate himself as the expert, but in a way that allowed himself to wash his hands clean of any responsibility, accountability, or accusations of self-aggrandizement. His carefully chosen words, his cautiously framed narratives, his use of "could," "maybe," "perhaps," "potentially," and the like to underscore the seriousness of the consequences that would befall those who disobeyed his recommended courses of action du jour—all were clever devices of control. All were evidence of his self-pride. All were displays of his disregard for American exceptionalism, based on individual liberties. All were weapons that he and his Big Government cronies wielded to seize power, clamp down human rights, steamroll in globalist agendas, and compel the free citizens of the United States to cower in the corners of their homes, socially distanced and awaiting the stimulus checks.

---

[31] Cory Stieg, "Dr. Fauci: Double-masking makes 'common sense' and is likely more effective," CNBC, January 25, 2021, https://www.cnbc.com/2021/01/25/dr-fauci-double-mask-during-covid-makes-common-sense-more-effective.html#:~:text=%E2%80%9CSo%20if%20you%20have%20a,a%20version%20of%20an%20N95.%E2%80%9D.

All are methods of the Marxists and collectivists of the world to drown the soul and kill the spirit, so as to shepherd individuals toward a mindset that says "state first."

But these three-plus years of Covid-19 clampdowns never would have happened if Americans had demanded their God-given liberties be respected and upheld. It couldn't have happened. A country with citizens who are grounded in God, trusting in His sovereignty and sensitive to the promptings of a Holy Spirit that gives the gift of discernment, would never have bought into the many, many lies of Fauci or his crowd.

Faith would have prevailed, not fear.

Cooler-headed thinking would have guided—not hysterical irrationalism.

Judeo-Christian wisdom based on Judeo-Christian values would have dominated, not secular instruction.

> From Colossians 2:8: "See to it that no one takes you captive through philosophy and empty deception, according to the tradition of men, according to the elementary principles of the world, rather than according to Christ."
>
> (Col. 2:8, NASB1995)

Science is great. But it's no substitute for the wisdom of God. And it should never be received as the be-all and end-all of truth. Godless science is untrustworthy science. Godless Fauci's science, therefore, was untrustworthy from the beginning, in need of challenges and checks—which made it all the more disastrous when social media and Big Tech decided to stifle all questions about government's response to Covid-19.

Only those who have something to hide resist transparency and flee challenges to their authority.

In June 2021, Fauci knocked on doors in the Washington, DC, neighborhood of Anacostia with Democrat mayor Muriel Bowser, a small gaggle of fellow bureaucrats, and at least one reporter, trying to convince residents to get the Covid-19 shots. Some of the discussions were enlightening, especially a couple of the offhand remarks captured on camera made by Fauci to Bowser about the reluctance of many to do the government's bidding.

One conversation, as PBS reported in a video clip, went like this:[32]

> "These people aren't really opposed," Bowser said, at the doorway of one homeowner who said she hadn't taken the shot. "But they do need a push."
>
> "They need a little push," Fauci agreed.
>
> "A push and a drag," Bowser added.
>
> "Yeah," Fauci said.

That's called "Government Knows Best." The nanny attitude of some in government to believe that they know better than the citizens how the citizens should behave, how the citizens should think, has no place in a free country like America. It has no place in a nation where liberties are inherent at birth—a gift of the Creator. It's elitism, arrogance, and derision dressed

---

[32] American Masters, "Dr. Fauci visits D.C. to battle vaccine hesitancy," PBS. org, S37, E2, video shot June 2021, released March 21, 2023, https://www. pbs.org/video/dr-fauci-visits-dc-battle-vaccine-hesistancy-nvc620/.

as concern, care, and compassion. In America, moral public servants don't "push and drag" the citizens who pay their salaries to get them to do something they have the lawful right to refuse. It's called the Constitution, not command and compel.

At another home, Fauci—after blowing a kiss to a woman on her porch who said she had taken the shot—expressed frustration, along with Bowser, with Republicans for refusing the shots:[33]

> "What are we gonna do about those other states?" Bowser was heard asking off-camera.

> Fauci responded, "Oh my God," as the camera lens panned to them standing in the street. "They're going to keep the outbreaks smoldering in the country. It's so crazy. I mean, they're not doing it because they say they don't want to do it. They're Republicans—they don't like to be told what to do."

> "Right," Bowser said.

> "And we got to break that, you know, unpack that," Fauci said.[34]

If any statement could summarize how the medical bureaucrats, nanny-state politicians, and globalist-minded Marxists looked upon the general American public during the Covid-19 years, it's that one: "We got to break that"—meaning, the spirit

---

33 American Masters, "Dr. Fauci visits D.C. to battle vaccine hesitancy," PBS. org, video shot June 2021, released March 21, 2023, https://www.pbs.org/ video/dr-fauci-visits-dc-battle-vaccine-hesistancy-nvc620/.
34 Ibid.

of independence. Challenge authority? Got to break that. Question the science? Got to break that. Demand the reopening of schools, businesses, and churches? Got to break that. Resist the stupid face masks and randomly applied social distance mandates? Got to break that.

Just because the message was relayed through lips that smiled doesn't change the tyrannical tone, tenor, or intent of the message.

When bureaucrats profess to love and care for the people, one has to wonder: At what price? And if the price is to take from one to give to another; to govern by force; and to drive out individualism, free thought, and the freedom of decision-making for collectivism, groupthink, and decision-making that benefits the state, first and foremost—then in America that price is too high.

In America, God-given liberties must prevail, because that's the protection that keeps Americans free. That's the ten-foot-thick, mile-high brick wall that stops tyrants in their tracks.

A nation with citizens who know that God is the provider, and that government is simply the protector of what God already provides, never would have allowed Fauci's lies to root and spread; they never would have so willingly bent and bowed to the daily whim of government and so-called science and exchanged liberties for a whiff of safety, security, and health. A country of people who understand biblical truths and teachings, who set God at the forefront, and who take their marching orders from above, not from Capitol Hill, would have discerned the many Fauci lies and spins from the very beginning—and would have resisted, rebelled, and outright bucked a government call for the closing of businesses, schools, parks, beaches, and communities. God-fearing Americans would have demanded answers to the swirl of questions about random policies, senseless science, and pseudoscience masked as truth. They would have stormed the halls of political offices, figuratively, and perhaps, as time wore on, even literally, until these conflicting mandates and illogical dictates were explained and clarified and, as necessary, tossed to the side.

A government that knows the citizens will fight for their God-given liberties is a government that doesn't even try to wrest control from the people; it's a government that fears the people, and as such, stays humble.

The problem in America, as showcased during Covid-19, is that too much emphasis has been placed on secular education and too much regard given to those with college degrees, to the point where the Bible is seen as a book of fairy tales and God as unimportant in the day-to-day matters. Degrees are great and college is wonderful—but only when they are subjugated to the authority of biblical teachings and godly virtues. Without—we get a Fauci. Without—we get the intelligentsia class acting as the gods of society.

This is a bad situation for Americans. Historically speaking, scientists and scholars haven't exactly been models of ethics.

- In 2012, Marc Hauser, a scientist and psychology professor at Harvard University, was forced to resign after a three-year investigation deemed him guilty of committing six instances of scientific misconduct in research work supported by the National Institutes of Health. He neither admitted nor denied guilt, but he did apologize, and one of his papers was outright retracted, while two others, corrected.[35]

- In 2015, Dong-Pyou Han, a biomedical scientist at Iowa State University, was sentenced to fifty-seven months behind bars and fined $7.2 million for fabricating and falsifying HIV vaccine trial data in lab work he conducted that was funded with National Institutes of Health grants. He had been forced by the university to resign a couple years earlier, after he was caught spiking samples of rabbit blood with HIV antibodies from humans to make it seem as if he had discovered an immunization against the virus.[36]

- In 2016, Bharat Aggarwal, formerly of the University of Texas MD Anderson Cancer Center, saw two of the papers he coauthored retracted for "inappropriate" or "unacceptable" image manipulation—and that was after seven others he coauthored were previously retracted for similar manipulations. Worse, these falsified findings had been cited dozens of times in other papers used to support tumor and cancer research.[37]

- In 2018, Ching-Shih Chen, a cancer researcher, resigned from The Ohio State University (OSU) in Columbus after administrators and investigators found that he had falsely reported findings in eight papers. His years-long

---

[35] Carolyn Y. Johnson, "Ex-Harvard scientist fabricated, manipulated data, report says," *The Boston Globe*, September 5, 2012, https://www.bostonglobe.com/news/science/2012/09/05/harvard-professor-who-resigned-fabricated-manipulated-data-says/6gDVkzPNxv1ZDkh4wVnKhO/story.html.

[36] Sara Reardon, "US vaccine researcher sentenced to prison for fraud," *Nature*, July 1, 2015, https://www.nature.com/articles/nature.2015.17660.

[37] Tanya Lewis, "More Retractions for Cancer Researcher," *The Scientist*, June 22, 2016, https://www.the-scientist.com/the-nutshell/more-retractions-for-cancer-researcher-33320.

research, published in two-hundred-plus papers, had been supported with more than $8 million from the National Institutes for Health, and he was so highly regarded for his studies that in 2010 he received the Innovator of the Year award from OSU.[38]

- In 2020, cancer researcher Andrew Dannenberg saw several of his papers retracted for evidence of data falsification or fabrication and, in early 2021, resigned from Weill Cornell Medical College. His coauthor, Kotha Subbaramaiah, had resigned a few weeks earlier. The 2020 retractions were just the latest in a long line of retractions for scientific misconduct tied to Dannenberg and Subbaramaiah.[39]

- In 2022, exosome biologist and former University of Louisville School of Medicine professor Douglas Taylor cited false data in thirteen different applications for grants from the National Institutes of Health and the National Cancer Institute, one of which was funded. He was also found to have cited false figures in at least one paper published years earlier.[40]

---

[38] Alison McCook, "Cancer researcher at The Ohio State University resigns following multiple misconduct findings," Retraction Watch, published by Science.org, March 30, 2018, https://www.science.org/content/article/cancer-researcher-ohio-state-university-resigns-following-multiple-misconduct-findings.

[39] Ellie Kincaid, "Former Weill Cornell cancer researcher up to 20 retractions; investigation's findings are with feds," Retraction Watch, June 3, 2022, https://retractionwatch.com/2022/06/03/former-weill-cornell-cancer-researcher-up-to-20-retractions-investigations-findings-are-with-feds/.

[40] Katherine Irving, "Exosome Scientist Douglas Taylor Stole and Mislabeled Images: Report," The Scientist, November 23, 2022, https://www.the-scientist.com/news-opinion/exosome-scientist-douglas-taylor-stole-and-mislabeled-images-report-70788.

This is just a tiny number of science and research misconduct cases that have come to light in recent years—a tiny slice of what an internet search reveals, a teeny glimpse into the thousands upon thousands of instances of fraudulent findings the scientific community has pushed onto an unaware public. And this is just a glimpse at America. Add in all the other countries, and volumes could be written about all the science misconduct that's been discovered. More examples?

The Office of Research Integrity (ORI), a government office under the Department of Health and Human Services, maintains a list of science-related misconduct cases that resulted in disciplinary actions. But the names of the researchers who received administrative actions are cleared after seven years. What a great blessing for the researchers.

In 2023, ORI listed the following:

- University of Pennsylvania research associate professor of anesthesiology and critical care William M. Armstead "engaged in research misconduct by knowingly and intentionally falsifying and/or fabricating fifty-one figures and the methods, data, result and conclusions."[41]
- University of Utah assistant professor in the department of internal medicine Ivana Frech, formerly Ivana De Domenico, "intentionally, knowingly, or recklessly falsified and/or fabricated...images to falsely report data

---

[41] ORI, "Case Summary: Armstead, William M.," The Office of Research Integrity, https://ori.hhs.gov/content/case-summary-armstead-william-m, published in Federal Register on July 7, 2020, https://ori.hhs.gov/sites/default/files/2023-07/William%20Armstead%2C%20Ph.D.%20FRN%202023-14426.pdf.

in eight figures included in...three PHS [US Public Health Service]-supported published papers..."[42]

- Rosalind Franklin University of Medicine and Science professor of microbiology and immunology Johnny J. He "engaged in research misconduct by intentionally, knowingly, or recklessly falsifying, fabricating, and plagiarizing experimental data and text that described the research from one pre-print and four published papers and represented the data and/or ideas as his own... in four NIH [National Institutes of Health] grant applications."[43]

- Baylor University assistant professor in the department of psychology and neuroscience Lara S. Hwa "engaged in research misconduct by knowingly or recklessly falsifying and/or fabricating data, methods, results, and conclusions in...experimental timelines, group conditions, sex of animal subjects, mouse strains, and behavioral response data in...two published papers and two PHS grant applications."[44]

- University of Alabama in Huntsville assistant professor of chemistry Surangi (Suranji) Jayawardena "engaged in research misconduct by intentionally, knowingly, or

[42] ORI, "Case Summary: Frech, Ivana," The Office of Research Integrity, https://ori.hhs.gov/content/case-summary-de-domenico-ivana, published in Federal Register on September 5, 2023, https://ori.hhs.gov/sites/default/files/2023-09/Frech%20FRN%202023-19086.pdf.

[43] ORI, "Case Summary: He, Johnny J.," The Office of Research Integrity, https://ori.hhs.gov/content/case-summary-he-johnny-j, published in *Federal Register* on May 3, 2023, https://ori.hhs.gov/sites/default/files/2023-05/FRN%202023-09355%20-%20Johnny%20J.%20He%2C%20Ph.D..pdf.

[44] ORI, "Case Summary: Hwa, Lara S.," The Office of Research Integrity, https://ori.hhs.gov/content/case-summary-hwa-lara-s, as of 2023 still awaiting publication in *Federal Register*.

recklessly falsifying and/or fabricating data in twelve figure panels in…four NIH grant applications."[45]

- Ohio State University postdoctoral fellow in the department of cancer biology and genetics Yiorgos (Georgios) I. Laliotis "engaged in research misconduct by intentionally and knowingly falsifying and/or fabricating data, methods, results, and conclusions…in three published papers, two NIH grant applications, and two unpublished manuscripts."[46]

- Yale University assistant professor of medicine in the department of digestive diseases Carlo Spirli "engaged in research misconduct by knowingly, intentionally, or recklessly falsifying and/or fabricating data included in…four published papers, two presentations, and three grant applications submitted for PHS funds."[47]

Then there were the separate listings for Dannenberg and Subbaramaiah, the Weill Cornell Medical College professor of medicine and professor of biochemistry research, respectively,

---

[45] ORI, "Case Summary: Jayawardena, Surangi (Suranji)," The Office of Research Integrity, https://ori.hhs.gov/content/case-summary-jayawardena-suranji, published in *Federal Register* on September 1, 2023, https://ori.hhs.gov/sites/default/files/2023-09/Jayawardena%20FRN.pdf.

[46] ORI, "Case Summary: Laliotis, Yiorgos (Georgios) I.," The Office of Research Integrity, https://ori.hhs.gov/content/case-summary-laliotis-yiorgos-georgios-i, published in *Federal Register* on June 29, 2023, https://ori.hhs.gov/sites/default/files/2023-06/Yiorgos%20%28Georgios%29%20I.%20Laliotis%20FRN%202023-13847.pdf.

[47] ORI, "Case Summary: Spirli, Carlo," The Office of Research Integrity, https://ori.hhs.gov/content/case-summary-spirli-carlo, published in *Federal Register* on April 13, 2023, https://ori.hhs.gov/sites/default/files/2023-04/FRN%202023-07850%20-%20Carlo%20Spirli%2C%20Ph.D..pdf.

both cited for "recklessly reporting falsified and/or fabricated data in…twelve published papers."[48]

That's just 2023.

That's just a handful of what ORI reports and subsequently publishes in the *Federal Register*, the official publication of the US government.

More importantly, perhaps, is the matter of accountability. So, what happens to these lying scientists and researchers? Well, by and large, they're not booted from their fields.

In Dannenberg's case, he "entered into a Voluntary Settlement Agreement" to "have his research supervised for a period of seven years," during which he would ensure that "any institution employing him submits, in conjunction with each application for PHS funds…a certification to ORI that the data are based on actual experiments or are otherwise legitimately derived." He was also to remove himself from all consideration for advisory or consulting positions tied to the US Public Health Service, again, for seven years.[49]

Subbaramaiah received a similarly sweet deal to sign a seven-year "Voluntary Exclusion Agreement" in which he promised not to contract or subcontract with any agency of the federal

---

footnotes
48 ORI, "Case Summary: Dannenberg, Andrew," The Office of Research Integrity, September 13, 2023, https://ori.hhs.gov/content/case-summary-dannenberg-andrew.

49 ORI, "Case Summary: Dannenberg, Andre," The Office of Research Integrity, https://ori.hhs.gov/content/case-summary-dannenberg-andrew, published in *Federal Register* on September 13, 2023, https://ori.hhs.gov/sites/default/files/2023-09/Dannenberg%20FRN%202023-19779_0.pdf.

government or to serve in any advisory or consultant role with the PHS.[50]

These are slaps on the wrist that not only are slaps to the faces of taxpayers but also make mockeries of law and morality. At the very least, the scientists and researchers who are found guilty of fraud and misconduct should have to return grant dollars that were used in their fraudulent scientific pursuits. The worst offenders, meanwhile, should lose their rights to continue in fields involving science and research. It's not just the original instance of scientific misconduct that's the problem. There's a ripple effect from bad science that occurs when other scientists, other researchers, and other medical professionals cite the original false findings to further their own research, leading to the potential for years and years of flawed and deceptive data being passed as true.

If attorneys are found guilty of certain offenses, they're disbarred. They lose their rights to practice law.

If private investigators are found guilty of certain offenses, they're stripped of their licenses or certifications. They lose their rights for private investigating.

If cashiers in retail are found guilty of certain offenses, they're fired, perhaps even arrested.

But cancer researchers who commit egregious and willful acts of deception? Scientists in the field of microbiology who falsify data to fraudulently obtain tax-funded grants?

---

[50] ORI, "Case Summary: Subbaramaiah, Kotha," The Office of Research Integrity, https://ori.hhs.gov/content/case-summary-subbaramaiah-kotha, published in *Federal Register* on September 13, 2023, https://ori.hhs.gov/content/case-summary-subbaramaiah-kotha.

Medical bureaucrats who use their positions of authority to force an entire nation into compliance and an entire country of free citizens to bend knee to the god of government?

That's a problem. That's the two-tiered system of justice America now allows.

Fauci got away with his tyranny because of a fear-filled populace, an incompetent and greedy corporate-owned media filled with members who failed to do their watchdog duties, and a corrupt world of science.

He got away with his tyranny because Americans forgot God and set government, science, politicians, and bureaucracies in place of God. And it's not like Americans didn't have a long, long list of warnings of all the science liars who've permeated and sullied the field for years.

> For if you cry for discernment, lift your voice for understanding; if you seek her as silver and search for her as for hidden treasures, then you will discern the fear of the Lord and discover the knowledge of God.... Discretion will guard you, understanding will watch over you, to deliver you from the way of evil, from the man who speaks perverse things.
>
> (Proverbs 2:3–5, Proverbs 2:11–12, NASB1995)

We didn't do that during Covid-19.
We need to do that going forward.

CHAPTER 3

THE EVIL ONE HAS THE FAMILY UNIT IN HIS CROSSHAIRS

I n October 2023, tens of thousands descended upon the festival grounds at Lake Eola in Orlando, Florida, for a "Come Out With Pride" day-long celebration of the LGBTQ lifestyle.[51]

The grand marshal was an eleven-year-old transgender child.[52] That is to say, the grand marshal was an eleven-year-old

---

[51] Brittany Caldwell, "Large crowds show up for this year's 'Come Out With Pride' festival in downtown Orlando," WFTV.com, October 21, 2023, https://www.wftv.com/news/local/large-crowds-show-up-this-years-come-out-with-pride-festival-downtown-orlando/26TVYORH4ZG7LMJFN6FU WRIEWU/.

[52] Aila Slisco, "Transgender 11-Year-Old Becomes Youngest Grand Marshal at Pride Parade," Newsweek, October 23, 2023, https://www.newsweek.com/transgender-11-year-old-becomes-youngest-grand-marshal-pride-parade-1837129.

boy who was pretending to be a girl. Where were his parents? Right next to him, beaming and smiling.[53]

This is where the evil really ratchets. It's one thing for members of the LGBTQ community to hold parades, protests, public rallies, and the like. That is their right; that is their constitutionally protected authority to peacefully assemble. But to rope in children to this madness and advance a narrative that boys can be girls, and girls can be boys, simply by personal whim, wish, and will—this is a new form of evil that's tantamount, in many instances, to the sexual grooming of minors. That parents would subject their own kids to such insanity shows how perilously close to doomsday America has moved. As Genesis 1:27 states, "So God created man in His *own* image, in the image of God He created him; male and female He created them." (NKJV) Anything else—anything outside the basic male-female structure—it's not of God.

It's from Satan.

And if we don't fight for the basic creations of God—the male; the female; the joining of a man and woman in marriage, where both leave their parents and cleave to each other; and the traditional family with a mother and father at the head of the home, raising virtuous children and teaching them the godly way to go—if we don't fight for this model, then American society is lost. Family is the foundation of community, and communities are what weave together to form a nation. It's not enough to simply go to church on Sunday and turn blind eyes

---

[53] Amanda Harding, "Trans-Identifying 11-Year-Old Becomes Youngest Grand Marshal At Orlando Pride Parade," The Daily Wire, October 23, 2023, https://www.dailywire.com/news/trans-identifying-11-year-old-becomes-youngest-grand-marshal-at-orlando-pride-parade.

to the moral depravity that's destroying children, families, and society Monday through Saturday.

We have to call out the evil for what it is—evil. We have to fight the evil as if our own lives depended upon it—because they do.

Pseudoscience is having its way with our world, and nowhere is that being felt with greater impact than on the youngest and most innocent of God's creations: the little children.

An article in the *Orlando Sentinel* describes this 2023 pride event:

> Eleven-year-old transgender girl Dempsey Jara, the youngest grand marshal in the history of Orlando's Come Out With Pride parade, had a message Saturday when she took the stage at Lake Eola Park. "Being transgender is not about a choice," Dempsey said while wearing a princess-style gown. "It's about being true to myself. It's about embracing who I am even when the world tries to tell me otherwise. It's about standing tall in my identity even when it's really hard." Her mother, Jaime Jara, 45, a schoolteacher, beamed beside her on stage. Off stage, she said her youngest child has always known who she was. "She's just always gravitated toward girl things, girls' toys. We didn't have any of that stuff at home. She has two older brothers," Jaime said. "She'd say, 'I'm a girl in my heart and my brain.' She's been on

this journey since she was 5 and she's living her best life."[54]

There's so much wrong there, it's tough to know where to start.

This little boy, since age five, according to his mother, has been living as a girl. His parents, instead of guiding and instructing and, gosh, how about this, parenting as they should, tossed aside their duties and responsibilities and threw in with the liars of the pack. They told the *Daily Mail*, in a 2019 interview, that their son had been drawn toward sparkling, feminine objects from about the age of eighteen months.

> "Dempsey has been gender non-conforming since the age of eighteen months old, basically since she was able to express herself. She always gravitated to dolls, dresses and sparkly objects," Jaime said…. "Dempsey would use her imagination to fashion items of clothing such as pajama trousers into long hair and shirts into skirts for dress-up. She would always draw herself as a girl with long blonde hair. She would ask for dolls and princess dresses as gifts for holidays. Knowing that these items were what she wanted, we bought them because we knew how happy they made her." Initially, Jaime and her husband, Dennis, thought it was just a phase that would pass, but over the

54 Stephen Hudak, "Trans girl, 11, leads Orlando Pride Parade: 'It's about being true to yourself,'" *Orlando Sentinel*, October 21, 2023, https://www.orlandosentinel.com/2023/10/21/trans-girl-11-leads-orlando-pride-parade-its-about-being-true-to-yourself/.

years Dempsey became increasingly angry at having to dress like a boy; she would bring back pictures she drew of herself as a girl with long blonde hair and would cry when she had her hair cut short.[55]

At the same time, Dempsey would still refer to himself as "he" at home.

Jaime and Dennis said their son was mocked at preschool for choosing to play with girls' toys and would often return home in tears. When he was four, they took their son to a therapist, who diagnosed gender dysphoria. That was after a previous pediatrician had told them Dempsey was simply going through a phase of adolescence and that transgenderism wasn't real.[56]

From the *Daily Mail* again: "'Dennis and I continued to follow Dempsey's lead, as was advised to us by her therapists,' Jaime said. 'She entered kindergarten using masculine pronouns but started to grow out her hair and [wear] feminine accessories to school.'"[57]

Ultimately, Jaime and Dennis posted their son's trans-journey on Instagram. They were flooded with messages and notes from others in the LGBTQ community offering support, as well as from parents who wanted advice on how to help their own similarly confused children.

---

[55] DailyMail.com reporter, "Mother reveals she has been accused of CHILD ABUSE and 'brainwashing' for raising her eight-year-old as a transgender girl—but she insists the youngster is happier living as a female," *Daily Mail*, November 14, 2019, https://www.dailymail.co.uk/femail/article-7673229/Mother-accused-CHILD-ABUSE-raising-daughter-transgender.html.

[56] Ibid.

[57] Ibid.

And one more remark from mom, Jaime: "A lot of people have commented that Dempsey is lucky to have me as her mom. I feel just the opposite. I feel lucky to have Dempsey as my child. She teaches me new things every day and has changed my perspective on so many things, many of which are about compassion and acceptance."[58]

Love is love.

If it feels good, if it feels right, if it gives a warm and happy feeling, then it must be right; it must be love; and since God is love, it must be godly.

With the LGBTQ attack on children, it's best to remember a few biblical truths. The first, from Jeremiah 17:9 (NKJV):

> The heart *is* deceitful above all *things*, And desperately wicked; Who can know it?

The second, from Psalm 12:8 (NASB1995):

> The wicked strut about on every side When vileness is exalted among the sons of men.

The third, from 1 Peter 5:8 (NKJV):

> Be sober, be vigilant; because your adversary the devil walks about like a roaring lion, seeking whom he may devour.

---

[58] DailyMail.com reporter, "Mother reveals she has been accused of CHILD ABUSE and 'brainwashing' for raising her eight-year-old as a transgender girl—but she insists the youngster is happier living as a female," *Daily Mail*, November 14, 2019, https://www.dailymail.co.uk/femail/article-7673229/Mother-accused-CHILD-ABUSE-raising-daughter-transgender.html.

The fourth, a warning right from God, in Matthew 18:6 (ESV):

> Whoever causes one of these little ones who believe in me to sin, it would be better for him to have a great millstone fastened around his neck and to be drowned in the depth of the sea.

Parenting is not simply about loving a child. That's cheap. That's easy. That's a cop-out and a derelict of duty. Parenting is about raising a child to be a moral, principled, productive member of society—and that's the hard part. It takes guts, courage, determination, and a willingness to stand firm in the face of tears and tempers. It also takes a commitment to truth and integrity so that when the fantasies of youth arise, as they undoubtedly will, parents can reel them in and, without dampening the imagination or creative drive, nonetheless point to the differences between myth and reality.

Jaime and Dennis let their son go off the deep end.

And they did so because they were more concerned with their child's fleeting feelings of happiness than with doing right by their child.

They could have said "no," but instead, in their own words, they "continued to follow Dempsey's lead." They probably wouldn't have allowed their son to suck down a fruity alcoholic drink or steal candy from a grocery store, no matter how much he begged and cried, no matter how instant the gratification would have been for him, and no matter how happy he may have seemed in the moment of fulfillment. They probably wouldn't have let it go unpunished, or at least undisciplined, if he smacked a kid in the face for taking his toy or stabbed him with a pencil or pair of scissors—no matter how righteously indignant he felt and how insistent he was on retaliation. They probably wouldn't let him wear a dolphin costume to school just because he imagined himself to be a dolphin and felt his happiest when he was wriggling on the floor like a dolphin in water—even if he shed tears every morning before school. But when he claimed to be a girl stuck in a boy's body?

That's when they gave in and let him have his way.

That's when they caved to the deceits of the heart, both his and their own.

And that's when they discovered that caving to these deceits was not only accepted but also rewarded and cheered by a growing segment of society—of the wicked who strut openly because their vileness is now moving mainstream.

This abuse of children must stop.

It's not a "journey"—a spiritual skip down Ethereal Lane. It's not a game—do not pass go, do not collect $200. It's a sacred life. It's not the child who is supposed to take the lead while the parents follow; it's the parents and caretakers who are supposed to lead while the child follows—and in cases where the child refuses to follow, they are then to use wisdom and discernment to determine whether to compel obedience. Parents have that right; they invoke it all the time. They make their kids go to school. They make them brush their teeth. They make them go to bed, eat vegetables, and tell them not to put the cat in the dryer or let the dog eat cotton candy, happiness be danged. Why not make them understand their God-given, biological sex? Parenting is not a popularity contest. And a happy child is not automatically the mark of good parenting. After all, a beastly, disobedient, rude, and obnoxious little boy can seem very happy when he gets his way. But he wouldn't be a badge of honor for the parents.

Happiness, as the world means it, is truly overrated—and underwhelming. It's fleeting, it's dependent on circumstances, and it's ever-changing. It should not be the driving force of parents to provide for their children. Rather, parents should be most concerned with not screwing up what God created—with raising their children to serve out the mission God made them for and in a way that honors and respects self, family, and society. Ultimately, it's God who should be glorified by His children, and parents play a big role in ensuring that outcome.

The day after serving as marshal of the pride parade in Orlando, Dempsey danced in a video on Instagram and said, "Yesterday was the best day of my life! It's not easy to be a constant target of hate, but I remain visible because I want other Trans kids to know there is such #joy in being your authentic self."[59]

This is the kind of confusion poor parenting brings. This is the door the LGBTQ community and incompetent parents open to wickedness. To call a lie a truth—to flout a deception as authentic—and to encourage the smallest and youngest of children to embrace those lies and deceptions as truths is evil personified.

Picture for the moment the statue of Baphomet commissioned by The Satanic Temple—the one where the goat-headed, winged demonic creature is seated upon a throne, on either side of which stand a small girl and a small boy, their heads tilted upwards as they gaze adoringly at their beastly master. That's the

59 Pink News, "#DempseyJara is the youngest grand marshal in the #Pride event's 18-year history," TikTok, October 24, 2023, https://www.tiktok.com/@pinknews/video/7293534306960559392.

perfect illustration of the evil the LGBTQ movement is thrusting onto the most innocent.

Simply put, little boys can't decide at the age of five that they're really girls.

They've only just passed the point of needing their meat cut for them. Some of them still wet the bed at night and their pants in the day. Others can't decide whether they want to be firemen when they grow up—or dinosaurs. Here's a checklist of physical, emotional, and social milestones for the average, normal five-year-old boy, from the website Verywell Family, in an article that was reviewed for accuracy by a medical doctor:

- They are becoming adept at climbing and somersaulting and should be able to stand on one foot for ten seconds.
- They are mostly potty trained.
- They can "hop"—and "may even be able to skip."
- They can remember their phone number, as well as their parents' names.
- They can recognize when words rhyme.
- They're learning to become quite the conversationalists and have a vocabulary of around two thousand words.
- They engage in more cooperative play with others and can help with simple household chores—like bringing their dishes to the sink.
- They're starting to lose their baby teeth—so "get your tooth fairy skills ready," the site suggests.[60]

Does any of that scream adult maturity?

---

[60] Wendy Wisner, reviewed for accuracy by Tyra Tennyson Francis MD, "5-Year-Old Child Development Milestones," Verywell Family, February 3, 2022, https://www.verywellfamily.com/5-year-old-developmental-milestones-620713.

And here's why Dempsey's parents are 100 percent complicit in the evil: they used their son, Dempsey, to bolster their own fame and celebrity status. From a Deadline report:

> Jaime Jara [is] a Florida mom and teacher who was featured in Season 3 of the Max reality series *We're Here* with her daughter Dempsey.... In the two-part finale, Jaime was recruited to participate in a drag show as the episodes explored how [Florida] is becoming increasingly hostile for LGBTQ+ people. Amid the joy of learning the art of drag, Jaime also spoke openly about her experience as the mother of a transgender daughter.... Jaime explained that, though Dempsey wasn't originally going to be part of the performance, the producers "realized that she is so much an integral part of the story." So, she and her dad took the stage with Jaime as she performed in drag to Katy Perry's "Roar."[61]

The *We're Here* show is about a trio of drag queens who travel the United States to promote the drag lifestyle and share stories with small-town residents. And season 3 included the Jara clan—mom, dad, and son-pretending-to-be-a-girl—all on stage, all forever memorialized for the viewing television audience. Again, from Deadline:

---

[61] Katie Campione, "'We're Here's' Jaime, Dempsey & DeBronski On Fighting For The LGBTQ Community And Finding Empowerment Through Drag—Deadline FYC House + HBO Max," Deadline, June 14, 2023, https://deadline.com/2023/06/were-here-interview-deadline-fyc-house-hbo-max-1235415987/.

Jaime said she only wanted to convey [that]…
"I'm just doing what a mom is supposed to do…
love our kid…and we just want her to live and
we just want her to be happy, and we just want
her to live the best life that she can." Dempsey
is hoping that audiences will see their story
and it will encourage other parents to be like
hers. "They are such loving parents. And like
without them, I wouldn't be here today. I hope
other parents just understand that kids like me
are really in danger right now. And they need to
be like, my mom and my dad," she said.[62]

Dempsey is going to face a hard time the rest of his life.
Either he will be forced to continue to live a lie, or he will one
day see the truth and utterly crumble. This is what makes the
transgender movement as it impacts kids so devastating, so abu-
sive: it inflicts permanent damage. It comes dressed as love—
cloaked in care, concern, and compassion—and is woven into
the culture as something good, all as it corrupts and destroys
God's most innocent. It is neither love nor understanding to lie
to children and tell them they were born into the wrong sex. It's
the ultimate in pride and rebellion.

Read Colossians 2:8 (ESV): "See to it that no one makes
a prey of you by philosophy and empty deceit, according to
human tradition, according to the elemental spirits of the world,
and not according to Christ."

Then recognize that this is what's happening in the LGBTQ
movement. As more and more lunacy and psychologically

---

disturbing and mentally ailing behaviors move mainstream, more and more self-professed, self-identifying LGBTQs seem to come out of the shadows, leading to more and more widespread acceptance of deviant behaviors and thought patterns—until the point where the LGBTQ lifestyle, deceitful as it is, contrary to God as it is, becomes the human tradition, that is, the norm. This is the path America is now walking.

Too many parents, who once were the gate-guards of their children's innocence, have bought into the philosophies and empty deceits of the LGBTQ crowd and are, with increasing and alarming frequency, offering up their own flesh and blood so the elemental spirits of the universe can have their wicked ways. These are ways that are not according to Christ.

These are ways that tear at the family foundation and utterly corrupt then capsize the culture and society. Dempsey's parents are not the only facilitators toward this demise of America. Just because someone says something is science or psychological truth or medical fact doesn't negate the responsibility to look first to the Bible for the real truth.

Type the words "men pregnant" into Google, and what that search produces is a page filled with articles and medical studies that, to various degrees, explain how men can indeed become pregnant. This is the whitewashing of truth. It's the Big Tech equivalent of Winston Smith in George Orwell's *1984* working tirelessly to toss words into the incinerator, thereby deleting them from the vocabulary.[63] Control the language, control the narrative, and soon enough, control the way people think.

---

[63] CourtneysThoughtCorner, "The Destruction of Language in George Orwell's '1984,'" The Essential Encounter, May 2, 2017, https://theessentialencounter.wordpress.com/2017/05/02/the-destruction-of-language-in-george-orwells-1984/.

Men cannot get pregnant. Men cannot deliver babies. Men cannot, by definition, be mothers. But as years go by, more and more truthful media on this commonsense fact will be pushed to the side, buried beneath the pseudoscience, "disappeared" from websites, journals, medical documentation, and even government records. Dempsey's parents changed their son's birth certificate in 2019 to reflect that he was a girl, and as such, in that official regard, he was erased from existence and replaced by a fabrication.[64] If it sounds horrifying, it's because it is. Removing offensive language, whether that offensive language be pronouns or narratives that counter leftists' desires, is a key method of Marxists to advance their anti-family, anti-God designs and bring about a society that is completely bendable, malleable, and programmable.

Look at the ways pseudoscience is being used to destroy traditional family:

The idea that men can breastfeed. "Some transgender men and nonbinary people use the term chestfeeding or bodyfeeding rather than breastfeeding. Chestfeeding can mean nursing at the breast, but it can also mean using a tube attached to the nipple to feed a baby formula or breast milk. Chestfeeding may also be used for non-nutritive sucking—in other words, for comfort rather than nutrition," BabyCenter reported.[65] Producing milk for babies to drink is a distinctly female operation. Men—being men—cannot naturally breastfeed, that is, produce and pro-

64 *The Pink Times*, "11-Year-Old Trans Girl Makes History as Orlando Pride Parade's Youngest Grand Marshal," *The Pink Times*, October 23, 2023, https://thepinktimes.com/11-year-old-trans-girl-makes-history-as-orlando-pride-parades-youngest-grand-marshal/.
65 Rebekah Wahlberg, "Can men and transgender people lactate?" BabyCenter, July 19, 2023, https://www.babycenter.com/baby/breastfeeding/can-men-breastfeed_8824.

vide the liquid food that is required to nurse a growing baby to health. They might be able to fake it by attaching tubes and bottles and cleverly designed appendages that are affixed to the chest. But that's not breastfeeding. One could just as easily clamp the tube creation to a pillow, or a board, or a sleeping puppy, and position the baby to feed—but that won't mean the pillow, board, or puppy is actually breastfeeding the baby. Here's the truer science, from an article by the *Daily Mail*:

> By using a regimen known as the Newman-Goldfarb protocol, originally developed in 2000 for adoptive mothers, the body can be tricked into lactating even if it's male. It works by mimicking the hormonal changes that take place naturally in the body of a woman who has just given birth, and involves several weeks of regularly using a pump to stimulate the breast, taking a combination of contraceptive hormones and the anti-nausea drug domperidone, which increases levels of the milk-producing hormone prolactin. But if that sounds simple, it really isn't. For a start, domperidone is banned in the U.S. over concerns it causes heart problems.[66]

So, there's that.

There's also the added complication of what exactly is being fed a baby suckling at an artificially created breast with artificially created milk. Men who think they can become

---

[66] Milli Hill, "Can a person who was born male REALLY breastfeed a baby? The answer will shock you," *Daily Mail*, July 6, 2023, updated July 7, 2023, https://www.dailymail.co.uk/femail/article-12272905/Can-person-born-male-REALLY-breastfeed-baby-answer-shock-you.html.

breastfeeding women by taking a few drugs and downing a few medicines ought to consider the chemicals they're passing along to the baby. Pregnant women—real women with real pregnancies—are already cautioned to avoid shellfish, wine, beer, liquor, tobacco, and certain medications during pregnancy and then after, while breastfeeding, to avoid passing along any poisons, contaminants, or ailments to their babies. Imagine now the unknowns with the antiandrogens, progesterone, and gonadotropin-releasing hormone (GnRH) agonists that are prescribed to men who want to change their appearance to become more feminine.[67]

The idea that men can become pregnant. Thomas Beatie made national headlines in 2008–9 when it was reported he gave birth to a baby—thereby proving what the LGBTQ crowd has insisted all along: that anyone can be whatever sex one wants, and sex is as changeable as clothing. Only problem is: that's a lie. Only women can become pregnant and give birth to babies. And Beatie, who was born a woman, even acknowledged that truth. From ABC News:

> Born a woman, Beatie, 34, who had had his breasts surgically removed and legally changed his gender from female to male, leaped to prominence around the world in April [2008] when the wispy bearded man revealed he was pregnant. Despite years of taking hormones and living outwardly as a man, Beatie maintained

---

67 Transline, "What are commonly used medications for transition?" Transline: Transgender Medical Consultation Service, undated, https://transline.zendesk.com/hc/en-us/articles/229373208-What-are-commonly-used-medications-for-transition-.

that he retained his female sex organs because he intended one day to get pregnant. "I actually opted not to do anything to my reproductive organs because I wanted to have a child one day. I see pregnancy as a process, and it doesn't define who I am," Beatie told Oprah Winfrey in April. "I feel it's not a male or female desire to have a child. It's a human need. I'm a person and I have the right to have a biological child," he said.[68]

What an astonishing rebellion against God. While it's not a male or female trait to desire a child, it is a matter of human biology—as ordained by God—that only females birth babies.

Worse was this headline, also in 2008, from *The Guardian*: "Childbirth: Transgender man has his baby, naturally."[69] No, there's nothing natural about a man birthing a baby. To think so is delusional. To believe so is evidence of mental illness. Yet that very notion is being normalized in this dark world.

The idea that males belong in women's athletic competitions. In November 2023, a Massachusetts female field hockey player suffered serious injuries, including some knocked-out teeth, when a male player pretending to be a female fired off a shot that struck her in the face.[70] In September 2022, a North Carolina female

68 ABC News, "'Pregnant Man' Gives Birth to Girl," ABC News, July 3, 2008, https://abcnews.go.com/Health/story?id=5302756&page=1.
69 Ed Pilkington, "Childbirth: Transgender man has his baby, naturally," *The Guardian*, July 4, 2008, https://www.theguardian.com/world/2008/jul/05/gender.usa.
70 Richard Pollina, "High school girls' field hockey player loses teeth, injured by shot from male opponent," *New York Post*, November 4, 2023, https://nypost.com/2023/11/04/news/massachusetts-high-school-field-hockey-player-loses-teeth-after-shot-from-male-on-womans-team/.

volleyball player suffered a concussion when a male pretending to be a female spiked the ball firmly into her face.[71] In 2017 and again in 2018, a Texas high school boy pretending to be a girl won the wrestling title in the girls' division after entering "the tournament with an undefeated 32-0 record," U.S. News & World Report wrote.[72] This is just the tip of the iceberg of the insanity of allowing men to play women's sports, while denying they are men. Gender identity should not be the deciding factor in determining sports teams and lineups. As Riley Gaines, the competitive swimmer at the University of Kentucky who watched, along with scores of other females, pretend female Lia Thomas break record after record, said through the Independent Women's Forum: "Allowing male-bodied athletes to participate in women's competitions will destroy the integrity of women's sports and leave women vulnerable."[73] It's common sense.

My body, my choice?

My body, mind your own business?

That only works if the lunatics and liars stay in their own lanes and don't insist on others participating in the lunacy and lies.

Children are not "born" in the wrong bodies. Maleness is not interchangeable with femaleness. Men and women are two

---

[71] Sports Litigation Alert, "After Suffering Concussion at the Hands of Transgender Athlete, High School Volleyball Player Becomes Spokeswoman," Sports Litigation Alert, May 5, 2023, https://sportslitigationalert.com/after-suffering-concussion-at-the-hands-of-transgender-athlete-high-school-volleyball-player-becomes-spokeswoman/.

[72] Alexa Lardieri, "Transgender Wrestler Wins High School Girls Title," U.S. News & World Report, February 26, 2018, https://www.usnews.com/news/national-news/articles/2018-02-26/transgender-wrestler-wins-high-school-girls-title.

[73] Riley Gaines, "I Just Got Beat By Someone Who Probably Didn't Have To Try," Independent Women's Forum, April 18, 2022, https://www.iwf.org/2022/04/18/i-just-got-beat-by-someone-who-probably-didnt-have-to-try/.

distinct sexes. And no matter what meds, pills, or procedures are given, prescribed, and undertaken, the fact is that males born males will stay males and females born females will stay females, until death do they part. Moreover, moving to a society where minor-age children are able to make medical decisions their young minds cannot possibly comprehend—in terms of safety, in terms of long-term health impacts, in terms of psychological soundness—is a horror, especially when pushed by those with political designs.

This is the way of Marxists.

It's not just the destruction of family, the foundation of any nation. With the LGBTQ madness, it's also an open attack on capitalism and the economic engine of a free America.

In a summary of the book *Transgender Marxism*, Pluto Press wrote:

> [This book] is a provocative and groundbreaking union of transgender studies and Marxist theory. Exploring trans lives and movements, the authors delve into the experience of surviving as transgender under capitalism. They explore the pressures, oppression and state persecution faced by trans people living in capitalist societies, their tenuous positions in the workplace and the home, and give a powerful response to right-wing scaremongering against 'gender ideology.' Reflecting on the relations between gender and labor, these essays reveal the structure of antagonisms faced by gender non-conforming people within society. Looking at the history of transgender movements, Marxist interventions

into developmental theory, psychoanalysis and workplace ethnography, the authors conclude that for trans liberation, capitalism must be abolished.[74]

Read that again: for transgenders to thrive, capitalism—the free market—must be abolished.

It's a mad scientist way of looking at things. But it's just part of the cycle of pseudoscience that's been making the rounds of modern America. And the LGBTQ movement doesn't want this quiet part said out loud—but here it is, clear and simple: at the root of all LGBTQ campaigns is a quest to destroy traditional family, to make the abnormal the norm. Why? To have a society where anything goes—where morals, virtues, and restraints are tossed to the winds—where those with the most disgusting and depraved ways of thinking and behaving are accepted and, eventually, embraced. Democrats love this cultural rot because it plays into their political designs to control the citizenry. They know the more chaotic a culture becomes, the more the people beg for a fix, and that's all the "in" the Democrats need to expand government.

Staying silent on the LGBTQ lies is to be complicit in the LGBTQ evils. Playing along with pronoun preferences, gender switches, sex-change surgeries—especially in minors—is to embolden the liars and destroy youth. God cannot be pleased with a country that grooms children to live as liars; He cannot be pleased with those who stand idly by as the grooming goes forth; and He cannot be pleased with adults who mock

---

[74] PlutoBooks.com, "Transgender Marxism," book edited by Jules Joanne Gleeson and Elle O'Rourke, Pluto Press, undated post, https://www.plutobooks.com/9780745341668/transgender-marxism/.

His creations—who thumb their noses at the idea of fixed sexes, male and female, formed wonderfully in the womb.

What of a country that continues its open rebellion of God? From Jeremiah 18:

> And if at any time I declare concerning a nation or a kingdom that I will build and plant it, and if it does evil in my sight, not listening to my voice, then I will repent of the good which I had intended to do to it. (Jer. 18:9–10, RSV)

The consequences are clear.

The LGBTQ lies must be stopped before families are destroyed, children are destroyed, and the building blocks of all of society are destroyed. And the main way to stop the lies is simple: quit fueling the liars by participating in their lies. If a waiter who's obviously a male is wearing a nametag at a restaurant that contains the pronouns "she/her" and then insists on being addressed as a female—refuse. Find another restaurant. Quit enabling lunacy and evil.

CHAPTER 4

IT'S REALLY LOOKING LIKE AN OLIGARCHY OUT THERE

The Founding Fathers warned that a limited form of government could only survive if the nation's people were moral and virtuous. The same holds true for a free market. A capitalist system cannot last if the people in charge of the system are immoral, rudderless, adrift on a sea solely of greed, all-consumed by lusts for money and material gain, and entirely devoid of virtue and biblical principles. Immoral capitalists are just as destructive to a free society as Marxists. As a matter of fact, a free market that's devolved into a winner-take-all, profit-at-all-costs type of system is one that works hand in hand with Marxists, ultimately leading to a plutocracy, an oligarchy, a corporatocracy—fascism.

The delicate balance is that business owners must be moral and conduct their businesses with principle and honor, but without going woke and succumbing to the secular wills of an increasingly demanding, politically charged, and angry consumer base. Just ask Bud Light how quickly a company's fortunes can change. When marketing executives for Anheuser-Busch decided to throw in with secular society and slap the face of a man pretending to be a woman, Dylan Mulvaney, on a beer can as a selling point, the company's profits plummeted.[75] This is a classic, textbook case of failed wokeism. Another way to look at it: companies, like countries, cannot mock God for long without facing consequences.

Business owners who are not virtuous, like politicians who are not virtuous, will constantly try to stretch the boundaries of their powers and become something they're not and seize positions of influence they don't deserve. They will try to become the arbiters of societal goods, of determining societal plusses versus minuses and goods versus evils, rather than remain in their more simplistic roles as material reflections of society at-large. In their arrogance, they will start to believe they hold the keys to a country's prosperity and success. In their prideful boasts of riches and wealth, they will start to see themselves as leaders of not just business but of an entire nation, including its government, culture, and citizens. They will get the idea that they are better than the average Joe and Jane Taxpayer because they have a talent for making money, and because they provide the average Joe and Jane Taxpayer with the means of making their own money.

---

[75] Dee-Ann Durbin, "Bud Light parent says US market share stabilizing after transgender promotion cost sales," Associated Press, August 3, 2023, https://apnews.com/article/bud-light-anheuser-busch-inbev-earnings-46b6412f84b5e8884caea941fc069d2f.

They will see themselves as sorts of gods, deserving of special treatment, entitled to special benefits. From 1 Timothy:

> As for the rich in this world, charge them not to be haughty, nor to set their hopes on uncertain riches but on God who richly furnishes us with everything to enjoy. They are to do good, to be rich in good deeds, liberal and generous, thus laying up for themselves a good foundation for the future, so that they may take hold of the life which is life indeed. (1 Tim. 6:17–19, RSV)

When capitalists go down this road—when business owners become so successful their pride dominates, their money becomes their manna, and their own minds turn into tools of self-worship—then it's a time of peril for the free market.

This is when the economic tools of freedom are turned into weapons of enslavement.

This is the time when capitalism crumbles and the same wicked entities who exploit government for personal power also use businesses to boot-stomp individual liberties. This is the time when the anti-American forces like Barack Obama and the socialists like Alexandria Ocasio-Cortez come out of their dark corners to rail against fat-cat capitalists and unfair, discriminatory business owners—and because the market has turned down a path of immorality, these anti-American forces and socialists actually start to have a valid point. They have their wedge issue. They have that crack in the door of capitalism that they can fling wide open with cries of equal wages for all, demands of redistributions of wealth, catcalls for more money for the poor, and insistence for government controls on the free market—so as to make it a fairer market for all.

You didn't build that.[76]

It's not yours; it belongs to us all.

America's free market is truly in this danger zone, tipping partway free and partway controlled. The future of capitalism depends entirely on the moral compass of American citizens, the ability of these morally compassed citizens to resist globalism, and the awareness of both elected leaders and the electorate to see how the free market is being eroded by Marxist international powers, one tame-sounding, seemingly kind and compassionate talking point at a time.

Much is taking place behind the scenes to move America from a sovereign nation—guided by the Constitution and a democratic republic form of government, where the citizens elect the leaders, but then the leaders are limited in their powers by a system of separate branches that emphasizes individualism and rule of law—into a state-run cesspool of collectivism, where businesses work not for owners and profits but for social justice, and where the economy is run entirely by communists.

They call this a democracy.

And that's the first of the tame-sounding, seemingly kind and compassionate talking points—the devil in disguise. America is not a democracy, nor should it ever become a democracy.

James Madison had much to say about the problems of a democracy versus the solution of a republic in his "Federalist No. 10," where he discussed the inevitable factions that would result from a free society. His basic argument was that a democratic

76 Aaron Blake, "Obama's 'You didn't build that' problem," *Washington Post*, July 18, 2012, https://www.washingtonpost.com/blogs/the-fix/post/obamas-you-didnt-build-that-problem/2012/07/18/gJQAJxyotW_blog.html.

form of government ultimately leads to various parties banding together in common interest—whether political, cultural, or personal—and that these factions then try to exert powers and controls in the political realms. Given the impossibility in removing factions from society, Madison instead recommended placing controls, or checks, on their abilities to sway government to bend to ever-changing wills.

Among his words:

> [A] pure democracy, by which I mean a society consisting of a small number of citizens, who assemble and administer the government in person, can admit of no cure for the mischiefs of faction. A common passion or interest will, in almost every case, be felt by a majority of the whole; a communication and concert result from the form of government itself; and there is nothing to check the inducements to sacrifice the weaker party or an obnoxious individual. Hence it is that such democracies have ever been spectacles of turbulence and contention... and have in general been as short in their lives as they have been violent in their deaths.... A republic, by which I mean a government in which the scheme of representation takes place, opens a different prospect, and promises the cure for which we are seeking.... The two great points of difference between a democracy and a republic are: first, the delegation of the government, in the latter, to a small number of citizens elected by the rest; secondly, the

greater number of citizens, and greater sphere of country, over which the latter may be extended.[77]

In other words: a democracy leads to mob rule, while a republic lays a foundation of laws and order that govern the masses.

Madison, in this same "Federalist No. 10," also gave this clear warning: "Theoretic politicians, who have patronized this species of government, have erroneously supposed that by reducing mankind to a perfect equality in their political rights, they would, at the same time, be perfectly equalized and assimilated in their possessions, their opinions, and their passions."[78]

That is the guiding theme of today's Democrats—a call to arms for an equality determined by a socially conscious government with politicians in power to distribute and redistribute as they see fit. This is what democracy breeds: socialism, and ultimately, communism. This is why Democrats and their partners in the globalist governments push democracy, democracy, democracy as the ideal and refuse to recognize that America is a republic and was always intended to stay a republic. Once leftists are able to kill the idea of America as a republic, they'll then be able to kill the idea of America as a free market—indeed, as even a free society.

Take note and beware. Behind the scenes, quietly, but determinedly, the Democrat Party has been working with governments of the world to mainstream democracy, remove the republic tag, and forge corporate-political partnerships dedicated to doing just that.

And nobody's been a better friend to globalists than the puppet president, Joe Biden.

In December 2021, Biden delivered remarks to open the first Summit for Democracy, a gathering of leaders from more than one hundred nations, to discuss ways of advancing democratic principles around the world.[79] In 2023, the second Summit for Democracy, cohosted by Biden and advocating for more of the same, took place.[80] Sounds great. But the fine print is revealing. This summit, this organization, and this entire campaign are simply an extension of the United Nations' sustainable development and 2030 Agenda goals. That it's hosted by an American president, and under the umbrella of the US State Department, speaks volumes.[81]

It says that America is ready to cede its sovereignty for global governance.

America, with the Constitution, with an ideal of exceptionalism that's encapsulated in the phrase "God-given individual liberties," does not need to band together with the likes of Colombia and the Czech Republic, Moldova and Nigeria, or Senegal and Tonga in order to govern with law and with order in

---

[79] President Joe Biden, "Fact Sheet: Announcing the Presidential Initiative for Democratic Renewal," The White House Briefing Room, December 9, 2021, https://www.whitehouse.gov/briefing-room/statements-releases/2021/12/09/fact-sheet-announcing-the-presidential-initiative-for-democratic-renewal/.

[80] U.S. Department of State, "Summit for Democracy 2023: The March 2023 Summit," U.S. Department of State, 2023, https://www.state.gov/summit-for-democracy-2023/.

[81] U.S. Department of State, "Declaration of the Summit for Democracy," U.S. Department of State Bureau of Democracy, Human Rights and Labor, March 29, 2023, https://www.state.gov/declaration-of-the-summit-for-democracy-2023/#:~:text=We%20believe%20democratic%20institutions%2C%20which,and%20live%20without%20fear%20of.

a way that upholds human rights, in a manner that guarantees equality for all.[82] America does not need to play host to a gathering of world leaders, either, who tie and bind US legislators, judicial officials, public servants, and, ultimately, free citizens to standards that are agreed upon by these world leaders—these unelected, unaccountable-to-the-American-voter world leaders. America's already in deep with the United Nations; Americans don't need another layer of global bureaucracy breathing hot demands for tax dollars, compliance, and obedience.

But this is what the Summit for Democracy advances—a global governance goal that's antithetical to individualism. And it comes with ongoing commitments and requirements for accountability. The 2021 summit provided the marching orders for 2022 action; the 2023 summit served as a check and fine-tuning for further action. All in the name of democracy. All in the name of a form of government that will destroy America, crumble capitalism, and cripple the Constitution.

From the 2023 "Declaration of the Summit for Democracy":

- "We, the leaders of the Summit for Democracy, reaffirm our shared belief that democracy—government reflecting the effective participation and will of the people—is humanity's most enduring means to advance peace, prosperity, equality, sustainable development and security."[83] No. This premise is flawed.

---

[82] U.S. State Department, "Summit for Democracy 2021: Invited Participants," U.S. State Department, 2021, https://www.state.gov/participant-list-the-summit-for-democracy/.

[83] U.S. Department of State, "Declaration of the Summit for Democracy," State Department Bureau of Democracy, Human Rights and Labor, March 29, 2023, https://www.state.gov/declaration-of-the-summit-for-democracy-2023/#:~:text=We%20believe%20democratic%20institutions%2C%20which,and%20live%20without%20fear%20of.

- "We recognize that democracy can take many forms, but shares common characteristics."[84] Actually, democracy is democracy; but that's the basic problem with democracy, as James Madison explained. It does indeed shift into many forms—all leading away from a government that's limited in power.

- "[Democracy] shares…free and fair elections that are inclusive and accessible; separation of powers; checks and balances; peaceful transitions of power; an independent media and safety of journalists; transparency; access to information; accountability; inclusion; gender equality; civic participation; equal protection of the law; and respect for human rights, including freedoms of expression, peaceful assembly, and association."[85] Read the following: America's Constitution and America's Declaration of Independence, based on the ideal of God-given rights and liberties, already offer these protections for citizens. Rather than committing America to the terms of the Summit for Democracy, the White House ought to have instead sent copies of the Constitution of the United States to all the various heads of state attending these summits. America is already the ideal: the shining city on the hill.

- "To meet the rising challenges to democracy worldwide, we commit to strengthen democratic institutions and processes and build resilience."[86] America, through a variety of public, private, and non-profit organizations and missions—and when necessary, through

---

[84] Ibid.
[85] Ibid.
[86] Ibid.

the military—already accomplishes this goal. In fiscal year 2022, American taxpayers provided $69 billion in foreign aid for 210 countries, according to ForeignAssistance.gov. Most of that money—$38.72 billion and $21.35 billion, respectively—was managed by the US Agency for International Development, or USAID, and by the State Department. The remaining were disbursed through a range of other agencies, including the departments of Treasury, Defense, Health and Human Services, Agriculture, Energy, and the Interior, as well as through the Millennium Challenge Corporation, the Peace Corps, and a handful of miscellaneous groups. More than $16 billion went for humanitarian assistance, nearly $16 billion for health aid, an estimated $12 billion each for peace/security and then for economic development; and the rest for a range of other activities, including to spread democracy and advance human rights. In fiscal year 2023, the monetary commitments from US taxpayers for 207 countries were similarly significant. By mid-November 2023, America had already disbursed $40 billion in aid for the same sorts of services, through the same federal agencies, and another $50 billion had already been requested by the White House, as part of the president's 2024 fiscal budget. In other words: the last thing American taxpayers need is to commit to yet another foreign aid slush fund for globalists promising to advance democracy.[87]

---

[87] ForeignAssistance.gov, databases on U.S. aid to foreign nations, accessed on November 24, 2023, updated on November 17, 2023, https://www.foreignassistance.gov/.

- "We acknowledge that freedom and democracy are strengthened through cooperation."[88] Actually, we don't—and by "we," of course, it's meant as American patriots who know history, specifically, the causes of the rising and falling of free societies, and who cherish the type of liberty that comes from the Creator. It's by an emphasis on individualism, God-given liberties, and a system of government that both recognizes and protects those concepts—primarily with a rule of law that's not easily shifted by ever-changing whims of democracy-clamoring mobs—that freedom is actually strengthened. Cooperation, as globalists mean it, is another word for collectivism. Take note. This is what the Summit for Democracy is all about: spreading collectivism, which is to say communism, which is to say, total top-down global governance, around the world—including in America.

And here's where the Declaration of the Summit for Democracy makes that clear:

> Globally, we commit to put the strength of our democracies into action to revitalize, consolidate, and strengthen an international rules-based order that delivers equitable, sustainable development for all people and to deepen international cooperation to accelerate progress on the 2030 Agenda for Sustainable Development

---

[88] U.S. Department of State, "Declaration of the Summit for Democracy," State Department Bureau of Democracy, Human Rights and Labor, March 29, 2023, https://www.state.gov/declaration-of-the-summit-for-democracy-2023/#:~:text=We%20believe%20democratic%20institutions%2C%20which,and%20live%20without%20fear%20of.

and the 17 Sustainable Development Goals. We acknowledge that eradicating poverty is critical to strengthening inclusivity and building confidence and stability in democracies globally. We recognize that democracies that respect human rights are the best means by which to solve the 21st Century's most critical challenges. We remain united in supporting one another in our efforts to bolster democracy domestically, regionally, and internationally, combat authoritarian trends, advance multilateral and multistakeholder dialogue and cooperation, and safeguard the full and effective exercise of human rights, including civil and political rights, as well as the progressive realization of economic, social, and cultural rights. We are determined to save the present and succeeding generations from the scourge of war. To this end we unite the strength of our democracies to secure and maintain domestic, regional, and international peace and security.[89]

If the Summit for Democracy participants were truly committed to respecting human rights, combating authoritarianism, and safeguarding civil and political rights, the declaration would have called for harsh actions against China. It would have named China, Iran, North Korea, or other dictatorial, tyrannical, and

---

[89] U.S. Department of State, "Declaration of the Summit for Democracy," State Department Bureau of Democracy, Human Rights and Labor, March 29, 2023, https://www.state.gov/declaration-of-the-summit-for-democracy-2023/#:~:text=We%20believe%20democratic%20institutions%2C%20which,and%20live%20without%20fear%20of.

terrorist-sponsoring regimes as enemies of the free world and called for partnering efforts to destroy the enemies. But the Summit for Democracy is not so much concerned with obliterating the evil as enriching the powers and pockets of the elite and elect—even if it means working with the evil, within the realms of evil, or, at the very least, ignoring the evil in order to achieve success for the elites and elect few.

The Summit for Democracy is simply another mechanism for fooling the sheeple and duping the masses into believing government is good and that the bigger the government, the more global the government, the more of this good that government can achieve. It's bureaucratic bullcrap, nothing more.

The United Nations' "17 Goals" of Sustainable Development are as follows:

1. No poverty
2. Zero hunger
3. Good health and well-being
4. Quality education
5. Gender equality
6. Clean water and sanitation
7. Affordable and clean energy
8. Decent work and economic growth
9. Industry, innovation, and infrastructure
10. Reduced inequalities
11. Sustainable cities and communities
12. Responsible consumption and production
13. Climate action
14. Life below water (taking care of sea life)
15. Life on land (taking care of mammal life)
16. Peace, justice, and strong institutions

17. Partnerships for the goals (forging successful, long-last-
ing collaborative ties)[90]

They're worthy pursuits—Christian pursuits, even. But not
if it means ceding freedoms—ceding sovereignty—to a global
governing board with members who will forever control human
behaviors. A free market is the solution to almost every issue
that presents on that list. Interestingly, and tellingly, the United
Nations does not call for freer markets as the solution but rather
collaborations among governments; greater powers for these
governments to exert controls on production, development, and
economies; broader reach for the specially selected bureaucrats
at the top of the government chain; redistribution of wealth,
material resources, and manpower; and open borders so that
those born in nations with fewer resources and opportunities
may travel and relocate to nations with greater resources and
opportunities—it's only fair and equitable, after all.

In America, churches and charities help with poverty eradi-
cation and hunger.

At the United Nations, churches and charities are the ways
of fools.

In America, capitalism and free markets allow for individuals
to use their talents, skills, experiences, education—their dreams,
purposes, and missions, as planted by God at birth—to build,
create, pursue, explore, and the like as a means of making money,
supporting their families, helping others, leaving legacies, contributing to humanity, and all along, living independently.

---

[90] United Nations Department of Economic and Social Affairs, Sustainable
Development, "The 17 Goals," United Nations, accessed November 24,
2023, https://sdgs.un.org/goals.

At the United Nations, the entrepreneurial spirit is only something to be subdued and twisted for the use of the state, for the betterment of the collective, for the exploitation of the select and elite. Why? Globalists' worst nightmare is an independent citizenry—a citizenry who does not need government, a citizenry of capable entrepreneurs, skilled workers, and proud patriots who shun entitlements because they don't need entitlements.

This is why America's capitalist system is constantly under attack.

This is why a properly morally compassed corporate world, where executives take their marching orders from God and biblical principles, is imperative: there are far too many devious globalist minds who are gunning for America's resources, and it takes a discerning businessman or woman to see all the strategic attacks on the capitalist system. If they can't see the attacks, they can't fight the attackers. If they can't see the battlefield, they can't win the battle.

They're coming for the young people.

"Welcome to Our Future Agenda, a new program by the UN Foundation that empowers young changemakers to be the agents of change for a sustainable 2100 world. UN Foundation's Our Future Agenda program offers a unique platform for young innovators, entrepreneurs, and champions to reimagine the UN for 21st-century needs. We tap into young people's energy, collectivism, and long-term vision, fostering collective action, building alliances, and fortifying support for the United Nations. It's all about fostering international cooperation to drive solutions to our shared challenges, something we need now more than ever."[91]

Train the children in the way of collectivism, and they will grow up and become the next generation of communist leaders.

They're coming for the business owners.

From Summit for Democracy's "Call to the Private Sector to Advance Democracy" early 2023 document on the US State Department's website comes the following:

> Democracy increases GDP [Gross Domestic Product], democratic governments pursue more economic reforms, reduce social unrest, and see higher business investment than non-democracies. Companies, therefore, have an incentive and vital role to uphold and protect democratic norms, principles, and institutions. Private sector impacts can be felt far beyond employees, extending to customers, suppliers, partners, and local communities. In advance of the Summit, the United States government invites private sector partners to join efforts to advance an affirmative agenda for democratic renewal and tackle the greatest threats faced by democracies today.[92]

91 United Nations Foundation, "Our Future Agenda: Unlocking the Power of Next and Future Generations," Our Future Agenda, accessed November 25, 2023, https://ourfutureagenda.org/.

92 U.S. Department of State, "Summit for Democracy: Call to the Private Sector to Advance Democracy," March 2023, accessed November 25, 2023, https://www.state.gov/wp-content/uploads/2023/02/Private-Sector-Call-to-Advance-Democracy-1.pdf.

What is that affirmative agenda? Again, it sounds worthy—combating corruption and the misuse of technology, protecting the public spaces, and advancing the rights of employees in the work force. But again, the devil's in the details. Employers and business owners who are moral and principled don't need government overseers who dictate how their businesses must operate. Employers and business owners who are rooted in biblical values don't require Big Government handlers regulating and controlling their operations. But this is what the Summit for Democracy seeks: control of the free market. The Summit for Democracy, for example, wants business owners to use only US State Department–approved surveillance technology—which is to say, technology that meets the "UN Guiding Principles on Business and Human Rights." What's that? From the US State Department's webpage on "Guidance on Implementing the 'UN Guiding Principles' for Transactions Linked to Foreign Government End-Users for Products or Services With Surveillance Capabilities" is this: "This guidance is a first-of-its-kind tool intended to provide practical and accessible human rights guidance to U.S. businesses seeking to prevent their products or services with surveillance capabilities from being misused by government end-users to commit human rights abuses.... This guidance also recommends human rights safeguards if a U.S. business considers proceeding with a transaction, such as developing a grievance mechanism, and publicly reporting on sales practices."[93]

---

[93] U.S. Department of State, "U.S. Department of State Guidance on Implementing the 'UN Guiding Principles' for Transactions Linked to Foreign Government End-Users for Products or Services with Surveillance Capabilities," U.S. Department of State Bureau of Democracy, Human Rights, and Labor, September 30, 2020, https://www.state.gov/key-topics-bureau-of-democracy-human-rights-and-labor/due-diligence-guidance/.

Since when do US companies in the business of making and selling spy gear have to obtain the OK of the United Nations to pitch their products overseas?

"Business enterprises should respect human rights," the "UN Guiding Principles on Businesses and Human Rights" states. "This means that they should avoid infringing on the human rights of others and should address adverse human rights impacts with which they are involved."[94]

Ostensibly, any surveillance could be argued as a privacy infringement—meaning, an infringement of human rights. See where this is headed? Meanwhile, the Biden administration is fully in favor of such globalist controls on America's free market.

When Biden opened the first Summit for Democracy in December 2021, he also announced his "Presidential Initiative for Democratic Renewal," a set of initiatives that builds on the very anti-America, pro-globalist agenda from the Summit for Democracy. Among the pages of its fact sheet was an announcement of a new Treasury Department program to increase "reporting requirements for those closest to real estate transactions"—aimed at fighting corruption in the real estate market; an announcement of a $6.5 million State Department fund for government and businesses to work together to fight corruption; and funding from USAID, the Labor Department, and the State Department in the total of $137 million to launch a

---

[94] U.S. Department of State, "U.S. Department of State Guidance on Implementing the 'UN Guiding Principles' for Transactions Linked to Foreign Government End-Users for Products or Services with Surveillance Capabilities," U.S. Department of State, published 2020, accessed November 25, 2023, p. 4, https://www.state.gov/wp-content/uploads/2020/10/DRL-Industry-Guidance-Project-FINAL-1-pager-508-1.pdf.

couple of social protest groups.[95]The exact words of the directive are as follows:

> USAID will provide up to $15 million to launch the Powered by the People initiative, which will assist nonviolent social movements by increasing coordination through exchanges, seed grants, and engagement with younger pro-democracy actors. Additionally, the Departments of Labor and State, and USAID, will provide up to $122 million to establish a Multilateral Partnership for Organizing, Worker Empowerment, and Rights (M-POWER), which will help workers around the world claim their rights and improve wages and conditions by strengthening democratic and independent worker organizations and supporting labor law reform and enforcement.[96]

That's social activism and union protesting, courtesy of the president of the United States—courtesy of the US taxpayers.

They're coming for the investment firms.

Like much within the halls of global governance, there are layers upon layers of committees, groups, task forces, summit organizers and organizations, associations, and the like. And they all carry their various acronym names—making it all the more difficult to track and trace their doings and goings-on and

---

[95] President Joe Biden, "Fact Sheet: Announcing the Presidential Initiative for Democratic Renewal," White House briefing room, December 9, 2021, https://www.whitehouse.gov/briefing-room/statements-releases/2021/12/09/fact-sheet-announcing-the-presidential-initiative-for-democratic-renewal/.

[96] Ibid.

hold them accountable for actions and expenditures. But alongside the Summit for Democracy, working again beneath the umbrella of the United Nations, comes this convoluted attack on free markets:

> On June 18, 2018, a group called the Global Impact Investing Network, or GIIN, hosted a webinar called, "IRIS Standards Series: The UN SDGs, IRIS, and the Investor Perspective." The webinar "addressed the United Nations Sustainable Development Goals' (SDGs) connection to IRIS, and shed light on how two different investors are integrating the SDGs into their impact measurement and management (IMM) practices. IRIS, managed by the GIIN, is leading an industry-wide effort to bring clarity to the myriad impact measurement and management metrics, tools, and methodologies available today.[97]

The takeaway is that the United Nations, GIIN, the SDGs, and IRIS are all linked. So, what's GIIN?

GIIN is a non-profit that aims to facilitate "impact investing," or socially conscious investing, and its call to action for corporations goes like this: "When it comes to corporate investing and asset management, companies can do more. With USD $2 trillion held by U.S. companies alone, corporations

[97] Global Impact Investing Network, "IRIS Standards Series Webinar: The UN, SDGs, IRIS and the Investor Perspective," GIIN, June 18, 2018, https://thegiin.org/iris-standards-series-webinar-the-un-sdgs,-iris,-and-the-investor-perspective/.

have enormous potential to leverage impact investments and partnerships toward addressing urgent environmental and social needs."[98]

The takeaway is that GIIN—like the World Economic Forum's Great Reset initiative (which will be discussed further in chapter 8), like the Biden administration's Build Back Better plan, like the radical environmental world's climate change activism and alarmism—is committed toward slipping and sliding far-leftist "woke" policies into all its civic, business, and political work, with the ultimate end game of controlling populations and bringing about global communism. GIIN's particular area of focus to accomplish this end game is the financial sector. So, what's IRIS? According to its webpage:

> IRIS+ is the generally accepted system for impact investors to measure, manage, and optimize their impact.... It is a free, publicly available resource that is managed by the Global Impact Investing Network (GIIN).... The GIIN offers the IRIS+ system to support the practice of impact investing and promote transparency, credibility, and accountability in the use of impact data for decision making across the impact investment industry.... Use of IRIS+ allows investors to focus their capital allocation decisions and drive greater impact on

---

[98] Global Impact Investing Network, "Join the Corporate Impact Investing Initiative," GIIN, accessed November 25, 2023, https://thegiin.org/corporate-impact-investing-initiative/.

the world's most pressing social and environmental issues.[99]

The takeaway is that companies within GIIN's circle are monitored by a GIIN-owned data collection and analysis system called IRIS+ that ensures compliance with GIIN's socially conscious investment standards—which, remember, are based on the United Nations' 17 Goals of Sustainable Development.

Companies and the free market: they're the frontier of the future for the control freaks of the world.

"Corporations are critical to scaling the most promising solutions for the pressing challenges in our local communities and around the world. By working with impact investors, companies can discover new possibilities to help build a sustainable, just, and inclusive future," said GIIN CEO and cofounder Amit Bouri, as reported by PYMTS in September 2022.[100]

They won't stop with a few corporations. They won't stop until the entire capitalist system has been completely overhauled and upended.

They're coming for capitalism itself.

Ultimately, GIIN, using its IRIS data system of accountability, will shift the free market into a new mold, one that serves those who play along with the UN quest for sustainable development—and one that leaves companies who don't play in the cold. It's called the GIIN New Capitalism Initiative, and it's designed "to transform economic systems…towards the future

---

[99] IRIS.TheGiin.org, "IRIS+System: About," IRIS+, accessed November 25, 2023, https://iris.thegiin.org/about/.

[100] PYMTS, "PayPal Partners With GIIN, Telus, Visa on Impact Investing Project," PYMTS, September 23, 2022, https://www.pymnts.com/partnerships/2022/paypal-partners-with-giin-telus-visa-on-impact-investing-project/.

of capitalism—the next normal," according to its website.[101] Here is more from the site:

> What might the future of capitalism look like? How can we reshape economic systems and capitalist societies to drive toward this next normal through efforts such as the New Capitalism Project?... The New Capitalism Project (NCP) was launched in February 2020 as an effort to explore how diverse stakeholders, such as members of the business and finance community, economists, policy makers, grassroots organizers and more, who have shared goals in building a more just, inclusive, and equitable economic system, can better align their work aimed at driving systemic change.... [GIIN and others] engage leaders from the fields of impact investing, sustainable business, economic justice.... These efforts are driven by the question, "How can we move from isolated interventions to aligned action, so that we can accomplish more together than we could by working alone?"[102]

The takeaway is this: collectivists are controlling the free market—which is to say, collectivists are turning capitalism into communism—and calling it the New Capitalism.

GIIN records its membership at 440 organizations in fifty-nine countries, including asset owners, asset managers, and

---

[101] Global Impact Investing Network, "New Capitalism Initiative," GIIN, accessed November 25, 2023, https://thegiin.org/new-capitalism/.
[102] Ibid.

service providers.[103] Among them? Bank of America. Citi. Deutsche Bank. JPMorgan Chase & Co. Morgan Stanley. CTBC Financial Holding. PayPal. Liberty Mutual Insurance Group. Prudential. MassMutual. The Mastercard Foundation. The Ford Foundation. The Heron Foundation. Rockefeller Brothers Fund. Soros Economic Development Fund. The Annie E. Casey Foundation. The Rockefeller Foundation. Visa Foundation. WHO Foundation. Deloitte. Microsoft. Catholic Relief Services. BlackRock. Village Capital. Vox Capital. And many, many, many more.

This goes beyond any ability to boycott.

This comes to the point where any business trying to do business will have to join in the business of social justice, woke, climate alarmist, elitist agenda warring—or not do business.

And that is what the globalists want. That has been their goal all along.

"In 2008, the Rockefeller Foundation gathered a group of pioneering impact investors to identify and being to address critical barriers to investing for social and environmental impact, while also expecting a financial return. These investors, many of whom became the founding members of the Global Impact Investing Network (GIIN) Investors' Council, identified a lack of transparency and credibility in how funds define, track, and report the social and environmental performance of their portfolios," the IRIS+ System webpage wrote.[104]

Control the money. Control the businesses. Control how the people buy and sell and save and invest. This is all just a

[103] Global Impact Investing Network, "About Membership," GIIN, accessed November 25, 2023, https://thegiin.org/about-membership/.
[104] IRIS.TheGIIN.org, "IRIS+ System: About," IRIS webpage, accessed November 25, 2023, https://iris.thegiin.org/history/.

small glimpse of how elites with little concern for American sovereignty, American entrepreneurial spirit, and American free markets are busily, behind the scenes and for the betterment of only their own pockets and self-pride, killing capitalism, one collectivist win at a time. The quest for money has become the quest for power.

"Put not your trust in princes, in a son of man, in whom there is no help. When his breath departs he returns to his earth; on that very day his plans perish," Psalm 146:3–4 (RSV) reminds.

Money is not evil. But money in the hands of immoral men and women can accomplish much evil. It's neither trite nor inaccurate to say that the fate of America's free market rests completely on the determination of American business owners to build first on biblical principles, and then from there, the rest may flow. Capitalism, like a republic, can only last so long as the people are moral and virtuous.

CHAPTER 5

THE CHIP WAR, AND THE GROWING NATIONAL SECURITY THREAT FROM RISING SECULARISM

I n the late 1950s, American companies were the leading producers of the world's microchips, the building blocks of technology.[105] But at the very same time, while computers were increasing in power in extraordinary amounts—by a trillion-fold between 1956 and 2015, according to one analysis—America was busily farming out its chip production to overseas spots.[106] Sad, meet sorry. In 1990, American-made chips fulfilled about 37 percent of the world's demand; currently, that figure is in the

---

[105] Don Clark and Ana Swanson, "U.S. Pours Money Into Chips, but Even Soaring Spending Has Limits," *New York Times*, January 1, 2023, https://www.nytimes.com/2023/01/01/technology/us-chip-making-china-invest.html.

[106] ASML, "The Basics of Microchips," ASML Holding, accessed November 30, 2023, https://www.asml.com/en/technology/all-about-microchips/microchip-basics.

range of 12 percent.[107] Taiwan, meanwhile, produces more than 60 percent of the world's semiconductors, most at the Taiwan Semiconductor Manufacturing Corporation, or TSMC, and 90 percent of the most advanced kinds.[108] But China is coming on strong. The communist country has a stated goal to become the global leader for chip production by 2030.[109]

The big deal is this: chips mean technology. Technology means power. The nation with the best technology is the nation that will dominate the world in the coming years—generations, even.

And right now, America's at a distinct disadvantage—and to China, no less. How did this happen? More specifically, how could those in US leadership positions in politics allow this to happen?

That's the question going forward because if Congress doesn't get its act together—if those who were elected to, first and foremost, defend this nation from all enemies, both foreign and domestic, don't get their butts in gear, along with whomever serves as president and in the executive agencies, both in the near and far futures—America the great will be America the servant.

---

[107] Katie Canales, "The US produces just 12% of the world's computer chip supply. Here's why it's trailing China when it comes to manufacturing and how it plans to get ahead," Business Insider, April 17, 2021, https://www.businessinsider.com/why-us-doesnt-make-chips-semiconductor-shortage-2021-4#:~:text=It%20became%20cheaper%20to%20build,regulation%20in%20places%20like%20Asia.

[108] *The Economist*, "Taiwan's dominance of the chip industry makes it more important," *The Economist*, March 6, 2023, https://www.economist.com/special-report/2023/03/06/taiwans-dominance-of-the-chip-industry-makes-it-more-important.

[109] Katie Canales, "The US produces just 12% of the world's computer chip supply. Here's why it's trailing China when it comes to manufacturing and how it plans to get ahead," Business Insider, April 17, 2021, https://www.businessinsider.com/why-us-doesnt-make-chips-semiconductor-shortage-2021-4#:~:text=It%20became%20cheaper%20to%20build,regulation%20in%20places%20like%20Asia.

America, on the technology front, will have been conquered by the Chinese Communist Party (CCP). And that means America, on the freedom front, will have been destroyed.

It's not as if we couldn't have seen this coming. Clearly, the dire situation America now faces was (a) entirely preventable, (b) due to curious failures on the part of either feckless, unconcerned, or outright unpatriotic politicians, and (c) a massive bureaucratic misstep that will prove a game changer on the geo-political front, potentially bringing ominous consequences for American sovereignty, American liberty, and truly, America as we know it.

Could this be a comeuppance for an America that's turned away from God?

From Isaiah 1, on God's handling of the wicked Judah:

> Ah, sinful nation, a people laden with iniquity, offspring of evildoers, sons who deal corruptly! They have forsaken the Lord, they have despised the Holy One of Israel, they are utterly estranged. Why will you still be smitten, that you continue to rebel? The whole head is sick, and the whole heart faint….Your country lies desolate, your cities are burned with fire; in your very presence aliens devour your land; it is desolate, as overthrown by aliens.
>
> (Isaiah 1:4–5; Isaiah 1:7, RSV)

America hasn't quite reached this stage of desolation, with foreign conquerors setting fire to the land. But that's not so much a sign of America's spiritual health and righteousness as it is a show of God's patience and grace. There's a reason America is waning in many respects while China is rising. If God judges nations, as the Bible makes clear He does, then the leaders, who are ambivalent about threats and careless with security, and the citizens, who are blinded to dangers and distracted with leisurely pursuits, are certainly evidences of His displeasure.

How this chip war plays out will serve as a pinnacle moment for America: either we lose to a godless communist country, due to our own godless government and society, or we recalibrate on a nationwide scale to a godlier culture, leading to godlier politics, leading to a nation where God leads, and subsequently, to a nation that God saves.

First, the background. America began to outsource its chip production for economic reasons.

"It became cheaper to build chip facilities in countries outside of the US," Business Insider wrote in 2021. "Those foreign governments offer more attractive financial incentives to construct semiconductor factories, like tax breaks and grants. There's also less regulation in places like Asia. On top of that, there aren't as many jobs in the US created to run such high-tech factories."[110]

Maybe. But those are all reasons tied to government failures.

It's government that controls the financial incentives, like favorable tax deals. It's government that inflicts burdensome regulations or eases regulations, thereby either stifling or opening the free market for production and development. It's government that impacts the ability of businesses to expand its hiring—or

<hr>

[110] Katie Canales, "The US produces just 12% of the world's computer chip supply. Here's why it's trailing China when it comes to manufacturing and how it plans to get ahead," Business Insider, April 17, 2021, https://www.businessinsider.com/why-us-doesnt-make-chips-semiconductor-shortage-2021-4#:~:text=It%20became%20cheaper%20to%20build,regulation%20in%20places%20like%20Asia.

not. It's government that sets the stage for public school successes or failures in the very fields necessary for skilled technological workers, that is, the fields of mathematics and sciences. America has moved from a nation of creators and producers to a nation that farms out its manufacturing. In the case of chips, American policy shifted from one of industry to one of science—where investments, both public and private, went toward the building and development of chips and toward the research necessary to stay ahead of the curve, where investment dollars instead fostered a more scholarly, collaborative environment.

Here's an excellent description from Employ America:

> Science policy focused on fostering public-private partnerships with individual firms, the closer integration of industry R&D with academic R&D, a broad division of research labor, and an industry structure that allowed innovative firms to run asset-light. The goal of policy shifted from creating a robust competitive ecosystem with strong supply chains, to creating public-private institutions to coordinate complex handoffs between researchers, fabless design firms, equipment suppliers and large-scale "champion firms." This way, no firms would need to spend more than absolutely necessary on R&D—preserving global cost

competitiveness—while the government would also avoid large-scale investment spending.[111]

In brief, America moved from making to not so much making. Why is that?

In the 1950s and 1960s, the US military demand for top technological developments led to a government flow of money for research and development in chips.[112] In the 1970s, the private sector latched on to the genius of semiconductors and seized on the technology, surpassing the government and military in terms of investment and development.[113] US private company innovation surged; America dominated the chip market globally until the 1980s and, after a couple of ebbs and flows, again in the early 1990s, but faced concerted struggles to stay at the top, particularly after Japan shifted into high gear and went into competitive mode.[114]

Japan's industrial policy focused on exploiting both the market and products America had already created. It identified the most sought after and easiest sale—in terms of making a layperson's case for its importance—of the various US-developed

[111] Alex Williams and Hassan Khan, "A Brief History of Semiconductors: How the US Cut Costs and Lost the Leading Edge," Employ America, March 20, 2021, https://employamerica.medium.com/a-brief-history-of-semiconductors-how-the-us-cut-costs-and-lost-the-leading-edge-c21b96707cd2.

[112] Don Clark and Ana Swanson, "U.S. Pours Money Into Chips, but Even Soaring Spending Has Limits," *New York Times*, January 1, 2023, https://www.nytimes.com/2023/01/01/technology/us-chip-making-china-invest.html.

[113] David Gewirtz, "Technology that changed us: The 1970s, from Pong to Apollo," ZDNET, June 28, 2019, https://www.zdnet.com/article/technology-that-changed-us-the-1970s/.

[114] Michaela D. Platzer, John F. Sargent Jr., and Karen M. Sutter, "Semiconductors: U.S. Industry, Global Competition, and Federal Policy," Congressional Research Service, October 26, 2020, https://crsreports.congress.gov/product/pdf/R/R46581.

products in the semiconductor field and put tremendous effort into creating and exporting this single item: the dynamic random access memory, or DRAM, the working memory chips that save data and speed up data-reading processes for devices in their "on" position.[115] American companies, specifically those with heavy concentrations on selling their own DRAM chips, were overwhelmed by the competition from Japan, and many closed while others banded together to lobby government for protection. In 1987, the federally funded SEMATECH, short for Semiconductor Manufacturing Technology, was formed to find new ways to build chip technology into American products.[116] Depending on who is asked, SEMATECH was either plagued by bureaucracy and infighting among contributing companies—T. J. Rodgers, chief executive of Cypress Semiconductor, called it an "exclusive country club" where large chipmakers refused to share their technology—or it was a model of public-private partnership that saved the American chipmaking industry.[117] Either way, SEMATECH helped curb costs, at least for a time.[118] In 2011, *MIT Technology Review* wrote the following:

[115] Editorial Team, "How Japan Beat the US in the First Chip War," Techovedas, August 19, 2023, https://techovedas.com/how-japan-beat-the-us-in-the-first-chip-war/.

[116] Alex Williams and Hassan Khan, "A Brief History of Semiconductors: How the US Cut Costs and Lost the Leading Edge," Employ America, March 20, 2021, https://employamerica.medium.com/a-brief-history-of-semiconductors-how-the-us-cut-costs-and-lost-the-leading-edge-c21b96707cd2.

[117] Robert D. Hof, "Lessons from Sematech," *MIT Technology Review*, July 25, 2011, https://www.technologyreview.com/2011/07/25/192832/lessons-from-sematech/.

[118] DARPA, "SEMATECH," Defense Advanced Research Projects Agency, various webpages, accessed December 2, 2023, https://www.darpa.mil/about-us/timeline/sematech.

[B]efore Sematech, it used to take 30 percent more research and development dollars to bring about each new generation of chip miniaturization, says G. Dan Hutcheson, CEO of market researcher VLSI Research. That increase dropped to 12.5 percent shortly after the advent of Sematech and has since fallen to the low single digits. Perhaps just as important, Sematech set a goal in the early 1990s of compressing miniaturization cycles from three years to two. The industry has done just that since the mid-1990s, speeding innovation throughout the electronics industry and, consequently, the entire economy.[119]

Remember, that analysis comes from 2011. So, yes, for a short period in the 1990s, America once again was a leading maker in the chip market. Since then, markets have changed considerably—and not in America's favor. Costs combined with ongoing competition from Japan and also South Korea have changed America's national policy on the semiconductor market. Post-1990s, the United States shifted from industrial policy to science policy.

These are the years of America's technology downfall.

These are the years America, in the chip industry, went from serving as a leader in innovation, and therefore sales, to an America that more cautiously weighed the balance of cost versus risk; more timidly formed partnerships and collaborations that

---

[119] Robert D. Hof, "Lessons from Sematech," *MIT Technology Review*, July 25, 2011, https://www.technologyreview.com/2011/07/25/192832/lessons-from-sematech/.

included bureaucratic and government efficiency experts and the like; and more disastrously set labor, skill, entrepreneurial pursuits, and competitive spirit as lower considerations than bottom-line dollars and cents. Government investment in this key area of technology plummeted.

Employ America wrote about the change in direction:

> Instead, the government would spend a much smaller amount of money, and attempt to inaugurate a division of labor that would allow all participants to cut costs in pursuit of profitability without sacrificing the technological frontier. To do this, it funded R&D in academic research laboratories on one side and industry groups to translate that research into commercial capabilities on the other. In a way, this further devalued the R&D investments of individual firms, as advancements created only minimal competitive advantages.[120]

Big bureaucratic science became the driver behind private market investment, resulting in little to no financial ability for private sector firms without government contracts to compete. Simultaneously, government policy opened wide the doors for America's foreign competitors to sell on the cheap in US markets and for US manufacturers to compete on the cheap against foreign competitors, further undercutting the ability of the best and brightest in America—particularly those with

---

[120] Alex Williams and Hassan Khan, "A Brief History of Semiconductors: How the US Cut Costs and Lost the Leading Edge," Employ America, March 20, 2021, https://employamerica.medium.com/a-brief-history-of-semiconductors-how-the-us-cut-costs-and-lost-the-leading-edge-c21b96707cd2.

smaller businesses—to both create and remain financially afloat. The dual whammy of bureaucratic controls—that is, science policy—and permissive trade deals actually worked for a time, meaning America saw an uptick in semiconductor revenues. But it didn't last.

"The goal," Employ America wrote, "was [for America] to recapture the technological frontier on the cheap for the public and private sector alike by solving a collective action problem and reducing redundancies in the system as a whole."[121]

And therein lies today's problem.

The further we move from a free market, the further we move toward a government-controlled economy, and the further we move toward putting politicians and their various friends—some of whom may be antithetical to America's own interests—in control of the means of supply and production. With chips, America's gone from that exciting individualistic quest to conquer, dominate, create, provide, problem-solve, and win, win, win—to a slog walk of defeatism, concession, collaboration, and cost-cutting, in soul-sucking, creativity-drowning lockstep with bureaucracy.

Analysis provides a slew of reasons and rationales for America's fall as semiconductor leader, and it's a complicated story that spans decades, but at least one basic takeaway of our demise is this: secular concerns superseded spiritual pursuits. Cost-cutting and profit margins became such the focus that the spirit of entrepreneurialism, the spirit of individualism, and the spirit of exceptionalism that comes from God—fueled by a force to create, and to create to the best of one's ability—were all tossed to the side. Cavalierly. Dangerously. On chips, circa 2023, science

---

[121] Ibid.

policy, not industrial policy, remains the national preference. This is giving rise to America's enemies seizing dominance of the chip market—and it's not as if American leaders couldn't see this coming.

"In the mid-1980s, President [Ronald] Reagan articulated the need to retain US global leadership in chips to counter the Soviet bloc's numerically superior military forces through 'smart' systems driven by semiconductors—satellites, stealth aircraft, cruise missiles, and the like," wrote the Center for Strategic and International Studies in 2022.[122]

Well, the face of the enemy has changed but not the battle.

"China's Share of Global Chip Sales Now Surpasses Taiwan's, Closing in on Europe's and Japan's," ran one headline in January 2022 from the Semiconductor Industry Association.[123]

The threat is real. Without a change in direction, the communists in China will eventually seize control of nearly every facet of human life.

Here's a list of industries and products that rely heavily on semiconductor chips, not including the military:

- Computers: Microprocessors and memory chips are the main components in computers, servers, data centers, and the like that are, in turn, used in almost all modern industries, from healthcare to military to manufacturing

---

[122] Sujai Shivakumar and Charles Wessner, "Semiconductors and National Defense: What Are the Stakes?" Center for Strategic & International Studies, June 8, 2022, https://www.csis.org/analysis/semiconductors-and-national-defense-what-are-stakes.

[123] Semiconductor Industry Association, "China's Share of Global Chip Shares Now Surpasses Taiwan's, Closing in on Europe's and Japan's," SIA, January 10, 2022, https://www.semiconductors.org/chinas-share-of-global-chip-sales-now-surpasses-taiwan-closing-in-on-europe-and-japan/.

to finance. What isn't run by computer nowadays? Chips
are the basic building blocks for computerized technology.

- Telecommunications: Everything from cells phones to
satellite systems, routers to pagers, network equipment
and data transmission hardware to answering machines,
and more—all rely on chips.

- Household appliances: Semiconductors power and reg-
ulate temperatures and timers on refrigerators, washers
and dryers, stoves, air conditioners, microwaves, coffee
pots, and more.

- Automotive and transportation sectors: Chips are used
in passenger cars and trucks, both electric and gas-pow-
ered, as well as in all forms of public transportation—
buses, subways, trains, and airplanes. Not only are these
systems guided mechanically by internal technology,
with many of the safety features stemming from chips,
but computers are responsible for providing riders and
travelers such services as GPS, Wi-Fi, and automated
announcements and alerts.

- Healthcare: Semiconductors have permeated the medical field, giving health professionals the ability to provide highly accurate imaging, offer top-notch diagnos-
tics, and perform risky operations with precision. Chips
are used in everything from pacemakers to monitoring
devices, so that physicians can record everything from
blood pressure to cell counts with speed, patient comfort, and accuracy.

- Security: Chips have advanced security and surveillance
in the field by providing better photographic imagery,
more accurate recording of times and dates, and more
sensitive responses to motion and light infringements,

as well as boosting crime fighting and spy capabilities in the cybersecurity realm.

- Banking and finance: These sectors don't just rely on computers for data collection, storage, communications, and both short- and long-term accounting and bookkeeping; they rely on chips for advanced security technology for ATMs, cameras, locks, and keys.

As if those fields weren't enough to demonstrate the importance of semiconductors, there's this: artificial intelligence chips. This is where the chip wars get really dangerous. Specialty AI chips can perform a variety of different and complicated tasks with great speed and efficiency. They're generally the building blocks of smartphones, self-driving cars, and much of the robotics technology that's underway. Crucially, they're the golden egg of surveillance technology too. The website OurCrowd states:

> By leveraging parallel processing capabilities, AI chips can quickly and effectively deal with large datasets. This form of computing allows multiple tasks to be executed simultaneously. It also means that networks driven by Artificial Intelligence can utilize available information when learning or completing certain activities. For example, AI can use inference—like in the human realm a combination of reasoning and decision-making based on available information—to apply real-world knowledge for facial recognition, gesture identification,

natural language interpretation, image searching and much more.[124]

It's eerie enough to imagine America's government possessing and using, say, facial recognition technology on a widespread basis. But to imagine the bulk of these types of AI chips in the hands of communists from China, who want nothing but to control the masses, including Americans—it's unthinkable. Now consider the military and the fact that who controls the AI chips controls the world.

The Potomac Institute for Policy Studies wrote in 2022 that the "Communist Party of China (CPC) Central Committee has established the goal of building a 'fully modern military' by 2027." It also mentioned a report on China's military developments that discussed "a focus on the People Liberation Army's (PLA's) strategy to use science and technology for military purposes."[125]

The technological revolution that's already here promises to render ineffective militaries and military equipment as we now know them. In 2021, the National Security Commission on Artificial Intelligence (NSCAI) presented its 756-page "Final Report" to Congress, alerting, notably to the fact, that most Americans are unaware of the dangers due to artificial intelligence and technological developments that other nations, particularly China, might wield as tools to control and conquer

---

[124] OurCrowd, "What is an AI Chip? Exploring the Latest in Artificial Intelligence Technology," OurCrowd, September 19, 2023, https://www.ourcrowd.com/learn/what-is-an-ai-chip#:~:text=These%20specially%2Dcrafted%20pieces%20of,that%20would%20otherwise%20be%20impossible.

[125] The Honorable Zachary J. Lemnios, "US National Security in a New Era of Intense Global Competition," Potomac Institute for Policy Studies, accessed December 3, 2023, https://www.potomacinstitute.org/index.php/featured/us-national-security-in-a-new-era-of-intense-global-competition

in the very near future. A few pertinent quotes from this NSCAI report:

- "China possesses the might, talent, and ambition to surpass the United States as the world's leader in AI in the next decade if current trends do not change."[126]
- "This is not a time for incremental toggles to federal research budgets or adding a few new positions in the Pentagon for Silicon Valley technologists. This will be expense and require a significant change in mindset. America needs White House leadership, Cabinet-member action, and bipartisan Congressional support to win the AI era."[127]
- "Our armed forces' competitive military-technical advantage could be lost within the next decade if they do not accelerate the adoption of AI across their missions."[128]
- "The race to research, develop, and deploy AI and associated technologies is intensifying the technology competition that underpins a wider strategic competition. China is organized, resourced, and determined to win this contest. The United States retains advantages in critical areas, but current trends are concerning."[129]
- "We know adversaries are determined to turn AI capabilities against us. We know China is determined to surpass us in AI leadership. We know advances in AI

---

[126] The National Security Commission on Artificial Intelligence, "Final Report," NSCAI, March 2021, pp. 1–30, https://www.nscai.gov/wp-content/uploads/2021/03/Full-Report-Digital-1.pdf.

[127] Ibid.

[128] Ibid.

[129] Ibid.

build on themselves and confer significant first-mover advantages. Now we must act."[130]

Of course, the NSCAI commission members may or may not have carried conflicts of interest in terms of what they proposed Congress should do—in large part, infuse the AI world with billions of dollars, meaning taxpayer dollars—and what they themselves do for work. NSCAI's chairman, for instance, is Eric Schmidt, former chief executive officer of Google, previously on the board of directors at Apple, and a billionaire software engineer and tech businessman.[131] On one hand, his knowledge of the technology sector is nearly unrivaled; on the other, his contacts, company alliances, and corporate interests could be seen as clouds on his judgments. Regardless, the "Final Report" carries weight. Politicians, including the Joe Biden White House, have taken action in recent times to address the growing divide between American and foreign semiconductor market shares.

Some actions have brought positive results.

In 2023, for instance, US news headlines rang of a decrease in China's imports and exports of chips, a condition that came about due to White House and congressional action directly aimed at slowing the CCP's market share of this technology.

But these headlines only tell part of the story. They show the one step forward America's taken toward fighting China's chip domination but not the two steps back that quickly followed. And they completely ignore some of the incestuous relationships American technology companies and politicians maintain with

---

[130] Ibid.
[131] The National Security Commission on Artificial Intelligence, "About Us," NSCAI, accessed December 3, 2023, https://www.nscai.gov/about/.

the communists who control corporations in China. It evokes the biblical warnings to God's people who failed to walk in the faith and obey His commands.

From Ephesians 4, a clear alarm for both people and nations:

> Now this I affirm and testify in the Lord, that you must no longer live as the Gentiles do, in the futility of their minds; they are darkened in their understanding, alienated from the life of God because of the ignorance that is in them, due to their hardness of heart; they have become callous and have given themselves up to licentiousness, greedy to practice every kind of uncleanness.

(Eph. 4:17–19, RSV)

Blind leading the blind. American leaders, blinded by unbelief, leading a nation that's growing in secularism and, therefore, a nation of people who are increasingly as blinded by unbelief as the leaders they elect—down a path of national security peril.

In October 2023, the Commerce Department unveiled new trade rules that cracked down on US exports to China of certain types of semiconductors and manufacturing equipment. This was an expansion of a crackdown the White House implemented a year earlier, both of which were aimed at slowing China's chip industry and preventing the CCP from obtaining technology that would boost its military and surveillance powers.[132] The new rules, said Commerce Secretary Gina Raimondo in a statement, "will increase effectiveness of our controls and further shut off pathways to evade our restrictions." She also vowed the Biden administration would "keep working to protect our national security by restricting access to critical technologies, vigilantly enforcing our rules, while minimizing any unintended impact on trade flows."[133]

Sounds wonderful. A White House that protects American national security is always a good thing. It'd be more wonderful if it were true, though.

From Reuters, in November 2023, came this headline: "China receives US equipment to make advanced chips despite new rules-report."[134]

The article cited the report from the U.S.-China Economic and Security Review Commission:

> Chinese companies are buying up U.S. chip-making equipment to make advanced semi-conductors, despite a raft of new export curbs

[132] Michelle Toh and Kayla Tausche, "US escalates tech battle by cutting China off from AI chips," CNN, October 18, 2023, https://www.cnn.com/2023/10/18/tech/us-china-chip-export-curbs-intl-hnk/index.html#:~:text=The%20Biden%20administration%20is%20reducing,existing%20regulations%20announced%20last%20year.

[133] Gina M. Raimondo, "Commerce Strengthens Restrictions on Advanced Computing Semiconductors, Semiconductor Manufacturing Equipment, and Supercomputing Items to Countries of Concern," Bureau of Industry and Security, U.S. Department of Commerce, October 17, 2023, https://www.bis.doc.gov/index.php/documents/about-bis/newsroom/press-releases/3355-2023-10-17-bis-press-release-acs-and-sme-rules-final-js/file.

[134] Alexandra Alper, "China receives US equipment to make advanced chips despite new rules-report," Reuters, November 14, 2023, https://www.reuters.com/technology/china-receives-us-equipment-make-advanced-chips-despite-new-rules-report-2023-11-14/.

> aimed at thwarting advances in the country's
> semiconductor industry…. China stockpiled
> equipment by taking advantage of the lagtime
> between the United States' October 2022 rules,
> and Japan and the Netherlands' similar moves
> in July and September of 2023 respectively.[135]

That lag time could explain how China's massive telecommunications firm Huawei was able to design and market a Mate 60 Pro smartphone powered by an advanced seven-nanometer chip, despite the fact Huawei and China's top chipmaker Semiconductor Manufacturing International Corporation (SMIC) had both been placed on trade restriction lists in 2019 and 2020.[136] So, how were they able to make such a top-of-the-line technological product? One theory is that SMIC may have created the chip using equipment that was purchased before the October 2022 rules went into play; another is that China bought massive amounts of advanced equipment from the Netherlands and other technologically developed countries to stockpile between the months that America's ban and the other nations' bans took effect. The stockpile theory seems to have substance.

The U.S.-China Economic and Security Review Commission found that between the months of January and August 2023—a time frame that coincides with America's rules preventing China from obtaining top-grade chips and equipment, and the months before the Netherlands' and Japan's similar bans were to take effect—China imported about $3.2 billion of

---

[135] Ibid.

[136] Eric Revell, "Huawei building secret chip network to dodge US sanctions: report," Fox Business, August 23, 2023, https://www.foxbusiness.com/politics/huawei-building-secret-chip-network-dodge-us-sanctions-report.

semiconductor manufacturing machines from the Netherlands alone.[137] That represents about a 96 percent increase of China's $1.7 billion purchase of the same type of equipment the previous year.[138]

Bans and rules and prohibitions and limits only work if they're able to be enforced.

Interestingly, the White House's November 2023 crackdowns on China—the ones so cheered by Commerce Secretary Raimondo as so protective of America's national security—weren't due to take effect until thirty days after they were announced. More lag time, more opportunity for China to exploit lag times. Even so, it's not as if the Biden White House was being taken seriously in the tech war against China, anyway. As *Investor's Business Daily* wrote in November 2023:

> A key question is just how determined the Biden administration is to keep advanced semiconductor technology out of China's hands. The Aug. 30 [2023] unveiling of a 5G smartphone by Chinese tech powerhouse Huawei, later confirmed to have a highly advanced chip, signaled that U.S. efforts to contain China's technology ambitions are failing. While the Biden administration responded by adopting still-tighter export restrictions for AI chips and

[137] U.S.-China Economic and Security Review Commission, "2023 Report to Congress," U.S.-China Economic and Security Review Commission, November 2023, pp. 5–12, https://www.uscc.gov/sites/default/files/2023-11/2023_Annual_Report_to_Congress.pdf.

[138] Alexandra Alper, "China receives US equipment to make advanced chips despite new rules-report," Reuters, November 14, 2023, https://www.reuters.com/technology/china-receives-us-equipment-make-advanced-chips-despite-new-rules-report-2023-11-14/.

advanced semiconductor-making equipment in October, those updated rules already appear to be falling short.[139]

How so? Well, for one, the new rules aimed at curbing China's chip technology tossed out a key accountability method—that of requiring companies with Chinese factories to obtain annual waivers from US authorities. South Korea's Samsung and SK hynix "will be allowed to ship U.S. semiconductor manufacturing equipment to their China factories indefinitely without separate U.S. approvals," CNBC reported in October 2023.[140] Oh, but South Korea is an American ally, so what could go wrong? Plenty.

The CCP has taken decided steps in the last couple years to place communists within the corporate structure of companies with physical presence in China, or at the least, compel those companies to adhere to communist ideals, support communist principles, and/or outright pay public homage to communist values. For an America that's supposedly free with a foundation that's supposedly built on God-given individualism, headlines such as this one, from *Forbes* in February 2023, are alarming:

---

[139] Jed Graham, "Taiwan Presidential Race Set: U.S.-China Chip War Nears Moment Of Truth For Nvidia, Apple And The World," *Investor's Business Daily*, November 24, 2023, https://www.investors.com/news/taiwan-presidential-race-set-us-china-chip-war-nears-moment-of-truth-for-nvidia-apple-and-the-world/.

[140] Sheila Chiang, "Samsung, SK Hynix to get indefinite waivers to ship U.S. chip equipment to their China factories," CNBC News, October 10, 2023, https://www.cnbc.com/2023/10/10/samsung-sk-hynix-get-indefinite-waivers-on-us-chip-equipment.html.

"Chinese Communist Party Demands Employees At Western Firm Show Their Support."[141] The story opens like this:

> When China began to require Western corporations to establish Chinese Communist Party (CCP) cells, businesses brushed off the move as benign. For example, when HSBC became the first international financial institution at which workers established a Chinese Communist Party cell in its investment banking venture in China in July, the bank stated that the CCP committee does not influence the direction of the firm and has no formal role in its day-to-day activities. But the CCP may have begun to flex its muscle in other ways. This week, the CCP cell inside the Beijing office of Big Four accounting firm EY demanded that party members wear CCP badges at work in the run-up to China's annual parliamentary meetings. The presence of CCP cells in Western financial institutions may not mean that communists are managing your money. However, they spell trouble for Western businesses operating in China.[142]

Well, there's a "no duh" moment, if ever there was one.

The Center for Strategic and International Studies (CSIS) warned in a 2021 analysis that the CCP was moving rapidly

[141] Jill Goldenziel, "Chinese Communist Party Demands Employees At Western Firm Show Their Support," *Forbes*, February 27, 2023, https://www.forbes.com/sites/jillgoldenziel/2023/02/27/chinese-communist-party-demands-employees-at-western-firm-show-their-support/?sh=73ea87a33804.
[142] Ibid.

toward strengthening the party's influences on private businesses—first, within China's own corporations, and then second, more slowly and subtly, into corporations that hail from outside China but that either operate or want to operate in the country. One warning from CSIS went like this: "Because the CCP might well attempt to extend this push into foreign private companies operating in China, these new [CCP] actions pose a very real threat to the operational independence of foreign-invested enterprises."[143] Notably, CSIS also offered advice for governments and businesses wishing to continue or start corporate ventures within China.

> To formulate an effective response, companies and governments in market economies should increase their understanding of how the CCP operates at the grassroots level and work to ensure greater transparency and understanding of the overall level of [CCP] influence within specific firms. To further this transparency, U.S. policymakers could consider requiring securities issuers in the United States provide enhanced disclosures relating to CCP activities within their firms. The U.S. government should also consider reviving open-source data collection initiatives to publish and translate key CCP regulations and [CCP] documents in order

---

[143] Scott Livingston, "The New Challenge of Communist Corporate Governance," Center for Strategic & International Studies, January 15, 2021, https://www.csis.org/analysis/new-challenge-communist-corporate-governance.

to increase understanding and spur further analysis of the [CCP] system.[144]

Given those recommendations, it would seem counterintuitive for Biden's administration to, say, grant a couple of the world's leading tech firms, Samsung and SK hynix, indefinite passes of automatic approval to ship semiconductor manufacturing equipment to the CCP-controlled China, thereby removing the annual waiver process—that is to say, US oversight. Commerce Secretary Raimondo may insist that all she wants is the White House to be "laser-focused" on preventing China from achieving a state of military might through technological dominance and on keeping the CCP from exploiting loopholes to become a world leader in semiconductors.[145] But talk is cheap, particularly when the enemies know talk rarely leads to a walk.

Look at this, from the earlier article by *Investor's Business Daily* in November 2023: "Now the U.S. has assembled a united front to deprive China of the world's most advanced chips and equipment to make them. Those cutting-edge technologies come from the U.S., U.K., the Netherlands, South Korea and Japan. Yet 90% of advanced chips designed by companies like Nvidia, Apple and Broadcom are made at the sprawling TSMC

[144] Ibid.

[145] Michelle Toh and Kayla Tausche, "US escalates tech battle by cutting China off from AI chips," CNN, October 18, 2023, https://www.cnn.com/2023/10/18/tech/us-china-chip-export-curbs-intl-hnk/index.html#:~:text=The%20Biden%20administration%20is%20reducing,existing%20regulations%20announced%20last%20year.

[Taiwan Semiconductor Manufacturing Company] factory campus on the island that China claims as its own [Taiwan]."[146]

The October 2023 Securities and Exchange Commission report that added controls from the Biden administration was targeted, in large part, at Nvidia, one of the biggest makers of advanced AI chips.[147]

But to see how well the crackdown worked—or more truthfully, to see how well-regarded the Biden administration is by companies and other countries' governments alike—see this headline from HotHardware in December 2023: "US Issues Apparent Warning to NVIDIA Over Redesigned Chip Shipments To China."[148] The story went on to report a response from Commerce Secretary Raimondo about NVIDIA's skirt of Team Biden's ban on sales of the advanced technology to China, just weeks after the administration supposedly closed all the loopholes. She said, at the Reagan National Defense Forum in California, "We cannot let China get these chips. Period. We're going to deny them our most cutting-edge technology."[149]

That's almost laughable.

Or it would be, if it didn't point to America's weakness under the feckless Joe Biden administration. And weakness breeds national insecurity. But Biden isn't just weak; his family is

---

[146] Jed Graham, "Taiwan Presidential Race Set: U.S.-China Chip War Nears Moment Of Truth For Nvidia, Apple And The World," *Investor's Business Daily*, November 24, 2023, https://www.investors.com/news/taiwan-presidential-race-set-us-china-chip-war-nears-moment-of-truth-for-nvidia-apple-and-the-world/.

[147] United States Securities and Exchange Commission, "Form 8-K, NVIDIA CORPORATION," SEC, October 17, 2023, https://d18rn0p25nwr6d.cloudfront.net/CIK-0001045810/6314522a-929c-470d-b67c-23fa99238516.pdf.

[148] Alan Velasco, "US Issues Apparent Warning To NVIDIA Over Redesigned Chip Shipments To China," HotHardware, December 4, 2023, https://hothardware.com/news/us-issues-warning-to-nvidia-over-chip-shipments.

[149] Ibid.

also tainted by corruption—making his White House dealings with China all the more suspect.

Nevertheless, the bigger lesson is one of spiritual decay.

If America hadn't turned down a path of secularism—if Americans hadn't pursued materialism to such a degree that businesses became about making more money, more money, more money, no matter the moral conflicts, regardless of the questionable partnerships, despite the dancing with evil, like the CCP—then perhaps the state of American liberties wouldn't depend so much on which way the chip war falls. Perhaps America's national security wouldn't be so intricately tied to the corporate world and, therefore, to the CCP. Perhaps America's politicians would have seen the peril before it arrived—would have listened to Reagan's concerns and carried forth the fight for global dominance in technology—and would have adopted long-term policies that favored US businesses, taught US school children well, kept the market free, invested tax dollars wisely, and favored more of an industrial policy over science policy, with an emphasis on good old-fashioned American entrepreneurial spirit and God-given talent.

So much goes awry when Americans fail to keep God first.

Priorities shift, eyes close to dangers, and attention turns to other matters. Evil very often exploits these distractions for gain. And an American loss in the chip war could bring an irreversible loss in individual liberties. Do we want to be America, or do we want to be an extension of China? The answer lies in whether or not and how quickly we turn back to God as a society.

CHAPTER 6

PROTECTING PEDOPHILES, PROSECUTING PRESIDENTS, AND POLITICS OF PURE EVIL

A nation that doesn't defend its most vulnerable, particularly the children, and that doesn't make sure the weakest of society are prioritized for protection is a nation that can hardly call itself in line with godly governance and values.

In August 2019, convicted sex offender and well-connected financier Jeffrey Epstein died in a New York jail cell, supposedly of suicide, while awaiting trial on child sex trafficking charges.[150] In June 2023, J.P. Morgan agreed to a $290 million payout to victims who accused the bank of ignoring Epstein's criminal

---

[150] Miles Clee, "Far Right Resurrects Jeffrey Epstein Conspiracy Theories," *Rolling Stone*, December 6, 2023, https://www.rollingstone.com/politics/politics-news/jeffrey-epstein-conspiracy-theories-israel-hamas-war-1234918631/.

behavior to the point of actually facilitating his sex trafficking.[151] In November 2023, Senator Marsha Blackburn, Tennessee Republican, put out this message on the social media platform X, formerly known as Twitter: "The American people deserve to know the names of every person who participated in Jeffrey Epstein's human trafficking ring. We need to see his flight logs. I've asked the Senate Judiciary Committee to authorize a subpoena to his estate so we can review these documents."[152] And finally, in December 2023, a federal judge ordered the unsealing of documents that would make public the names of scores of Epstein associates.[153] That order came as part of a settlement from a civil suit brought by Virginia Giuffre against Ghislaine Maxwell, who was sentenced in 2022 to twenty years in prison for sex trafficking and procuring young women for Epstein.[154] That civil suit was settled in 2017.[155] It took six years for the

[151] Ellen Cranley, Kenneth Niemeyer, and Benjamin Goggin, "The life of Jeffrey Epstein, the convicted sex offender and well-connected financier who died in jail awaiting sex trafficking charges," Business Insider, June 13, 2023, https://www.businessinsider.com/jeffrey-epstein-life-biography-net-worth-2019-7#epsteins-partner-ghislaine-maxwell-was-charged-in-july-2020-by-prosecutors-in-new-york-with-sexual-d%20whyabuse-crimes-15.

[152] Sen. Marsha Blackburn, "X" post, @Marsha Blackburn, November 8, 2023, https://twitter.com/MarshaBlackburn/status/1722763300629266562?ref_src=twsrc%5Etfw.

[153] James Hill and Aaron Katersky, "Federal judge orders documents naming Jeffrey Epstein's associates to be unsealed," ABC News, December 19, 2023, https://abcnews.go.com/US/federal-judge-orders-documents-naming-jeffrey-epsteins-associates/story?id=105779882.

[154] Nicholas Biase and Victoria Bosah, "Ghislaine Maxwell Sentenced To 20 Years In Prison For Conspiring With Jeffrey Epstein To Sexually Abuse Minors," United States Attorney's Office, Southern District of New York, June 29, 2022, https://www.justice.gov/usao-sdny/pr/ghislaine-maxwell-sentenced-20-years-prison-conspiring-jeffrey-epstein-sexually-abuse.

[155] James Hill and Aaron Katersky, "Federal judge orders documents naming Jeffrey Epstein's associates to be unsealed," ABC News, December 19, 2023, https://abcnews.go.com/US/federal-judge-orders-documents-naming-jeffrey-epsteins-associates/story?id=105779882.

order to come to unseal the names tied to a known sex offender. And when the documents were released—well, within these 4,553 pages of documents were roughly 150 names connected to Epstein, but these names "were largely known from previous public documents and interviews," as NBC News put it.[156] It was a nothingburger, in other words—making it all the more curious why it took six years to release them.

Six years.

Yes, legal matters frequently take years to wind through courts. But when it comes to Epstein, on any and all matters tied to Epstein, the wheels of justice have moved tortuously and curiously slow. After all, this was a guy who wasn't exactly hiding his crimes.

Officially, we know very little about the players who participated in Epstein's criminal sexual escapades with minor-age girls and with lured, captured, and trafficked women, or about all the activities on his Little St. James–island estate. Unofficially, though—due to rumors, innuendos, whispers, open secrets, and leaked information, combined with witness and victim reports and Epstein's own past sexual offender court conviction—we know plenty. We know enough. We know enough to see that evil went forth—that young women were harmed; that young women and minor-age females were used, exploited, and treated as dirt by some of the world's most powerful and influential and elite; and that most of the offenders have yet to be held accountable.

---

[156] Adam Reiss, Tom Winter, and Sarah Fitzpatrick, "Last batch of unsealed Jeffrey Epstein documents released," NBC News, January 10, 2024, https://www.nbcnews.com/news/us-news/last-batch-unsealed-jeffrey-epstein-documents-released-rcna132936.

Why is that? Politics, no doubt. The politically powerful protecting the politically powerful, and the wealthy and elite shielding their fellow wealthy and elite. That's the secular explanation, and it makes sense. But from a biblical perspective, from a deeper dive to the root of the sickness of those who shield evil and shun accountability, here's a thought—Psalm 36:

> Transgression speaks to the wicked deep in his heart; there is no fear of God before his eyes. For he flatters himself in his own eyes that his iniquity cannot be found out and hated. The words of his mouth are mischief and deceit; he has ceased to act wisely and do good. He plots mischief while on his bed; he sets himself in a way that is not good; he spurns not evil.

(Psalm 36:1–4, RSV)

Evil flourishes when there is no fear of God.

The wicked don't care. The evil don't worry about what others think. The wicked and evil don't fear a label of liar. They aren't concerned with an accusation of hypocrite. And they won't be much bothered by whispers, innuendos, and pointed fingers—so long as they're never put in positions of having to admit with their own lips their own wicked and evil acts.

They can boldface lie but still look at themselves in the mirror and go about their days.

They can casually and, without missing a beat, cover up the lie but still lay their heads on soft pillows at night and sleep.

The fact that such an open evil as Jeffrey Epstein has taken place in America, though, is a ringing alarm to the sickness of America's soul. Where is our light on a hill? Has it indeed gone so dark as to allow the barely disguised sexual abuse of young girls, minor-age girls, and innocent young females to go forth for years, all while people in the positions to put a stop to it turned blind eyes? America is supposed to be a nation of equal protection under the law, where the justice system favors no rank, no title, no position, and no status over another—sort of like how Jesus sees Jews and Gentiles alike, all equal in His eyes. We haven't just strayed from that Judeo-Christian principle. We've tossed it in the trash bin.

Vanity Fair reported this in 2019:

> Ever since billionaire Jeffrey Epstein was arrested on July 6 [2019] on charges of sex trafficking, the media have been scrambling to make sense of what happened on Little St. James, his 70-acre private island in the Caribbean. But on nearby St. Thomas, locals say Epstein continued to bring underage girls to the island as recently as this year—a decade after he was forced to register as a convicted sex offender—and that authorities did nothing to stop him.[157]

The magazine went on to write how two airport employees at the nearby St. Thomas island said they saw Epstein on several occasions board or exit his jet or helicopter "in the company of girls who appeared to be under the age of consent."[158] Flight records for Epstein's jets show he flew frequently to Paris, London, Slovakia, Mexico, and Morocco, sometimes stopping in

---

[157] Holly Aguirre, "'The Girls Were Just So Young': The Horrors of Jeffrey Epstein's Private Island," *Vanity Fair*, July 20, 2019, https://www.vanityfair.com/news/2019/07/horrors-of-jeffrey-epstein-private-island.
[158] Ibid.

these spots for only a few hours—as if to pick up or drop off passengers.[159]

Here are the statements these two employees, both anonymous, made to *Vanity Fair* in this same 2019 article:

- The first, a former air traffic controller: "On multiple occasions I saw Epstein exit his helicopter, stand on the tarmac in full view of my tower, and board his private jet with children—female children. One incident in particular really stands out in my mind, because the girls were just so young. They couldn't have been over 16. Epstein looked very angry and hurled his jacket at one of them. They were also carrying shopping bags from stores not on the island. I remember thinking, 'Where in the world have they been shopping?'"[160]
- The second, also an employee of the airstrip, on witnessing Epstein land at St. Thomas about twice a month: "There'd be girls that look like they could be in high school. They looked very young. They were always wearing college sweatshirts. It seemed like camouflage, that's the best way to put it."[161]

Other media picked up the reports.

The *Daily Mail*, tailing off *Vanity Fair*'s article, wrote this in 2019:

[159] J.K. Trotter, "Flight data from Jeffrey Epstein's private jets show a lavish travel schedule as the walls closed in," Business Insider, July 12, 2019, https://www.insider.com/jeffrey-epsteins-private-jet-flight-data-2019-7.

[160] Holly Aguirre, "'The Girls Were Just So Young': The Horrors of Jeffrey Epstein's Private Island," *Vanity Fair*, July 20, 2019, https://www.vanityfair.com/news/2019/07/horrors-of-jeffrey-epstein-private-island.

[161] Ibid.

The [airstrip] employee said he and colleagues would joke…saying [of Epstein's flights], "How many kids are on board this time?" because of Epstein's apparently brazen attitude. They also said they felt "pure disgust" that he was allowed to get away with it and claimed the alleged abuse [of girls] was ignored because "he tipped well." "The fact that young girls were getting out of his helicopter and getting into his plane, it was like he was flaunting it," the employee says.[162]

The abuse of young women was an open secret. His plane was the *Lolita Express*. His island was known as a place of pedophilia.

The *Daily Mail* article also included the locals' description of Epstein's seventy-acre Caribbean property: "Everybody called it 'Pedophile Island,'" said Kevin Goodrich, who is from St. Thomas and operates boat charters. 'It's our dark corner,'"[163]

How can it be that in America—in a nation where citizens have the final word on how politics run and how politicians serve, in a nation where voters and taxpayers have the final voice in guiding how government operates and ensuring that law

[162] George Martin, "'It was like he was flaunting it': Airport employees in Caribbean say they saw 'girls who couldn't be older than 16' en route to Jeffrey Epstein's 'pedophile island' as recently as last month," *Daily Mail*, July 22, 2019, https://www.dailymail.co.uk/news/article-7271703/Airport-employees-saw-girls-en-route-Jeffrey-Epsteins-pedophile-island.html.

[163] George Martin, "'It was like he was flaunting it': Airport employees in Caribbean say they saw 'girls who couldn't be older than 16' en route to Jeffrey Epstein's 'pedophile island' as recently as last month," *Daily Mail*, July 22, 2019, https://www.dailymail.co.uk/news/article-7271703/Airport-employees-saw-girls-en-route-Jeffrey-Epsteins-pedophile-island.html.

and order are actually equally applied to all—there was open pedophilia in a US–owned Virgin Island property. This—in a country with a legal system of supposed blind justice. How can it be that that years after Epstein's death, mysterious in itself— supposedly suicide in a jail cell at the exact blink in time when guards had conveniently turned from their watch—that we know so little about his life?

It's a question of priorities.

It's a matter of what society considers most worthy of pursuing.

Somebody, or a group of somebodies in very powerful positions, must be purposely hiding the truths of Epstein's sex trafficking. Otherwise, Senator Blackburn wouldn't have had to press for the most basic of information, the flight logs on this famous *Lolita Express*, to find out exactly who was aboard and why when Epstein was allegedly flying around underage girls as sexual playmates for his guests. In November and December 2023, Blackburn sent out another round of social media posts, expressing frustration with what she characterized as a stalled investigation.

From Fox News: "Sen. Marsha Blackburn, R-Tenn., criticized Sen. Dick Durbin, D-Ill., for allegedly blocking her request to file a subpoena for Jeffrey Epstein's flight logs. '@SenatorDurbin BLOCKED my request to subpoena Jeffrey Epstein's flight logs. What are Democrats trying to hide?' Blackburn posted on X."[164]

---

[164] Adam Sabes, "Jeffrey Epstein flight log subpoena denied by Democrat-led Senate Judiciary Committee, Blackburn says," Fox News, November 30, 2023, https://www.foxnews.com/politics/jeffrey-epstein-flight-logs-denied-democrat-led-senate-judiciary-committee-blackburn-says.

From Blackburn's X feed on December 1: "We need to uncover the names of every individual who participated in Jeffrey Epstein's horrific human trafficking ring. I'm calling to subpoena his flight logs."[165]

More from Blackburn's X feed on December 4: "I want to know the names of every single person who may have taken Jeffrey Epstein's private plane and participated in his human trafficking ring. RT if you do too."[166]

And even more from Blackburn's X feed a day later: "I'm not stopping until the names of every person on Epstein's flight log are released to the public. The American people deserve transparency. Let's see if [FBI Director] Christopher Wray will give us any during today's Senate Judiciary Hearing."[167]

And did Wray? No.

The *Tennessee Star* reported on Blackburn's peppery December 5 questioning of FBI Director Christopher Wray on the status of the Epstein investigation during the Senate judiciary hearing:

> "Senator Marsha Blackburn…grilled [Wray] about what she said she believes is a lack of thorough investigation into an alleged high-profile sex trafficking ring run by billionaire Jeffrey Epstein. 'The last few weeks I've been demanding some answers on Jeffrey Epstein's crimes, and trying to get these flight

165 Sen. Marsha Blackburn, "X," @MarshaBlackburn, December 1, 2023, https://twitter.com/MarshaBlackburn/status/1730591938879865052.
166 Sen. Marsha Blackburn, "X," @MarshaBlackburn, December 4, 2023, https://twitter.com/MarshaBlackburn/status/1731735177607401827.
167 Sen. Marsha Blackburn, "X," @MarshaBlackburn, December 5, 2023, https://twitter.com/MarshaBlackburn/status/1732045644108636247.

records,' said Blackburn.... 'I've kind of been stonewalled on it.... [I]n looking at some of the survivors of the Epstein issues, there are disturbing allegations that the FBI failed to investigate the sex trafficking allegations and indeed one survivor says that the FBI, even after she brought forward repeatedly content about his conduct, that the FBI refused to investigate her claims, even though she said the allegations were there on both the sex trafficking and the child sexual abuse material,' she said. 'I want to know why, or what awareness you have of the FBI's failure to investigate these claims and I want to get you on the record since numerous survivors have said the FBI did not show up to help them, what specifically has the FBI done to investigate the claims that Epstein and others participated in, produced, possessed and distributed [child sexual abuse material].'"[168]

A very excellent question. A very direct question. A very important and clear question—to which Wray basically replied this: I don't know.

"It's been a while since I looked at that case," Wray said.[169]

Boom. Once again, it's a matter of priorities.

[168] Peter D'Abrosca, "Blackburn Grills FBI Director on Epstein Logs," *Tennessee Star*, December 6, 2023, https://tennesseestar.com/news/blackburn-grills-fbi-director-on-epstein-flight-logs/pdabrosca/2023/12/06/.
[169] Ibid.

Few details are known about Epstein's accomplices in sexual deviancies because America's investigative focus has been on the wrong thing.

The FBI, for example, has been busily investigating Donald Trump for first, fake Russia collusion charges, followed by fake pee tape prostitution accusations, followed by fake Steele dossier allegations, followed by hyped-up Ukraine telephone call hysteria—it's more "he said, he said" nonsense that unfolded in typical Marxist propaganda style: all emotion, light on fact.

For instance, from the *New York Times* in 2019:

> A White House official who listened to President Trump's July phone call with Ukraine's leader described it as "crazy," "frightening" and "completely lacking in substance related to national security," according to a memo written by the whistle-blower at the center of the Ukraine scandal, a C.I.A. officer who spoke to the White House official. The official was "visibly shaken by what had transpired," the C.I.A. officer wrote in his memo, one day after Mr. Trump [allegedly] pressured President Volodymyr Zelensky of Ukraine in a July 25 phone call to open investigations that would benefit him politically.... Little, if any, of the [unnamed] whistle-blower's complaint has been disproved, though Mr. Trump has sought to discredit him. The White House transcript largely affirmed his account of the call, and [inspector general Michael] Atkinson deemed

his complaint credible, saying he interviewed others who corroborate it.[170]

Gotta love the unnamed whistle-blowers who are "visibly shaken" to the point of running to a CIA officer, who in turn pulls out a napkin and pen from their pocket, or the equivalent, writes down the reaction, adds a little hype here, a little hyperbole there, and voila!—an investigation based on a memo is born, an impeachment hails, and another unnamed source is afforded such credibility that the word of the president of the United States is deemed immaterial. Former FBI chief James Comey loved memos too. It was Comey's little notes to self about his self-proclaimed private meetings with then president Donald Trump—before Trump fired him in May 2017—that helped launch the mass media frenzy about obstruction of justice over fired White House aide Michael Flynn; and that fueled the press pool's titterings and twitterings of prostitutes peeing on mattresses, as well as the president's quote, unquote, "scandalous expressions of hope of jailing reporters who used leaked information."[171] Those memos caused quite a stir among the staid establishment of Washington, DC.

CNN ran with this racy headline—"The James Comey memo is an existential threat to Donald Trump's presidency"[172]—followed by these racy opening paragraphs:

---

[170] Nicholas Fandos, "Trump's Ukraine Call Was 'Crazy' and 'Frightening,' Official Told Whistleblower," *New York Times*, October 8, 2019, https://www.nytimes.com/2019/10/08/us/politics/trump-ukraine-whistleblower.html.

[171] Kevin Breuninger, "James Comey's Trump memos: Here are the takeaways," CNBC, April 20, 2018, https://www.cnbc.com/2018/04/20/james-comey-memos-give-new-insights-into-trump-interactions.html.

[172] Chris Cillizza, "The James Comey memo is an existential threat to Donald Trump's presidency," CNN, May 17, 2017, https://www.cnn.com/2017/05/16/politics/trump-comey-fbi/index.html.

The reporting coming out of The New York Times and CNN is explosive: Deposed FBI Director James Comey wrote a memo following a February 14 meeting with Donald Trump in which he says the president told him, "I hope you can let this go," in regard to fired aide Michael Flynn's role in the ongoing investigation into Russia's efforts to influence the 2016 campaign. If true, that is almost the textbook definition of obstruction of justice, a charge that could well lead to impeachment proceedings. "Reluctantly, I have to say yes," independent Maine Sen. Angus King told CNN's Wolf Blitzer Tuesday night about the prospect of impeachment if the claims in the Comey memo are true.[173]

So, in America, it's accepted that a member of government can simply scribble a note and from that, a president might be impeached? It just sounds beyond stupid that one person, no matter his or her title, could hold such power—could be seen as so above suspicion—that the press, the Fourth Estate, the watchdog of the people and the check on politician power, could jump right on an impeachment bandwagon. It is beyond stupid that an America born of God-given rights and liberties, and with a government that is subservient to the citizens, would oh-so-cavalierly nod and smile at the concept of a hastily scribbled note serving as sacrosanct truth. Comey wrote at least one

---

[173] Chris Cillizza, "The James Comey memo is an existential threat to Donald Trump's presidency," CNN, May 17, 2017, https://www.cnn.com/2017/05/16/politics/trump-comey-fbi/index.html.

memo in his FBI car—in his car!—giving rise to an unflattering image of him darting from the president's side like a juiced-up gossip to hurry and tap his tale into print.[174]

And for what? In the end, it was all for naught.

In August 2019, Justice Department inspector general Michael Horowitz found that Comey violated policy in the way he handled his memos—specifically, that he arranged with a friend to give some of the memos to a *New York Times* reporter, and also that he discussed them with attorneys in his home, without the knowledge of the FBI and before the FBI even knew their contents. Turns out, some of the information in Comey's memos were deemed "confidential" by the FBI.[175] Accountability for Comey?

Nope.

Horowitz referred his findings to prosecutors.

"After reviewing the matter," Horowitz's office said in a statement, "the DOJ declined prosecution."[176]

We went from hastily scribbled notes to hysterical headlines and public pundit chatter about impeachment, to the finding of the accuser's malfeasance—to zero accountability for the accuser. That's hardly American justice; it's barely the American way. But neither is a system that allows a government bureaucrat to be deemed automatic truth-teller just because he writes a memo or two. The American public wouldn't defer in such manner to

[174] Philip Ewing, "DOJ: Comey Violated Policy On His Trump Memos—But Won't Be Prosecuted," NPR, August 29, 2019, https://www.npr.org/2019/08/29/755402701/doj-comey-violated-policy-on-his-trump-memos-but-wont-be-prosecuted.

[175] Philip Ewing, "DOJ: Comey Violated Policy On His Trump Memos—But Won't Be Prosecuted," NPR, August 29, 2023, https://www.npr.org/2019/08/29/755402701/doj-comey-violated-policy-on-his-trump-memos-but-wont-be-prosecuted.

[176] Ibid.

a president—witness Trump's many political and legal battles, despite his claims of innocence and despite, even, prior findings of his innocence.

Why would anyone, regardless of political affiliation, defer so automatically to an FBI agent?

> Beloved, do not believe every spirit, but test the spirits to see whether they are from God, for many false prophets have gone out into the world. By this you know the Spirit of God: every spirit that confesses that Jesus Christ has come in the flesh is from God, and every spirit that does not confess Jesus is not from God. This is the spirit of the antichrist, which you heard was coming and now is in the world already.

(1 John 4:1–4, ESV)

As Christians, as patriotic Americans, and as members of a free society, questioning, testing, and questioning more ought to be as natural as breathing and eating. When we fail on this—when we fall into a more passive style of letting government be or into a more self-absorbed way of pursuing personal and perhaps more materialistic goals at the expense of civic responsibilities and spiritual attainment—then those in positions of power are emboldened to act in ways they wouldn't dare if they expected accountability, if they feared the people.

America's government no longer fears the people.

Too many American citizens nowadays actually fear the government.

This is a situation that has led government, along with their minions in most of the media outlets, to twist the Constitution into tortured bits of misguided, misdirected, and mistaken logic—and sadly, too few see the propaganda as its being pushed.

From the earlier 2019 *New York Times* quote, on the media-hyping of Trump's telephone call with Ukraine's leader, Zelensky, this line: "Little, if any, of the [unnamed] whistle-blower's complaint [about Trump] has been disproved, though Mr. Trump has sought to discredit him."[177]

Think about that for a moment.

In America, it's not the job of the accused to prove innocence; it's the job of the accuser to prove guilt. In America, too, it's the right of the accused to face the accuser. These are cherished and basic rights that help keep government and the judicial system free of corruption. Accusations from anonymous accusers lend themselves well to political hitmen and to political hitjobs.

Enter: Representative Adam Schiff, California Democrat.

"Schiff slammed for chalking up 'disturbing' fictional account of Trump-Ukraine call to 'parody,'" Fox News wrote in a headline in September 2019, after Schiff, then House Intelligence Committee chairman, took to the congressional floor and explained the Trump-Zelensky phone call in his own words, which happened to be lies that he later defended as a parody.[178] Just a joke—see? Nothing to see here—see?

From Fox News: "'I have a favor I want from you,' Schiff said while appearing to read from a paper [appearing to quote Trump's own words to Zelensky]. 'And I'm going to say this only seven times, so you better listen good. I want you to make up

[177] Nicholas Fandos, "Trump's Ukraine Call Was 'Crazy' and 'Frightening,' Official Told Whistleblower," *New York Times*, October 8, 2019, https://www.nytimes.com/2019/10/08/us/politics/trump-ukraine-whistleblower.html.

[178] Brian Flood, "Schiff slammed for chalking up 'disturbing' fictional account of Trump-Ukraine call to 'parody,'" Fox News, November 26, 2019, https://www.foxnews.com/media/schiff-parody.

dirt on my political opponent, understand? Lots of it, on this and on that.'"[179]

Bring me the heads of Joe and Hunter Biden on a plate—see? The mafia mock may have been entertaining to Democrats and anti-Trumpers. But politically speaking—because it was spoken from the House floor by the House Intelligence chairman, who appeared to read quotes from a written document, all while Trump was facing nonstop attacks and accusations from a host of enemies, including Schiff, who hated his White House and Make America First Again policies—even after the so-called joke was outed as a joke, the damage to the president was already done. Yes, Trump called out Schiff and demanded he resign from Congress because "he lied" to the American people.[180] Yes, some in the media expressed outrage at Schiff's circus show; some even agreed with Trump and Trump supporters that it was a curiously scripted, purposely worded, politically weaponized speech. But Trump's haters continued to use the occasion to paint the president as thuggish, tyrannical, unconstitutional— needful of impeachment. The Democrat Party's mouthpieces in the media quickly swung into gear.

PolitiFact rushed to give the "in context" look at Schiff's "joke," concluding it really wasn't all that untruthful.[181] CNN rushed to do the "fact check" of the matter, deciding that while, yes, Schiff may have "confused" viewers, regardless, "we can't

---

[179] Brian Flood, "Schiff slammed for chalking up 'disturbing' fictional account of Trump-Ukraine call to 'parody,'" Fox News, November 26, 2019, https://www.foxnews.com/media/schiff-parody.

[180] Yaron Steinbuch, "Trump calls on Adam Schiff to resign for allegedly lying to Congress," New York Post, September 27, 2019, https://nypost.com/2019/09/27/trump-calls-on-adam-schiff-to-resign-for-allegedly-lying-to-congress/.

[181] Bill McCarthy, "In context: Adam Schiff's dramatized version of the Trump-Zelensky call," PolitiFact, September 30, 2019, https://www.politifact.com/article/2019/sep/30/context-adam-schiffs-dramatized-version-trump-zele/.

endorse Trump's claim that Schiff 'lied,' since Schiff introduced his comments…by saying he would be outlining 'the essence of what the president communicates,' not providing 'the exact transcribed version of the call.'"[182] The *New York Times*, meanwhile, did a total redirect with its own "fact check" headline from September 2019: "Examining Trump's Claims About Democrats and Ukraine," rather than something less accusatory of Trump and more indicative of Schiff's obvious deceptions— such as "Examining Schiff's 'Lies' About Trump and Ukraine Call," or even a down-the-middle "Examining Trump's Claims of Schiff's 'Lies.'" The *New York Times* went on to find Trump guilty of exaggeration, even while acknowledging Schiff did deceive the public.

> Mr. Schiff, the chairman of the House Intelligence Committee did not claim to be reciting from the reconstructed transcript of the call and said he was conferring "the essence" of the conversation, "shorn of its rambling character and in not so many words." But he did speak in first person, leaving an impression that he was quoting Mr. Trump.[183]

In other words: Schiff gave a false impression. But he didn't lie. It's Trump who's really to blame for failing to understand the

[182] Daniel Dale, "Fact check: Breaking down Adam Schiff's account of Trump's Ukraine call," CNN, September 27, 2019, https://www.cnn.com/2019/09/27/politics/fact-check-adam-schiff-trumps-ukraine-call/index.html.

[183] Linda Qiu, "Examining Trump's Claims About Democrats and Ukraine," *New York Times*, September 30, 2019, https://www.nytimes.com/2019/09/30/us/politics/trump-ukraine-fact-check.html.

context—and all those Trump supporters too similarly stupid to see that Schiff's intents were pure.

It's incredible how some in America are given free passes, while others are figurately torn into two, while still others are draped in guilt but never targeted for investigations, while even still others are investigated into financial and political distress over entirely fabricated and falsified charges. To say there's a two-tiered system of justice in America is to downplay the problem. There's actually a class of "Innocent at All Costs" filled with elites, specially chosen favorites and carefully selected tools of the elites—and then there's the rest of America, "Guilty Until Proven Innocent."

Senator Blackburn, hammering for truth on Epstein, has exposed this corrupt system well.

As *Newsweek* reported in November 2023:

> During a Senate Judiciary Committee hearing...related to the authorization of subpoenas for [US Supreme Court] Justices Samuel A. Alito Jr. and Clarence Thomas as part of a Supreme Court ethics probe, Blackburn voiced her resistance to the subpoenas and mentioned Jeffrey Epstein. "Since we're in the business of issuing subpoenas now, here are a few more that I've filed," Blackburn said. "A subpoena to Jeffrey Epstein's estate to provide the flight logs for his private plane. Given the numerous allegations of human trafficking and abuse surrounding Mr. Epstein, we've got to identify everyone who could have participated in his horrific conduct."

Blackburn continued: "So, Mr. Chairman, I think there are real issues that we should be talking about. Social media is destroying our kids' lives, the southern border is wide open, and President Biden has lost track of 85,000 precious children. The world is on fire, but you've chosen to launch an assault on the Supreme Court's legitimacy. If you want to take up our time and go there, Mr. Chairman, we can go there. This is a sad day in the history of this prestigious committee, but I'm confident that the American people see this sham for what it really is."[184]

Senator Dick Durbin, in the face of Republican backlash, withdrew his push for the subpoenas, which were for Leonard Leo, a legal expert who helped President Donald Trump compile a list of potential Supreme Court justices to nominate, and Harlan Crow, a billionaire with ties to Justice Thomas—and who represented the hopes of the Democrats in the party's political takedown of the Supreme Court.

The *New York Times* in November 2023 stated:

> The fight over the [SCOTUS-tied] subpoenas is the result of a longstanding push by Mr. Durbin and Senate Democrats to persuade the Supreme Court to adopt a binding ethics code at least commensurate with one followed by

184 Anne Commander, "Jeffrey Epstein Plane Passenger Details Could Be Released," *Newsweek*, November 10, 2023, https://www.newsweek.com/jeffrey-epstein-plane-passenger-details-could-released-1842783.

judges on the lower federal courts. The effort gained new momentum in recent months after multiple reports by ProPublica and other news outlets about Justices Thomas and Alito taking private jet trips for stays at exclusive lodges and other luxury spots without revealing them on their financial disclosures. Mr. Leo, who has played a central role in pushing federal courts to the right, reportedly helped arrange an Alaskan fishing trip for Justice Alito while Mr. Crow also purchased real estate from Justice Thomas."[185]

But curiously missing from Durbin's righteous indignation about court ethics was his railing against Justice Sonia Sotomayor's staff and the fact they "prodded colleges and libraries to buy her books," as the Associated Press reported.[186]

Ethical behavior—it's all relative in the political realm.

But this is what happens when a nation turns from God and instead governs with a moral compass of human and earthly design. Priorities shift. Matters at first considered crucially important to pursue can so easily fall by the wayside. Winds can blow, whims can change, and in a flash, the wiles of just one can scatter the noble purposes and intents of others.

Pedophiles can go free while former presidents campaigning for second terms are unjustly prosecuted.

---

[185] Carl Hulse, "Senate Panel Punts Effort to Force Testimony in Supreme Court Ethics Inquiry," *New York Times*, November 9, 2023, https://www.nytimes.com/2023/11/09/us/politics/senate-supreme-court-ethics.html.

[186] Brian Slodysko and Eric Tucker, "Supreme Court Justice Sotomayor's staff prodded colleges and libraries to buy her books," Associated Press, July 11, 2023, https://apnews.com/article/supreme-court-sotomayor-book-sales-ethics-colleges-b2cb93493f927f995829762cb8338c02.

CHAPTER 7

THE FALSE PROPHET CALLED BILL GATES

I t's no secret the globalists want us to eat insects. So, when cow-hating, communist-adoring, climate change alarmist Bill Gates spends $113 million in a single six-year period buying up farmland in one state alone, then it's time to take notice.[187] He has a vision for manufacturing meat and for using bugs as sources of protein for people. And once again, as leftists love to tout, he says it's all for the good of the world.

"Put simply, there's no way," Gates wrote years ago on his Gates Notes blog, "to produce enough meat for 9 billion people. Yet we can't ask everyone to become vegetarians. That's why we

---

187 Destiny Herbers, "Spilling Bill's Beans: Tech billionaire spent $113 million on Nebraska farmland," Flatwater Free Press, December 21, 2023, https://flatwaterfreepress.org/spilling-bills-beans-tech-billionaire-spent-113-million-on-nebraska-farmland/.

need more options for producing meat without depleting our resources."[188]

Who died and put Gates in charge? And here you thought the feeding and caring for the people was God's role. This is the pride problem with Gates and his kind: They think they know best how the world should operate. They think they know better than God how to feed the masses—despite the fact that it's God who provides the food in the first place. They don't believe in the sovereignty of God, so they think they have to fill the role of God—with hope of receiving the glory that rightly belongs to God. The Bible is filled with evidence of God's ability and willingness to provide.

- In Exodus 15, as Moses was leading the Israelites, who God had freed from the Egyptians, away from the Red Sea and into the wilderness, the people began to complain. "When they came to Marah," Exodus 15:23–24 (RSV) states, "they could not drink the water of Marah because it was bitter; therefore it was named Marah. And the people murmured against Moses, saying, 'What shall we drink?' And he cried to the Lord; and the Lord showed him a tree, and he threw it into the water, and the water became sweet." So, the Israelites were provided water by God.

- In Exodus 16, as Moses was continuing to lead the Israelites away from their Egyptian bondage and deeper into the wilderness, the people began again to

[188] Bill Gates, "Future of food," GatesNotes.com: The blog of Bill Gates, March 18, 2013, https://www.gatesnotes.com/Future-of-Food#:~:text=Put%20simply%2C%20there's%20no%20way,meat%20without%20depleting%20our%20resources.

complain, this time from hunger. Exodus 16:2–5 (RSV) states, "And the whole congregation of the people of Israel murmured against Moses and [his brother] Aaron in the wilderness, and said to them, 'Would that we had died by the hand of the Lord in the land of Egypt, when we sat by the fleshpots and ate bread to the full; for you have brought us out into this wilderness to kill this whole assembly with hunger.' Then the Lord said to Moses, 'Behold I will rain bread from heaven for you; and the people shall go out and gather a day's portion every day, that I may prove them, whether they will walk in my law or not. On the sixth day, when they prepare what they bring in, it will be twice as much as they gather daily.'" So, the Israelites were provided by God both meat and manna, as well as a means of storing enough food so as to still honor the Sabbath as a day of rest. "In the evening," Exodus 16:13–15 (RSV) states, "quails came up and covered the camp; and in the morning dew lay round about the camp. And when the dew had gone up, there was on the face of the wilderness a fine, flake-like thing, fine as hoarfrost on the ground. When the people of Israel saw it, they said to one another, 'What is it?' For they did not know what it was. And Moses said to them, 'It is the bread which the Lord has given you to eat.'" So, the Israelites were provided by God the promised bread.

- In Exodus 17, as Moses and the Israelites continued their journey through the wilderness, the people began once more to complain. What was the problem this time? Again, they found no water. From Exodus 17:3–6 (RSV): "[A]nd the people murmured against Moses, and said, 'Why did you bring us up out of Egypt, to kill us and our children and our cattle with thirst?' So Moses cried to the Lord, 'What shall I do with this people? They are almost ready to stone me.' And the Lord said to Moses, 'Pass on before the people, taking with you some of the elders of Israel; and take in your hand the rod with which you struck the Nile, and go. Behold, I will stand before you there on the rock at Horeb; and you shall strike the rock, and water shall come out of it, that the people may drink.'" So, Moses did, and the people drank, and once again, it was all at God's provision.

Those are but a few of the examples of how God provides for the most basic of needs for His people. In the New Testament, Jesus fed thousands from five small loaves of bread and two fish (Matthew 14:13–21). He also turned water into wine—and not just any old wine, but the finest of wine—to provide for a party of wedding guests in Galilee (John 2:1–11). A nation that turns from God is a nation that forgets it's God who is the source of all—of food, of water, of drink, of all resources needed to survive and even thrive. And a nation that forgets God and instead looks elsewhere for basic needs is a nation that opens the door wide for enemies of God to become the providers and to bring with this provision an agenda, demand, or influence that is antithetical to godly principles, Judeo-Christian ideals, constitutional boundaries, and individual liberty.

This is where we get billionaire so-called philanthropists who don't see their roles as simply giving in line with God's command, freely and without strings. They act secretly, so that one hand does not know what the other hand has done—rather, giving in a manner they deem proper in their own minds, which very often leads to controlling in a manner they determine as suitable for their own strategized ends.

Gates may have been married to a church-going Catholic woman.[189] He may also profess a belief in God—sort of, anyway. On that, he's said, "I think it makes sense to believe in God, but exactly what decision in your life you make differently because of it, I don't know."[190] But his admiration for China's communists, as well as his all-court press for all-things-climate-change control and his flagrant disregard for American concepts of individualism and God-given liberties, make his hold over American farmland a matter of concern for individual freedom, and possibly national security. His farmland purchases are suspicious too, because he's not being entirely open and transparent about his intents.

Between 2017 and 2022, Gates spent $113 million buying farmland in Nebraska, which also gives him ownership of the precious water beneath the land.[191] He owns agricultural properties in at least seventeen other states, and as of 2023, he was the

---

[189] Terry Mattingly, "Religion ghosts in Bill and Melinda Gates split? There are some old questions to ask…," GetReligion.org, May 10, 2021, https://www.getreligion.org/getreligion/2021/5/10/any-religion-ghosts-in-the-bill-and-melinda-gates-split-there-are-questions-to-ask-.

[190] Stoyan Zaimov, "Bill Gates Reveals Family Goes to Catholic Church: 'It Makes Sense to Believe in God,'" The Christian Post, March 14, 2014, https://www.christianpost.com/news/bill-gates-reveals-family-goes-to-catholic-church-it-makes-sense-to-believe-in-god-116166/.

[191] Destiny Herbers, "Spilling Bill's beans: Tech billionaire spent $113 million on Nebraska farmland," Flatwater Free Press, December 21, 2023, https://flatwaterfreepress.org/spilling-bills-beans-tech-billionaire-spent-113-million-on-nebraska-farmland/.

largest private farmland owner in America.[192] Gates downplays
his farmland acquisitions. In a January 2023 "Ask Me Anything"
session on Reddit, a participant asked Gates about his land buys.
And this, in essence, is how Gates answered: "It wasn't my decision—it was my professional investment team's decision—and
besides, it's not really that much land, anyway."[193] "It's all about
increasing productivity," he added.[194] "It's all about creating
more jobs."[195]

It's all for the good of the people, he might as well have
added. Isn't that the usual and customary phrase of the left?

Gates could very well possess interest in creating models of
farming efficiency that provide jobs, increase food stocks for the
world, decrease pollutants, generate profits, boost economies,
and sharpen bottom lines. But he also has interest in matters
that will, if achieved, destroy economies, job opportunities,

[192] AgTecher, "Unveiling the Strategy: Why is Bill Gates Investing Massively in
Farmland?" AgTecher.com, March 15, 2023, https://agtecher.com/unveil-
ing-the-strategy-why-is-bill-gates-investing-massively-in-farmland/#:~:tex-
t=The%20Facts%3A%20Bill%20Gates%20and%20His%20Farmland%20
Empire&text=His%20most%20extensive%20holdings%20are,Let's%20
explore%20the%20possible%20reasons.

[193] Sarah Jackson, "Bill Gates responds to skepticism about him owning 275,000
acres of farmland: 'There isn't some grand scheme involved,'" Business Insider,
January 11, 2023, https://www.businessinsider.com/bill-gates-defends-farm-
land-purchases-there-isnt-some-grand-scheme-2023-1#:~:text=in%20the%20
US.-,Gates%20owns%20roughly%20275%2C000%20acres%20of%20farm-
land%20in%20the%20US,from%20the%20Department%20of%20
Agriculture.

[194] AJ Fabino, "Bill Gates Finally Explains Why He's Buying So Much U.S.
Farmland," Yahoo! Finance, February 27, 2023, https://finance.yahoo.com/
news/bill-gates-finally-explains-why-194910939.html?guccounter=1&guce_
referrer=aHR0cHM6Ly93d3cuZ29vZ2xlLmNvbS8&guce_referrer_sig=AQ
AAAJMjNrz8qqMwUwlmjYbWUrw4MsNNp6NKfAj3TNTSyX4jdDz9ytP
3PH3AXt3zuCJ8XFqfo1dxlB6mzYkmw8S5e1BOfE0z1cBq6mQxO8XBfz7
RextW8ViZIcBa7QmrMzJk1aWzDJ1bTRO-Jy2TBVimLhJAEjz7sixm8mN
z8rUAo1M5.

[195] Ibid.

and natural food sources. In other words, Gates has interest in advancing his own will, even at the displeasure of a reluctant world, and absent limits from a higher power—absent any spiritual grounding and yes, fear, of the eventual day of reckoning from a higher authority—it's unlikely his stated interest for humanity takes, or will take, priority over his oft-concealed interest for self. And what is that self-interest? Money, of course—but he has more than enough. Power and control too—but again, he already checks those columns. The true aim of Gates is glory; in the end, he wants to be remembered and regarded as someone who saved the world from demise. If that weren't so, if self-glorification was not his goal, he wouldn't fight too hard to put into place mandates, policies, agendas, and political ideas that are so truly secularist at root.

"Bill Gates Gives $4.8 Million To Develop Gas Masks For Cows To Fight Climate Change," one early-2023 heading from Cowboy State Daily read. The story went on to report:

> The Bill and Melinda Gates Foundation awarded a $4.8 million grant this [March] to London-based Zelp, a company developing a face mask for cattle designed to capture the methane produced by animal burps and turn it into carbon dioxide. Contrary to popular belief, it's not the gas coming out the back end of a cow that's a problem for the planet. Most of a bovine's methane is belched.... Methane is estimated to cause 85 times more warming than carbon dioxide, thereby the Zelp device

will reduce the threat cows pose to life on this planet.[196]

God's not smart enough to create animals that don't destroy the planet with their gaseous emissions?

As CNN reported in January 2023:

> Gates has announced an investment in Australian start-up Rumin8, which is developing a seaweed-based feed to reduce the methane emissions cows produce through their burps and, to a lesser extent, farts.... A spokesperson for Gates' fund, Breakthrough Energy Ventures, which led the $12 million investment round, told CNN: "Although cows are a significant [greenhouse gas] source, livestock agriculture remains one of the cheapest protein sources globally, which means technologies that can reduce emissions from the existing cattle supply chain today and in the future are critical.[197]

Rumin8 uses a bioactive ingredient found in red seaweed to make the methane-emission-lowering cow feed. But rather than spending the money and manpower to scoop up actual seaweed, the company produces the active ingredient in a lab.

[196] Cowboy State Daily, "Bill Gates Gives $4.8 Million To Develop Gas Masks For Cows To Fight Climate Change," Cowboy State Daily, February 23, 2023, https://cowboystatedaily.com/2023/03/23/bill-gates-gives-4-8-million-to-develop-gas-masks-for-cows-to-fight-climate-change/.

[197] Laura Paddison, "Bill Gates backs start-up tackling cow burps and farts," CNN, January 24, 2023, https://www.cnn.com/2023/01/24/world/cows-methane-emissions-seaweed-bill-gates-climate-intl/index.html. Brackets in original.

Rumin8 has plans to cut costs even further, and simultaneously expand distribution, by developing a capsule from the seaweed for farmers to give their bovines.[198]

Gas masks for cattle? Lab-developed food to cut down on bovine burps? Holy cow. Have we really come to this, America?

It's not Gates's dollar investments in these endeavors that matter; $4.8 million and $12 million are pennies in a billionaire's pockets. What matters more is the mainstreaming of such ideas. Just a few short years ago, the idea of stuffing cows' faces into masks to swish away their burps would have been laughable. Talk of cow farts as environmental hazards would have been ridiculous. That Gates has been able to move the ridiculous to an actual stage of development is one giant step toward a world he envisions under his thumb.

Of course, all the world's elites want a piece of the climate change pie.

Breakthrough Energy Ventures (BEV), founded by Gates in 2015, is an investment firm for massive environmental projects that all share the common mission of bringing the globe to a state and standard of zero greenhouse gas emissions.[199] Among the thirty-four names of board members and investors listed on BEV's website are Jack Ma, the Chinese business magnate and cofounder of the technology conglomerate the Alibaba Group; Jeff Bezos of Amazon CEO fame; Saudi billionaire Al Waleed bin Talal; German billionaire businessman and SAP SE software company cofounder Hasso Plattner; and Cari Tuna, philan-

---

[198] Oliver Milman, "Bill Gates backs new startup aiming to reduce emissions from cow burps," *The Guardian*, January 24, 2023, https://www.theguardian.com/us-news/2023/jan/24/bill-gates-startup-cow-burps-methane-emissions.

[199] Breakthrough Energy, "Our Approach: Letting Science Lead the Way," BreakthroughEnergy.org, accessed January 9, 2024, https://breakthroughenergy.org/our-approach/.

thropic organizer, and Dustin Moskovitz, Facebook cofounder, who married and then went on to establish the Good Ventures Foundation, Good Ventures LLC, Open Philanthropy, and the Open Philanthropy Project Fund and who donate millions of dollars to Democrat candidates and causes.[200] It's a veritable feast of far-leftist, globalist-thinking 1-percenters who see environmentalism as their next meal ticket. And why shouldn't they? Climate touches upon every aspect of human existence, from driving cars to flying planes to building homes to farming fields.

BEV seeks to control five key areas of life, according to their website:

1. "How We Make Things: Manufactured goods and materials—the cement in our buildings, the steel in our appliances, the clothes we wear, the books we read, the plastic in the device you're using to read this sentence—account for nearly one-third of emissions worldwide. To bring this sector to net zero, we need to use clean electricity and production processes whenever possible."[201]

2. "How We Get Around: From electric vehicles to low-carbon fuels, getting transportation to zero [emissions] will require a complete transformation of the way we move goods and people from place to place."[202]

3. "How We Plug In: We need to find new ways to generate, store, and use low-carbon electricity while scaling

200 Breakthrough Energy, "Breakthrough Energy Ventures: Board and Investors," BreakthroughEnergy.org, accessed January 9, 2024, https://breakthroughenergy.org/our-work/breakthrough-energy-ventures/bev-board-and-investors/.
201 Breakthrough Energy, ""How We Make Things," BreathroughEnergy.org, accessed January 9, 2023, https://breakthroughenergy.org/our-approach/grand-challenges/.
202 Ibid.

up existing technologies like wind and solar, advanced nuclear power, geothermal energy, and thermal generation with carbon capture."[203]

4. "How We Live: From greener materials to cleaner industrial processes, we must find ways to build and use buildings without emitting carbon."[204]

5. And finally—"How We Grow Things: Bringing these emissions to zero while still meeting a growing global demand for food will require us to make significant changes to the ways we farm and eat: reducing the use of fertilizers, improving soil management, cutting methane emissions from livestock, and minimizing the consumption and waste of high-carbon foods by scaling up technologies like plant-based meat and dairy products."[205]

These are the stated goals of Gates and his BEV partners.

Suddenly, his interest in farmland starts to make perfect sense. Consider this, though: The Environmental Protection Agency tracks greenhouse gas emissions by sector, and for 2021, the latest year available, America's agricultural sector was responsible for 11 percent of the total, including that generated by electricity use; for commercial and residential, 30 percent; for transportation, 29 percent; and for industry, 30 percent.[206] Put that in context of the world's greenhouse gas emissions—and it's not America that tops the list. China emits twice what

---

[203] Ibid.
[204] Ibid.
[205] Ibid.
[206] U.S. Environmental Protection Agency, "Sources of Greenhouse Gas Emissions," EPA.gov, updated November 16, 2023, accessed January 9, https://www.epa.gov/ghgemissions/sources-greenhouse-gas-emissions.

America does; third and fourth in line are India and the European Union.[207] China, of course, gets a free pass because the globalists are actively trying to buoy the communist country's economy and influence while depressing America's one regulatory control at a time, one shaming tactic at a time.

This is the danger Gates represents.

This is the enemy that has set up shop within America's gates.

"As of today," AgTecher wrote in March 2023, "Bill Gates is the largest private farmland owner in the United States, with a staggering 242,000 acres of agricultural land spread across 18 states. His most extensive holdings are in Louisiana (69,071 acres), Arkansas (47,927 acres), and Nebraska (20,588 acres)."[208] The acreage represents only a tiny fraction of America's vast farmlands—about 1/4,000th, according to Gates's estimation as cited by AgTecher. But it isn't necessary to hold a majority to exert an influence. As AgTecher also noted, "Gates' farmland investments might also have an impact on the agricultural industry and the environment, and it remains to be seen how they will unfold and what kind of impact they will have on the world."[209]

In the meantime, Gates gets yet another way to pad his pockets—and in a manner that skirts public scrutiny.

The Flatwater Free Press wrote in December 2023:

---

[207] U.S. Environmental Protection Agency, "Global Greenhouse Gas Emissions Data," EPA.gov, updated February 15, 2023, accessed January 9, 2024, https://www.epa.gov/ghgemissions/global-greenhouse-gas-emissions-data.

[208] AgTecher, "Unveiling the Strategy: Why is Bill Gates Investing Massively in Farmland?" AgTecher.com, March 15, 2023, https://agtecher.com/unveiling-the-strategy-why-is-bill-gates-investing-massively-in-farmland/#:~:text=The%20Facts%3A%20Bill%20Gates%20and%20His%20Farmland%20Empire&text=His%20most%20extensive%20holdings%20are,Let's%20explore%20the%20possible%20reasons.

[209] Ibid.

Gates' farmland is held by more than 20 shell
companies spread across the country. Some lead
back to a P.O. Box in Kirkland, Washington,
the city where Cascade Asset Management,
which manages all Gates' investments, is head-
quartered. Others are linked to Lenexa, Kansas,
and Monterey, Louisiana, population 371,
where reporters have previously traced Gates'
operations. These limited liability companies,
buried under layers of business names, overlap-
ping employees and addresses in at least three
states, form a network more tangled and opaque
than the one created by the Church of Jesus
Christ of Latter-day Saints, which is buying a
giant amount of Nebraska ranch land. Because
it's hidden, Nebraskans living and farming in
communities where Gates is among the largest
landowners are often unaware that one of the
world's richest men owns the cornfield down
the road.[210]

Or the fields of carrots and onions that find their way onto
Americans' dinner tables—or the potatoes that go into making the famous fries at McDonald's fast-food restaurants: few
know Gates owns these farm properties.[211] So why the secrecy?

---

[210] Destiny Herbers, "Spilling Bill's beans: Tech billionaire spent $113 million
on Nebraska farmland," Flatwater Free Press, December 21, 2023, https://
flatwaterfreepress.org/spilling-bills-beans-tech-billionaire-spent-113-million-
on-nebraska-farmland/.

[211] April Glaser, "McDonald's french fries, carrots, onions: all of the foods that
come from Bill Gates farmland," NBC News, June 9, 2021, https://www.
nbcnews.com/tech/tech-news/mcdonald-s-french-fries-carrots-onions-
all-foods-come-bill-n1270033.

Why the shell companies and network of tangled enterprises all invested in farmland on behalf of Gates?

Two reasons jump to mind—one, finances; the other, public relations.

Gates may be one of the wealthiest men in the world, estimated by *Forbes* in January 2024 to have a net worth of nearly $119 billion.[212] But he doesn't like paying taxes any more than the average American earner. ProPublica found that between 2013 and 2018, Gates's average annual income was about $2.85 billion, due in large part to sales of his Microsoft stock.[213] At the same time, his federal tax rate was only 18.4 percent, ProPublica reported.[214] How can that be? Simply put, it's a benefit of being a 1-percenter.

"The top 400 earners pay noticeably lower tax rates than the merely rich," ProPublica reported. "[A]nd, if you include payroll taxes, a married couple making $200,000 a year could end up paying higher tax rates than a person making $200 million a year."[215]

Gates and his billionaire cronies aren't breaking any laws by paying less tax than those who earn substantially less, but their strategic game does send a certain kind of message to the public—and it's not one of altruists at work. Moreover, in Gates's

---

[212] *Forbes*, "Profile: Bill Gates: Cochair, Bill and Melinda Gates Foundation, Real Time Net Worth," *Forbes*, January 9, 2024, https://www.forbes.com/profile/bill-gates/?sh=60a7366f689f.

[213] ProPublica, "America's Top 15 Earners and What They Reveal About the U.S. Tax System," ProPublica.org, April 13, 2022, https://www.propublica.org/article/americas-top-15-earners-and-what-they-reveal-about-the-us-tax-system.

[214] ProPublica, "America's Top 15 Earners and What They Reveal About the U.S. Tax System," ProPublica.org, April 13, 2022, https://www.propublica.org/article/americas-top-15-earners-and-what-they-reveal-about-the-us-tax-system.

[215] ProPublica, "America's Top 15 Earners and What They Reveal About the U.S. Tax System," ProPublica.org, April 13, 2022, https://www.propublica.org/article/americas-top-15-earners-and-what-they-reveal-about-the-us-tax-system.

case, he seeks to lower his already lowered tax rate even more. Enter: farmland. He takes out bank loans on his real estate assets so as to delay, or even avoid, paying tax.

From the Flatwater Free Press article again:

> Gates doesn't simply receive rent checks from his Nebraska farmland. He's also using it to borrow staggering sums of money. Three days before Christmas 2021, Mt. Edna Farms [owned by Gates] filed paperwork with Dawson County, clearing the path to use a part of Gates' land as collateral. Gates' LLC then took out two loans against his Nebraska farmland. The total of those loans: $700 million.[216]

It's a tax scheme—again, legal—that allows the super-rich to establish a corporate structure granting them the ability to borrow against appreciating assets and live tax-free off the loan dollars. Then, depending on the circumstances, these aging wealthy could even pass those assets, like land, along to inheritors, who could sell them off and pay back the loans—all the while, continuing the cycle of avoiding tax payments. Maybe that's why Gates prefers to purchase farm properties in America, rather than elsewhere in the world, where tax laws may not offer such opportunity.

Yet ask Gates about his interest in farmland, and it's all shoulder-shrugging.

---

216 Destiny Herbers, "Spilling Bill's beans: Tech billionaire spent $113 million on Nebraska farmland," Flatwater Free Press, December 21, 2023, https://flatwaterfreepress.org/spilling-bills-beans-tech-billionaire-spent-113-million-on-nebraska-farmland/.

As mentioned earlier in the chapter, Gates was asked a question about his farmland purchase by a Reddit user. He was asked, "Why are you buying up so much farmland, do you think this is a problem with billionaire wealth and how much you can disproportionally acquire?" And Gates answered, as Business Insider noted, "I own less than 1/4000 of the farmland in the US. I have invested in these farms to make them more productive and create more jobs. There isn't some grand scheme involved—in fact all these decisions are made by a professional investment team." He then went on to add this somewhat transparent attempt at care for the less financially fortunate: "In terms of the very rich I think they should pay a lot more in taxes and they should give away their wealth over time. It has been very fulfilling for me and is my full time job."[217]

Well, bully for Gates. But if he truly wants to pay more in taxes, why doesn't he? He could start by paying off his Nebraska land loans, living off his true income—and paying the IRS based on this actual asset income. But that's just one not-so-publicly discussed benefit Gates derives from his farm properties. The other is more stomach-churning.

In August 2021, the Bill & Melinda Gates Foundation announced on its website a $2.2 million grant for Insecti Pro Limited "to establish a commercially-viable business for sustainable insect production for food and feed products in East and

217 Sarah Jackson, "Bill Gates responds to skepticism about him owning 275,000 acres of farmland: 'There isn't some grand scheme involved,'" Business Insider, January 11, 2023, https://www.businessinsider.com/bill-gates-defends-farmland-purchases-there-isnt-some-grand-scheme-2023-1#:~:text=in%20the%20US.-,Gates%20owns%20roughly%20275%2C000%20acres%20of%20farmland%20in%20the%20US,from%20the%20Department%20of%20Agriculture.

Central Africa."[218] That came after a separate $100,000 foundation grant in 2012 to All Things Bugs, LLC "to develop a method for the efficient production of nutritionally dense food using insect species," according to the online announcement of award.[219] Disgusting. It's one thing to have to eat bugs because of starvation; it's another thing entirely to invest in a system that pressures people to eat insects because elites have convinced themselves that cows will destroy the planet.

"We are changemakers," Insecti Pro states on its website. "[I]nsects are the missing piece in our food and value chains."[220] As such, the company produces black soldier flies to pull "protein and fat from the larvae, chitin [used for biomedical applications] from the pre-pupals and organic fertilizer from the left overs," the website states.[221] Insecti Pro reports it also farms crickets, to be "consumed whole and as a powder…to be incorporated in many meals."[222]

It's a growing business.

"There are almost 2,000 insect species in the world that are considered edible, and each species has its own nutritional characteristics. Those more widely used to produce flours are crickets, mealworms, buffalo worms and grasshoppers," wrote

[218] Bill & Melinda Gates Foundation, "InsectiPro Limited, Committed Grants," Bill & Melinda Gates Foundation, August 2021, https://www.gatesfoundation.org/about/committed-grants/2021/08/inv032416.

[219] Bill & Melinda Gates Foundation, "All Things Bugs, LLC, Committed Grants," Bill & Melinda Gates Foundation, May 2012, https://www.gates-foundation.org/about/committed-grants/2012/05/opp1044748.

[220] InsectiPro, "We Are Changemakers," InsectiPro.com, accessed January 12, 2024, https://insectipro.com/meet-the-changemakers/.

[221] Ibid.

[222] Ibid.

21bites, in an article entitled "How to use insects flour" that was published in 2019.[223]

It's a growing, gross business.

And it's one that figures into Gates's announced climate change, emission-controlling intents to change the eating habits of the world, force people to eat what they don't want, and force the field of farming to move from God's natural grounds to laboratories run by chemical researchers who spend their time attempting to replicate the tastes of real food.

"Bill Gates: Rich nations should shift entirely to synthetic beef," ran one *MIT Technology Review* headline in February 2021.[224] The piece was a journalist-directed, question-answer session with Gates about his book *How to Avoid a Climate Disaster* that at one point included this brief back-and-forth:

> Q. In the book you cover a broad array of hard-to-solve sectors. The one I still have the hardest time with, in terms of fully addressing it, is food. The scale is massive. We've barely begun. We fundamentally don't have replacements that completely eliminate the highly potent emissions from burping livestock and fertilizer. How hopeful are you about agriculture?

[223] 21Bites, "How to use insects flour," 21Bites blog, February 19, 2019, https://21bites.com/blogs/blog/how-to-use-insects-flour#:~:text=It's%20 fairly%20simple%2C%20we%20only,according%20to%20taste%20 and%20needs.

[224] James Temple, "Bill Gates: Rich nations should shift entirely to synthetic beef," *MIT Technology Review*, February 14, 2021, https://www.technology review.com/2021/02/14/1018296/bill-gates-climate-change-beef-trees-microsoft/?gad_source=1&gclid=EAIaIQobChMIh4T62tXYgwMVVVtHA R28GgAYEAAYASAAEgL1K_D_BwE.

A. There are [companies], including one in
the [Breakthrough Energy Ventures] portfolio
called Pivot Bio, that significantly reduce
the amount of fertilizer you need. There are
advances in seeds.... In terms of livestock, it's
very difficult. There are all the things where
they feed them different food, like there's this
one compound that gives you a 20% reduction
[in methane emissions]. But sadly, those
bacteria [in their digestive systems that produce
methane] are a necessary part of breaking down
the grass. And so I don't know if there'll be some
natural approach there. I'm afraid the synthetic
[protein alternatives like plant-based burgers]
will be required for at least the beef thing.[225]

Arrogance, meet cavalier. Gates tosses out his decrees like
he's king and the citizens of the world were simply placed on the
planet to meet his wish and demand. He's sad that cows have
digestive systems that produce methane, and because he hasn't
thought of a way to beat back God's design on that, he's going
to force citizens to give up their steaks and burgers. Another
question-answer from this same *MIT* interview:

Q. Do you think plant-based and lab-grown
meats could be the full solution to the protein
problem globally, even in poor nations? Or do
you think it's going to be some fraction because
of the things you're talking about, the cultural

---

[225] Ibid. Brackets in original.

love of a hamburger and the way livestock is so central to economies around the world?

A. For Africa and other poor countries, we'll have to use animal genetics to dramatically raise the amount of beef per emissions for them.... So no, I don't think the poorest 80 countries will be eating synthetic meat. I do think all rich countries should move to 100% synthetic beef. You can get used to the taste difference, and the claim is they're going to make it taste even better over time. Eventually, that green premium is modest enough that you can sort of change the [behavior of] people or use regulation to totally shift the demand.[226]

Animal genetics? Synthetic beef? Regulatory controls on what foods are available to people so as to "shift the demand" and force them to eat what they don't currently want? It's already in the works. Gates in 2018 donated $40 million to the Edinburgh-based Global Alliance for Livestock Veterinary Medicines, GALVmed, for research that would produce a genetically altered cow that could better withstand hotter climates.[227] Why? The public message was to bring to poorer countries like Africa, where summer temperatures soar, the opportunity for beef and dairy in equal amounts to what European countries, with more temperate climates, can produce. On the surface, that seems a noble goal. But Gates has been interested in genetic engineering

---

[226] Ibid. Brackets in original.
[227] Alexandra Ma, "Bill Gates is funding genetic research into how to create the perfect cow," Business Insider, January 26, 2018, https://www.businessinsider.com/bill-gates-dfid-investment-galvmed-perfect-cow-edinburgh-2018-1.

for a long time. Given his hope to shift tastebuds toward lab-pro-duced meat, it's questionable whether his quest for hardier cows is solely an altruistic endeavor to feed the poor or, once again, rooted in the pursuit of power, control, and glory.

Smart money's on the bet that he's using the altruistic endeavor as a cover to experiment with genetics for his lon-ger-term aspirations with climate change and vaccines.

"By isolating desirable genetics traits from European and African cow breeds, geneticists hope to design a cow that produces high quantities of milk and is also able to withstand exceptionally high temperatures," Futurism wrote in January 2018. "'You can have a cow that is four times as productive with the same survivability,' Gates [said]."[228]

You could. Perhaps.

Or, you could get this, as described by a headline from *MIT Technology Review* in August 2019: "Gene-edited cattle have a major screwup in their DNA."[229]

The St. Paul, Minnesota, gene-editing company Recombi-netics claimed that by tinkering just a bit with the DNA of dairy cattle, they could bring to life a hornless breed. They did. But the Food and Drug Administration (FDA) found a problem—a bit of "unintended" bacterial DNA within the genome sequence of an edited bull, as *MIT Technology Review* reported.[230] Here's more from this *MIT* article:

---

[228] Lou Del Bello, "Bill Gates Is Working With Geneticists to Create the 'Perfect' Cow," Futurism, January 29, 2018, https://futurism.com/bill-gates-working-geneticists-create-perfect-cow.

[229] Antonio Regalado, "Gene-edited cattle have a major screwup in their DNA," *MIT Technology Review*, August 29, 2019, https://www.technologyreview.com/2019/08/29/65364/recombinetics-gene-edited-hornless-cattle-major-dna-screwup/.

[230] Ibid.

[G]ene editing isn't yet as predictable or reliable as promoters say. Instead, the procedure, meant to make pinpoint changes to DNA, can introduce significant unexpected changes without anyone noticing. "As genome-editing technology evolves, so does our understanding of the unintended alterations it produces," wrote the FDA scientists, led by Alexis Norris and Heather Lombardi, in a paper they released in July. They think gene-editing errors "are under reported" and a "blind spot" for scientists. The risk of haphazard engineering isn't just to barnyard animals. Genome-editing treatments to cure rare diseases are being tested on people and it is possible that patients will end up with unplanned genetic mutations.[231]

This is what happens when people like Bill Gates think they know better than God how to provide for humanity. A fine line separates good from evil, and what sometimes begins with honorable intentions can be corrupted and used for nefarious designs by others; more than that, what sometimes is presented as good is really window dressing to conduct evil. When altruistic intentions are driven by ego and pride and not by the love of Christ and a desire to obey His commandments, then wickedness is the result.

In 2015, China researchers used the gene-editing tool CRISPR to alter genes of human embryos in a lab dish, which

---

[231] Ibid.

were then implanted into two women.[232] One of the women gave birth to twin girls in November 2018.[233] About a year later, China quietly announced that the other woman had delivered a baby too.[234] The news horrified much of the world, sparking legal backlash. Scientist He Jiankui eventually pleaded guilty to "illegal medical practices" in court in Shenzhen, where he was sentenced to three years in prison and fined three million yuan, or about $429,000.[235] His collaborators, Zhang Renli and Qin Jinzhou, also pleaded guilty and received lesser prison sentences and fines.[236] These were essentially wrist slaps.

In 2023, a freed He was back at it.

"Controversial scientist He Jiankui proposes new gene editing research," CNN wrote in a headline dated July 2023. The story went on to state:

> [H]e again courted controversy by posting a new research proposal that experts say is reminiscent of his earlier work, which scientists broadly decried as unethical and dangerous—with the potential to impact human DNA across generations. In a succinct, one page

---

[232] Dennis Normile, "CRISPR bombshell: Chinese researcher claims to have created gene-edited twins," *Science*, November 26, 2018, https://www.science.org/content/article/crispr-bombshell-chinese-researcher-claims-have-created-gene-edited-twins.

[233] Tim Newcomb, "The First Gene-Edited Babies Are Supposedly Alive and Well, Says Guy Who Edited Them," *Popular Mechanics*, February 7, 2023, https://www.popularmechanics.com/science/health/a42790400/crispr-babies-where-are-they-now-first-gene-edited-children/.

[234] Ibid.

[235] Dennis Normile, "Chinese scientist who produced genetically altered babies sentenced to 3 years in jail," *Science*, December 30, 2019, https://www.science.org/content/article/chinese-scientist-who-produced-genetically-altered-babies-sentenced-3-years-jail.

[236] Ibid.

document, He proposed research that would involve gene-edited mouse embryos and then human fertilized egg cells, or zygotes, in order to test whether a mutation "confers protection against Alzheimer's disease."[237]

He spoke of the need to help the elderly, address China's rapidly aging population, and ease the country's financial burden as it relates to Alzheimer's patients. And away we go. Here we go again. It's for the good of humanity.

Or is it? From the same CNN article:

> "The whole thing is, to put it bluntly, insane," said Peter Dröge, an associate professor at the Nanyang Technological University in Singapore, who focuses on molecular and biochemical genetics. The proposed research could be seen as a step to explore if such a method of genetic editing could be used in a viable embryo in [the] future, according to Dröge. Apart from ethical considerations, gene-editing an embryo to address a complex disease that affects people toward the end of their life and doesn't have a clear, single genetic cause is "highly questionable," he said. "He basically wants to genetically modify the human species so they don't get Alzheimer's," he said.[238]

---

[237] Simone McCarthy, "Controversial Chinese scientist He Jiankui proposes new gene editing research," CNN, July 3, 2023, https://www.cnn.com/2023/07/03/china/he-jiankui-gene-editing-proposal-china-intl-hnk-scn/index.html.

[238] Ibid.

Someone somewhere listening to or reading Dröge's criticisms of He's proposal might say—so what? Eradicating Alzheimer's would be a good thing.

That's true; it would be. But with medical research—with scientific inquiry, development, and creation—the intended good must always be considered with a view toward unintended consequences. Adolf Hitler and his Nazi regime wanted to create a master race—a perfect race. Gene-editing to eradicate Alzheimer's could quickly jump to territories of gene-editing that wouldn't bring so welcome of results. The human heart and will must be subservient to God, else the chance for wickedness and evil is near certain.

Scientists and researchers—and so-called philanthropic billionaires—who aren't called to humble service to God first are frankly dangerous. Their motivations aren't pure, and because of their deep pockets and their public displays of charity, they too often fall beneath the radar of suspicion. Their love of self is easily packaged and presented as love for humanity. It takes discernment and understanding of God's intents for humanity—for each and every individual He created—to see the evil from the stated good.

It takes a belief in the spiritual realm and in an eternal afterlife to resist the power of the well-padded purse here on Earth and realize that billionaires may not care about humanity as much as they publicly put forth—and that they certainly don't care about humans as much as God does. Control and collectivism are not tenets of God, and always, the glory is supposed to go to Him, not self.

Beware the false idol of Bill Gates.

From his Gates Notes on June 16, 2023:

- "I just had a meeting with President Xi [Jinping], in which we discussed the importance of addressing global health and development challenges, like health inequity and climate change, and how China can play a role in achieving progress for people everywhere."[239]

- "One highlight was my visit to the Global Health Drug Discovery Institute, an organization our foundation helped establish six years ago in partnership with the Beijing Municipal Government and Tsinghua University. GHDDI represents a productive way for public and private partners to work together on discovering new medicines for diseases that disproportionately impact the world's most vulnerable populations but have applications for the world.... [We] extended our partnership over the next five years."[240]

Yes. *Forbes* reported it.

"Gates Foundation To Donate $50 Million, Partner With Beijing And Tsinghua To Fight Infectious Diseases," the news organization reported on June 15, 2023.[241]

Back to the June 2023 Gates Notes:

- "I also got to visit the National Crop Genebank of China. This facility is a prominent crop research center and also serves as a long-term preservation storage space

[239] Bill Gates, "Back In China: I'm visiting the country after four years away," GatesNotes.com, June 16, 2023, https://www.gatesnotes.com/Visiting-China.

[240] Ibid.

[241] Russell Flannery, "Gates Foundation To Donate $50 Million, Partner With Beijing And Tsinghua To Fight Infectious Diseases," *Forbes*, June 15, 2023, https://www.forbes.com/sites/russellflannery/2023/06/15/gates-foundation-to-donate-50-million-partner-with-beijing-and-tsinghua-to-fight-infectious-disease/?sh=7ea19dd54465.

for seeds so that scientists around the world have access to important genetic data."[242]

- "The genebank and GHDDI are just two examples of the promising work the foundation has seen in China in the more than 15 years we've been partnering here. And there will be more opportunities for China and others to step up."[243]

Why is Bill Gates meeting with President Xi to discuss ways the human-rights-destroying communists in China can make the world—can make America—a better place for all? Why is Bill Gates funding communist China's research into drugs, medicines, and health treatments to fight infectious diseases around the world—when it was the communist country who brought the world the Wuhan virus and then lied about it? Why is Bill Gates partnering with an enemy of America—communist China—on genetic-based research that could one day fuel the development of mass databases, mass surveillance, and mass controls? There's more. From the Daily Caller in January 2024:

> The Bill and Melinda Gates Foundation paid out or approved for future payment roughly $23 million in grants to Chinese government organizations during its 2022 reporting period, tax documents show. The nonprofit listed grants to over 20 different Chinese entities, including Chinese government agencies, labeled as "foreign government" on its 2022 tax forms. The

---

[242] Bill Gates, "Back In China: I'm visiting the country after four years away," GatesNotes.com, June 16, 2023, https://www.gatesnotes.com/Visiting-China.
[243] Ibid.

majority of the grants were for projects related to public health research and analysis, including several projects involving diseases and vaccine delivery…. Moreover, the Gates Foundation funded Chinese universities that regularly perform defense work for the Chinese military.[244]

Billionaires who use the American capitalistic system to grow their money ought to at least stay true to American principles, instead of selling the nation down the river to the communists. But immoral capitalists—a label that applies to Gates—always exploit the systems for personal gain and then use their successes and fat wallets to keep out the rest from similarly succeeding. They want to keep their elite status and don't want a flood of peons mucking their society of 1-percenters with their own financial wizardries. The more people who make money like Gates does, the less elite Gates's class becomes and the more threatened Gates becomes. Elitism only works, after all, when there are large classes to shut out and segregate.

Gates always pretends his motive is altruism, though. From the June 2023 Gates Notes, once more:

I'm convinced that if the world works together to address climate change, health inequity and food security we can make extraordinary progress. And I'm looking forward to exploring new

[244] Robert Schmad, "Bill Gates' Foundation Poured Millions Into Chinese Government Orgs in 2022," The Daily Caller News Foundation, January 7, 2024, https://dailycaller.com/2024/01/07/bill-gates-foundation-poured-millions-into-chinese-government-orgs-in-2022/.

opportunities for collaboration and innovation that will make a better future for everyone.[245]

The truth, however, is much darker.

Bill Gates works with China because he can pursue his scientific and research discoveries outside the boundaries of godly morals, constitutional laws, and concerns of individual liberties. Communism gives Gates a free pass on personal pursuits because, in the end, the goals of communists and Gates are one and the same: to control the populations of the world and dictate how all must live, eat, work, and travel.

Communists are just branded with a more negative label.

And that's what makes Gates all the more dangerous. He works hand in hand with the CCP but keeps one foot in America, exploiting the very freedoms he then seeks to undercut and destroy for everyone else—and all along, he receives kudos, respect, admiration, and fawning from the press, public, and people who don't see or care about his communist ties.

"Bill Gates Is the Most Interesting Man in the World," one writer in the *New York Times* opined in May 2020.[246]

"Coronavirus: Bill Gates as prophet predicted pandemic in 2015," Eudebates.tv wrote in March 2020.[247]

The adoration of a moneymaker is a danger to free society. It's capitalism without a moral compass. It's capitalism of the ungodly. It's worship of materialism.

---

245 Bill Gates, "Back In China: I'm visiting the country after four years away," GatesNotes.com, June 16, 2023, https://www.gatesnotes.com/Visiting-China.

246 Timothy Egan, "Bill Gates Is the Most Interesting Man in the World," *New York Times*, May 22, 2020, https://www.nytimes.com/2020/05/22/opinion/bill-gates-coronavirus.html.

247 Eudebates team, "Coronavirus: Bill Gates as prophet predicted pandemic in 2015," Eudebates.tv, March 30, 2020, https://eudebates.tv/debates/world-debates/coronavirus-bill-gates-as-prophet-predicted-pandemic-in-2015/.

Worse still, Gates is hardly the only elitist who gets a free pass on his Marxist ways. The communist capitalist model—yes, they're trying to pretend that's actually a thing—has seeped into America and is spreading fast.

CHAPTER 8

LIVING IN GREAT RESET TIMES

We are living out the Great Reset right now. What's that? It's the World Economic Forum's way of ushering in a total top-down communist control of all the countries, all the governments, and all the citizens of the globe. They don't want their designs known. They want to work in secret. The elites at the WEF and their partners and collaborators would much rather quietly steal sovereignty, instead of openly fight for it; they'd much rather the takeover of all individual liberties be accomplished by stealth, in the shadows, completely hidden from view. It's easier that way. It's much easier to conquer those who don't even know they're in a war.

"'The Great Reset' Conspiracy Flourishes Amid Continued Pandemic," ADL wrote in December 2020.[248]

But now the jig's up. Word's out. The Great Reset is a published "initiative"—taken from the WEF's economic recovery plan of 2008, called the Global Redesign Initiative,[249] as well as a published book, *COVID-19: The Great Reset*, by the WEF's founder, Klaus Schwab, and Thierry Malleret, founder of the Monthly Barometer.[250]

Calling it conspiracy theory any longer is nonsense.

But so is denying that it's going forth, as we live and breathe.

And so is denying that despite the detestable communist nature of its intents, despite the fact that much has been publicized about the inherent anti-American bent of its goals, despite the backlash that's come from what's been publicized and what's been revealed about its despicable Marxist ways—that despite all this, the Great Reset is actually underway. It's not been stopped. It's not been reversed. It's barely been slowed. Simply reporting on the truths of the Great Reset has not served to halt its inception.

These Great Resetters are neither ashamed nor afraid.

---

[248] Anti-Defamation League, "'The Great Reset' Conspiracy Flourishes Among Continued Pandemic," ADL.org, December 29, 2020, https://www.adl.org/resources/blog/great-reset-conspiracy-flourishes-amid-continued-pandemic?gad_source=1&gclid=EAIaIQobChMIwsiN1ZbsgwMViUhHAR0VkAbmEAAYASAAEgIMUvD_BwE&gclsrc=aw.ds.

[249] Ivan Wecke, "Conspiracy theories aside, there is something fishy about the Great Reset," openDemocracy, August 16, 2021, https://www.opendemocracy.net/en/oureconomy/conspiracy-theories-aside-there-something-fishy-about-great-reset/.

[250] Yann Zopf, "Klaus Schwab and Thierry Malleret Release 'COVID-19: The Great Reset,' the First Policy Book on the COVID Crisis Globally," World Economic Forum Media Releases, July 14, 2020, https://www.weforum.org/press/2020/07/klaus-schwab-and-thierry-malleret-release-covid-19-the-great-reset-the-first-policy-book-on-the-covid-crisis-globally/.

America, open wide your eyes and see that the Great Reset has been moving at a rapid pace through both country and culture, and soon enough it won't even matter who sits in the White House; it won't matter who's elected to Congress; it won't make a difference if Republicans versus Democrats versus card-carrying socialists serve in public office. Soon enough, the real movers and shakers will be working outside the confines of elected office and above and beyond the reproach of angry or disgruntled voters.

Legally speaking, they will be the untouchables.

Many are already in place. Many of the world's systems have been infiltrated and corrupted by Great Reset collaborators. They're busily at work exploiting America's Constitution for communist gain, turning America's freedoms into weapons to control. They hate Donald Trump because he represents all that threatens their global designs. They hate "America First" patriots, especially the Bible-thumping kind, because they cannot sustain their takeover so long as this spirit of individualism based on God-given liberty remains. Christian nationalists, the building blocks of American exceptionalism—the beacons who remind all that it's God who makes this country great and that it's God who grants individuals their freedoms—are their enemies, and they work hard to degrade the "Christian nationalism" label and turn it into a negative, a shame, a horror.

Yes, indeed. We are living out the Great Reset right now.

In August 2021, United Airlines, under the leadership of CEO Scott Kirby, told employees to either get the Covid-19 vaccine shots or face firings.[251] In September 2021, the company reported about 99 percent of its sixty-seven thousand or so US-based work force had complied, but another six hundred had refused and would be terminated.[252] In October 2021, a federal judge put a temporary halt to United's attempt to put on leave two-thousand-plus employees who had requested and received religious and medical exemptions to the Covid-19 shots.[253] A month later, a federal court in Texas granted United the ability to do just that.

"The Court appreciates the difficulty conscientious employees face when asserting their religious rights," wrote US district judge Mark T. Pittman in his November 2021 ruling. "But that difficulty does not demonstrate irreparable harm."[254]

United swung into gear, and hundreds of employees with exemptions for the Covid-19 shots were placed on unpaid leave and stripped of their company medical benefits—Kirby's way of granting so-called reasonable accommodations. Several of those

[251] Katherine Hamilton, "Lawsuit: United Airlines Mocked and Shamed Vaccine Mandate Holdouts—CEO Accused of Floating 'Scarlet Letter' On ID Badges," Breitbart, January 13, 2024, https://www.breitbart.com/law-and-order/2024/01/13/lawsuit-united-airlines-mocked-and-shamed-vaccine-mandate-holdouts-ceo-accused-of-floating-scarlet-letter-on-id-badges/.

[252] Coral Murphy Marcos, "United Airlines to Fire Workers Who Refused to Get a Vaccination," New York Times, September 29, 2021, https://www.nytimes.com/2021/09/29/business/united-airlines-vaccine-mandate.html#:~:text=United%20Airlines%20to%20Fire%20Workers,vaccinated%20after%20the%20company%20deadline.

[253] Jemima McEvoy, "United Airlines Firing 232 Employees Who Refused Covid Vaccine, CEO Says," Forbes, April 21, 2022, https://www.forbes.com/sites/jemimamcevoy/2021/10/13/united-airlines-firing-232-employees-who-refused-covid-vaccine-ceo-says/?sh=129723884399.

[254] Andrea Hsu, "Court rules United Airlines can put workers with vaccine exemptions on unpaid leave," NPR, November 9, 2021, https://www.gpb.org/news/2021/11/09/court-rules-united-airlines-can-put-workers-vaccine-exemptions-on-unpaid-leave.

filed lawsuits against United, alleging violations of Title VII of the Civil Rights Act and of the Americans with Disabilities Act.[255]

They also sent a letter in December 2021 to the United Airlines Holdings board of directors to step in and put a stop to "needless litigation" due to Kirby's burdensome mandates.[256] In March 2022, United finally announced an end to the stay-at-home orders for the medically and religiously exempted.

"United Airlines Holdings Inc. will allow workers who haven't been vaccinated against Covid-19 for religious or medical reasons to return [to work] at the end of this month," the *Wall Street Journal* wrote in March 2022. "The move permits staffers with exemptions from the carrier's vaccination requirement for its U.S. employees to return from unpaid leave."[257]

But the damage was done. Either employees had been forced to take shots they may not have wanted, or they had been forced to lose their livelihoods, including medical coverages, for the so-called crime of exercising their free choice. Practically overnight, private market employers had been handed the power to decide on medical treatments for their employees. United certainly wasn't the only business exercising such powers; Kirby certainly wasn't the only executive taking such liberties.

United was the first airline, though, and one of the largest American companies to impose this Covid-19 shot on its

---

[255] Ibid.

[256] Samuel Dorman, "United Airlines employees rail against CEO's handling of vaccine mandate in new letter," Fox Business, December 21, 2021, https://www.foxbusiness.com/politics/united-airlines-letter-scott-kirby.

[257] Alison Sider, "United Airlines to Let Unvaccinated Workers Return," *Wall Street Journal*, March 9, 2022, https://www.wsj.com/articles/united-airlines-to-let-unvaccinated-workers-return-11646869723.

employees.[258] It was also the strictest and most uncompromising in terms of punishing those who disobeyed. And on January 12, 2024, a legal brief was filed against United in the US District Court for the Northern District of Texas as part of a larger lawsuit over the Covid-19 shot mandates that made clear exactly how strict and uncompromising.

The lawsuit, *David Sambrano, individually and on behalf of all others similarly situated, et al., v. United Airlines, Inc.*, included the fifty-seven-page "Plaintiffs' Memorandum in Support of Motion for Class Certification and Appointment of Counsel."

The first section in the background to this memorandum was called "United Imposed a COVID-19 Vaccine Mandate for Marketing Purposes." The document summarized it as follows:

> This case arises out of United Airlines' strategic, company-wide campaign to coerce its employees to violate their religious beliefs and ignore their health. To accomplish this goal, United refused to provide any reasonable accommodations to its COVID-19 vaccine mandate. Instead, United told every employee who requested an accommodation—whether the employee requested a religious or medical accommodation and whether or not the employee was "customer facing"—that they would be effectively terminated by being placed on indefinite, unpaid leave.... Worse, discovery confirmed that United imposed

---

[258] David Koenig, "United Airlines will require US employees to be vaccinated," Associated Press, August 6, 2021, https://apnews.com/article/united-airlines-vaccine-mandate-employees-frontier-e8eef8e8f11d4924b81768484e5401a1.

this pressure campaign so that it could advertise a 100% vaccination rate after deciding that marketing was more important than its employees' civil rights.[259]

Kirby continued to claim the reason for the mandates was safety. Yet, several of his actions and statements contradict a strict safety-first argument.

In January 2021, and to the surprise of some on United's executive team, Kirby rocked national headlines by saying United ought to mandate the Covid-19 shots for all employees and that all other corporations should "require the vaccines and…make them mandatory" as well.[260] Then in August, according to the legal brief, when he did push through the mandate—despite the reluctance of some of his fellow executives—Kirby notified the then director of the Centers for Disease Control and Prevention, Rochelle Walensky, of his plans before even United's own employees.[261] According to the legal brief, he wrote to Walensky: "Sending a quick note to give you a personal heads up that tomorrow morning we will be informing United employees that we will be requiring our employees to be vaccinated by this fall."[262] Was he looking for head pats?

---

[259] *David Sambrano v. United Airlines*, "Case 4.21-cv-01074-P, Document 239," U.S. District Court for the Northern District of Texas, January 12, 2024, p. 6, https://sigforum.com/movedimages/para/238_Mot._to_Certify.pdf.

[260] Reuters, "United Airlines CEO calls on companies to mandate COVID-19 vaccination," Reuters, January 22, 2021, https://www.reuters.com/article/idUSKBN29R2GE/.

[261] *David Sambrano v. United Airlines*, "Case 4.21-cv-01074-P, Document 239," U.S. District Court for the Northern District of Texas, January 12, 2024, pp. 4–5, https://sigforum.com/movedimages/para/238_Mot._to_Certify.pdf.

[262] Ibid, p. 5.

Finally, Kirby may have imposed Covid-19 shots on all US company employees, but he left alone plenty of others who flew or worked on United. Among those who were not subjected to the mandate were "passengers," "pilots or flight attendants from other airlines who flew in United jump seats," "international United employees," "United employees residing in Montana," and "United's vendors and contractors," the legal brief stated.[263] If safety were the top concern, then it would seem the safety measures would apply to all, equally, without compromise or exemption. Kirby also made these curious remarks: as a persuasion tactic to press the need for the vaccine mandate, he said an unvaccinated individual was "nearly 300 times more likely to die" from Covid-19 than a vaccinated individual—a curious and utterly erroneous figure.[264] And to Congress, he doubled down on the cleanliness of United's cabins, bragging that the air infiltration system is so effective that "sitting next to a passenger in a United plane is equivalent to sitting 15 feet from the person in a typical building," the legal brief recounted of his statements.[265] So why the need for the Covid-19 shot mandate then?

The second section in the background was called "United Discouraged Employees from Requesting an Accommodation," with a summary as follows:

---

[263] *David Sambrano v. United Airlines*, "Case 4.21-cv-01074-P, Document 239," U.S. District Court for the Northern District of Texas, January 12, 2024, p. 6–7, https://sigforum.com/movedimages/para/238_Mot._to_Certify.pdf.

[264] *David Sambrano v. United Airlines*, "Case 4.21-cv-01074-P, Document 239," U.S. District Court for the Northern District of Texas, January 12, 2024, p. 6, https://sigforum.com/movedimages/para/238_Mot._to_Certify.pdf.

[265] *David Sambrano v. United Airlines*, "Case 4.21-cv-01074-P, Document 239," U.S. District Court for the Northern District of Texas, January 12, 2024, p. 7, https://sigforum.com/movedimages/para/238_Mot._to_Certify.pdf.

From the outset, United's CEO Scott Kirby made clear that he would not allow United to provide any reasonable accommodation to its vaccine mandate, despite United's legal obligations to do so. Kirby did not believe any such accommodations were necessary because, in his mind, United employees were making up their beliefs and "all [of a] sudden decid[ing] I'm really religious." That disdain for United employees of faith flowed directly from Kirby to those in Human Resources charged with reviewing accommodation requests who followed their CEO's lead and openly criticized the faith and medical conditions of employees seeking accommodations.[266]

In December 2021, Senator Ted Cruz, R-Texas, then member of the Commerce Committee and ranking member of the Aviation Subcommittee, listed several allegations of fired United employees against Kirby, all of whom claimed they were mistreated for their religious and medical beliefs. Cruz said:

> I have been literally inundated with United employees complaining about United's callous disregard for the rights of the pilots. One of the messages was from a pilot who flew for United for more than two decades, who applied for and received an exemption from [United's]

---

[266] *David Sambrano v. United Airlines*, "Case 4.21-cv-01074-P, Document 239," U.S. District Court for the Northern District of Texas, January 12, 2024, p. 6, https://sigforum.com/moveimages/para/238_Mot._to_Certify.pdf. Brackets in original.

vaccine mandate on religious grounds and was subsequently placed on leave with no pay and no benefits, including no medical insurance. Now his wife, who relies on her husband's insurance, has had to postpone a necessary surgery with no idea when her husband will be able to fly again. You're simultaneously enforcing a non-compete [contract clause], so this pilot can't even go work for your competitors.[267]

Cruz also spoke of another pilot who had flown for United for nearly thirty years, but after receiving an exemption from the shot, "found himself on indefinite unpaid leave" with an uncertain future and loss of all company benefits including "medical, dental, vision, insurance, disability, travel privileges, crew member access to jump seats" and the denial of access to his retirement savings.[268]

There was yet another United employee—a flight attendant with ten years' experience with United—a "woman [whose] name is Adrianna Uballe, who is a single mom…who you fired,"

---

[267] Sen. Ted Cruz, "Sen. Cruz Grills United CEO Over Mistreatment of Employees Seeking Religious Exemptions to the Company's Vaccine Mandate," Ted Cruz Senate website, press release page, December 16, 2021, https://www.cruz.senate.gov/newsroom/press-releases/sen-cruz-grills-united-ceo-over-mistreatment-of-employees-seeking-religious-exemptions-to-the-companys-vaccine-mandate.

[268] Sen. Ted Cruz, "Sen. Cruz Grills United CEO Over Mistreatment of Employees Seeking Religious Exemptions to the Company's Vaccine Mandate," Ted Cruz Senate website, press release page, December 16, 2021, https://www.cruz.senate.gov/newsroom/press-releases/sen-cruz-grills-united-ceo-over-mistreatment-of-employees-seeking-religious-exemptions-to-the-companys-vaccine-mandate.

Cruz said to Kirby. "She received her termination notice tied in a trash can to her front gate."[269]

Meanwhile, the legal brief went on to report: "Kirby even proposed requiring accommodated employees to walk around with special stickers on their badges broadcasting their vaccination status. Unsurprisingly, United's lawyers shot down this idea.... In fact, even some [Human Resources] employees were taken aback by Kirby's proposal, stating that putting stickers on unvaccinated employees' badges is 'like the scarlet letter.... Oh my goodness. Who are we???'"[270]

Another United practice to discourage employees from seeking the exemption?

According to the legal brief, United in August 2021 sent out postcards with text in bright bold red letters to all employees who had not yet taken the Covid-19 shot to remind them of the deadline for compliance and warn of termination for those who failed to obey.[271] Why postcards and not letters with envelopes? It's the same reason for the bright red text: to ensure the employees' spouses would see the warning and exert pressure at home.[272]

---

[269] Sen. Ted Cruz, "Sen. Cruz Grills United CEO Over Mistreatment of Employees Seeking Religious Exemptions to the Company's Vaccine Mandate," Ted Cruz Senate website, press release page, December 16, 2021, https://www.cruz.senate.gov/newsroom/press-releases/sen-cruz-grills-united-ceo-over-mistreatment-of-employees-seeking-religious-exemptions-to-the-companys-vaccine-mandate.

[270] *David Sambrano v. United Airlines*, "Case 4.21-cv-01074-P, Document 239," U.S. District Court for the Northern District of Texas, January 12, 2024, pp. 8–9, https://sigforum.com/movedimages/para/238_Mot._to_Certify.pdf

[271] *David Sambrano v. United Airlines*, "Case 4.21-cv-01074-P, Document 239," U.S. District Court for the Northern District of Texas, January 12, 2024, pp. 9–10, https://sigforum.com/movedimages/para/238_Mot._to_Certify.pdf.

[272] Ibid, p. 10.

The third section in the legal brief's background was called "United Made the Accommodation Process Purposefully Difficult," described as follows:

> This was all part of United's campaign to coerce compliance and ignore United's legal obligations to provide reasonable accommodations. That is no doubt why United designed a purposely vague and coercive accommodation process, imposed unreasonable and arbitrary deadlines, subjected employees to hostile and invasive questions criticizing their beliefs and health, and failed to engage in any discussion with employees about their job duties or the types of accommodations that would allow the employees to continue working.... United had already decided to offer only the accommodation of indefinite, unpaid leave. This universal accommodation plan sent a clear punitive message to coerce employees: acquiesce or be functionally terminated.[273]

Among the questions that United asked those seeking religious exemptions was this one, described in the legal brief: "Do your religious beliefs or practices prevent you from getting vaccinated for the sake of helping others avoid COVID-19?"[274] Eventually, United abandoned such questions due to their harassing

[273] *David Sambrano v. United Airlines*, "Case 4.21-cv-01074-P, Document 239," U.S. District Court for the Northern District of Texas, January 12, 2024, pp. 6–7, https://sigforum.com/movedimages/para/238_Mot._to_Certify.pdf.

[274] *David Sambrano v. United Airlines*, "Case 4.21-cv-01074-P, Document 239," U.S. District Court for the Northern District of Texas, January 12, 2024, pp. 13–14, https://www.scribd.com/document/698688409/Sambrano-v-United-Airlines-238-Motion-to-Certify-Class-Action#from_embed.

nature. But in the footnote section, the document also goes on to note United advised employees that "getting vaccinated was about 'loving your neighbor and colleague as yourself.'"[275]

Also in the footnoted section was this: "That hostility continued during litigation, with United's counsel asking parties and non-parties offensive and irrelevant questions, including asking [one employee] whether she would 'donate to a group that believed that gay and lesbian parents shouldn't be able to adopt children,' asking [another employee] whether he believes his drinking alcohol conflicts with [his] Buddhist precepts, and asking non-party [individual] whether he uses Johnson & Johnson soap on his grandchild."[276]

Meanwhile, look at this headline from Breitbart in June 2023: "Vax Lawsuit: United Airlines Demands Employees' Private Communications With Pastors and Priests to Prove Religious Exemption." Say what? The story goes on to report how United attorneys "made the demand in the discovery phase of a lawsuit filed in September 2021, in which eight United Airlines employees [who were] forced onto unpaid leave [were] sued on behalf of 2,000-plus workers seeking exemptions from the company's coronavirus vaccine mandate."[277] Wow. Intrusive is an understatement.

[275] *David Sambrano v. United Airlines*, "Case 4.21-cv-01074-P, Document 239," U.S. District Court for the Northern District of Texas, January 12, 2024, p. 14, https://sigforum.com/movedimages/para/238_Mot._to_Certify.pdf.

[276] *David Sambrano v. United Airlines*, "Case 4.21-cv-01074-P, Document 239," U.S. District Court for the Northern District of Texas, January 12, 2024, p. 14, https://sigforum.com/movedimages/para/238_Mot._to_Certify.pdf.

[277] Katherine Hamilton, "Vax Lawsuit: United Airlines Demands Employees' Private Communications With Pastors and Priests to Prove Religious Exemption," Breitbart, June 20, 2023, https://www.breitbart.com/politics/2023/06/20/united-airlines-demands-access-to-employees-private-conversations-with-pastors-in-vaccine-mandate-lawsuit/.

Those seeking medical exemptions were similarly burdened by United's bureaucratic and tyrannical approach, though. Aside from requiring employees with disabilities to navigate a complicated and lengthy medical documentation submission system, United cut out the corporate medical director from the decision-making process.

"[T]o [corporate medical director Pat] Baylis's disbelief," the legal brief reported, "United relied solely on HR and in-house counsel to make those medical determinations."[278]

"United Offered a Uniform and Unreasonable Accommodation" was the fourth section in the memorandum's background. The legal brief had this to say about it:

> Only after Plaintiffs filed this lawsuit did United start making changes for some employees. But even then, employees could not escape United's coercion. Rather, United adopted a uniform, discriminatory approach, dividing everyone who requested accommodations into just two groups: (1) those placed on indefinite, unpaid leave, consisting mostly of employees United deemed customer facing; and (2) all other "accommodated" employees, whom United subjected to a harsh masking-and-testing accommodation, which required wearing a respirator at all times, even while sitting alone outside, and taking frequent tests for COVID-19, even while on vacation or extended

---

[278] *David Sambrano v. United Airlines*, "Case 4.21-cv-01074-P, Document 239," U.S. District Court for the Northern District of Texas, January 12, 2024, pp. 14–15, https://sigforum.com/movedimages/para/238_Mot._to_Certify.pdf.

absence.... Kirby demanded that this policy sound "very serious" and impose harsh consequences, including immediate termination for any infractions.[279]

According to the document, there was no discussion about what types of jobs the requesters performed and how best to tailor the exemptions to fit their company roles, and no opportunity to discuss options. It was "unpaid leave for all"—or nothing.[280] Those granted medical benefits could use their paid sick days, but once those were burned through, any other out-of-work days would be unpaid; those granted religious exemptions were placed immediately on unpaid personal leave.[281]

"In reaching this decision," the legal brief stated, "United confirmed that safety was not a motivator. In fact, United did not even involve its head of safety, Sasha Johnson, in the decision to place all accommodated employees on unpaid leave. As Johnson explained, United's Safety and Medical teams were heavily involved in developing general masking-and-testing protocols, but they were not consulted about unpaid leave, which were not 'safety measures.'"[282]

---

[279] *David Sambrano v. United Airlines*, "Case 4.21-cv-01074-P, Document 239," U.S. District Court for the Northern District of Texas, January 12, 2024, p. 7, https://sigforum.com/movedimages/para/238_Mot._to_Certify.pdf.

[280] *David Sambrano v. United Airlines*, "Case 4.21-cv-01074-P, Document 239," U.S. District Court for the Northern District of Texas, January 12, 2024, p. 16, https://sigforum.com/movedimages/para/238_Mot._to_Certify.pdf.

[281] Ibid.

[282] *David Sambrano v. United Airlines*, "Case 4.21-cv-01074-P, Document 239," U.S. District Court for the Northern District of Texas, January 12, 2024, p. 17, https://sigforum.com/movedimages/para/238_Mot._to_Certify.pdf.

Under duress about the loss of income, many employees rescinded their exemption requests, the brief stated.[283]

At one point, while facing litigation, United then reportedly required the accommodated and unvaccinated to wear N95/KN95 face masks unless "actively taking bites of food or drinking"—"even while eating alone outside"—while simultaneously allowing the vaccinated to wear cloth face masks. The legal brief stated, "Astonishingly, United even told accommodated employees to wear these respirators while on personal travel."[284]

This is what happens when a company becomes the arbiter of morality, replacing God as the head of society—replacing even government as the enforcer and protector of constitutional rights: you get pinhead executives overseeing and dictating the medical decisions of employees, seeing a moral duty in stripping dissenters of their ability to make money. You get pretentious corporate chiefs pretending—to the point of believing, to the point of convincing others to believe—that because they have a financial stake in their employees' abilities to show up for work, they therefore have carte blanche to dictate how these employees live their lives, even their personal lives, until the lines between professional and personal are so blurred as to be erased.

This is not capitalism. This is communism. And it manifests in a slew of corporate ventures.

"Chinese company links annual bonuses to how many miles a worker runs each month," the *New York Post* reported

---

283 *David Sambrano v. United Airlines*, "Case 4.21-cv-01074-P, Document 239," U.S. District Court for the Northern District of Texas, January 12, 2024, pp. 17–18, https://sigforum.com/movedimages/para/238_Mot._to_Certify.pdf.

284 *David Sambrano v. United Airlines*, "Case 4.21-cv-01074-P, Document 239," U.S. District Court for the Northern District of Texas, January 12, 2024, pp. 18–19, https://sigforum.com/movedimages/para/238_Mot._to_Certify.pdf.

in December 2023.[285] Why? To push employees to live healthier so that, ultimately, the company's insurance costs are lower and that payouts for sick days are kept to a minimum. Those participating in the bonus program have to track their miles by app and submit the data to the company—giving the corporate world even more insight and control into employees' personal lives.[286]

A healthy employee is a productive employee.

"The song-and-exercise routines of the modern Chinese workplace have revolutionary roots," Quartz reported in 2017. The story went on to state: "Employees exercising collectively at the boss's orders is an important part of the landscape of work in contemporary China—but rather than a penalty, it's used far more often as a tool to boost team spirit."[287]

We're all in this together. We're all family. We're all pulling for the same team. Your health is our concern.

"Hospitals Shift Smoking Bans to Smoker Ban," the *New York Times* wrote in a 2011 headline about an emerging trend of US health facilities. The story stated:

> More hospitals and medical businesses in many states are adopting strict policies that make smoking a reason to turn away job applicants, saying they want to increase worker productivity,

---

[285] Chris Nesi, "Chinese company links annual bonuses to how many miles a worker runs each month," *New York Post*, December 18, 2023, https://nypost.com/2023/12/18/news/chinese-company-links-annual-bonuses-to-how-many-miles-a-worker-runs-each-month/.

[286] Ibid.

[287] Visen Liu, "The song-and-exercise routines of the modern Chinese workplace have revolutionary roots," Quartz, June 6, 2017, https://qz.com/996047/the-song-and-exercise-morning-routines-of-modern-chinese-offices-have-revolutionary-roots.

reduce health care costs and encourage healthier living. The policies reflect a frustration that softer efforts like banning smoking on company grounds, offering cessation programs and increasing health care premiums for smokers have not been powerful-enough incentives to quit.[288]

The problem isn't a company that cares about employee health; the problem isn't corporate executives who want to keep their workers healthy so as to lower insurance costs, boost profitability, and even hike morale. The problem is when incentives turn into mandates. The problem is when corporations become so involved in the health and well-being of employees that executives believe they have a right to control lives outside the office and to actually withhold salaries based on employees' undesirable but otherwise legal behaviors. Certain job standards and practical workplace requirements are necessary, of course; it's ridiculous to hire a grossly obese man as a firefighter if he can't perform the life-saving duties the role demands, for instance. But common sense, combined with a healthy and humble respect for individual choice—the very kind that God grants; it's called free will—are crucial to keep the wall that separates liberty from tyranny both intact and strong. This is why America's employers must be grounded in faith. Without a proper moral compass and an attitude of humility and true reverence for American freedom, it's all too easy for those with the means to do so to impose their wills on others. It's all too easy for bosses

[288] A.G. Sulzberger, "Hospitals Shift Smoking Bans to Smoker Ban," *New York Times*, February 10, 2011, https://www.nytimes.com/2011/02/11/us/11smoking.html.

to broaden their powers to the point where they forget their number one role is to make money—and not dictate morality.

But here we are in the age of woke corporatism. America's free markets are crumbling.

We've shifted from true capitalism, where profit is the goal—where dollars and cents and supply and demand are the clean, pure, and honest assessments of a company's growth, decline, success, or failure—and instead, we've moved into a more imaginary sphere of doing business. Instead of pleasing shareholders, or those with financial investment in the company, we're trying to please stakeholders, defined as anybody and everybody who could possibly have a stake in the business—like the Black Lives Matter activists, or the climate change alarmists, or the polar bear protectionists. Or whomever. Or whatever. With stakeholder capitalism, it's not money that matters most, but rather social justice, social governance, and social change.

This is pure Great Reset in motion.

From the UK-based international independent media platform, openDemocracy:

> The magic words are "stakeholder capitalism," a concept that WEF [World Economic Forum] chairman Klaus Schwab has been hammering for decades and which occupies pride of place in the WEF's Great Reset plan from June 2020. The idea is that global capitalism should be transformed so that corporations no longer focus solely on serving shareholders but become custodians of society by creating value for customers, suppliers, employees, communities and other "stakeholders." The way the WEF

sees stakeholder capitalism being carried out is through a range of "multi-stakeholder partnerships" bringing together the private sector, governments and civil society across all areas of global governance.... The idea of stakeholder capitalism and multi-stakeholder partnerships might sound warm and fuzzy, until we dig deeper and realize that this actually means giving corporations more power over society, and democratic institutions less.... Governments would be just one stakeholder in a multi-stakeholder model of global governance.[289]

One immediate effect of such a system is that elections won't matter.

If corporations are considered to be just another piece of the custodian-of-society pie, alongside governments, advocacy groups, nonprofits, and other civil organizations, then what's the point of Congress? What's the point of the "of, by, and for" system of governance in America, where legislators are elected to make laws, the judiciary is in place to decide constitutionality of laws, and the executive is in place to defend and enforce laws? Why vote if, say, Scott Kirby, CEO of United Airlines, can just make his own policies and press them on the citizens he employs with the force of law?

---

[289] Ivan Wecke, "Conspiracy theories aside, there is something fishy about the Great Reset," openDemocracy, August 16, 2021, https://www.opendemocracy.net/en/oureconomy/conspiracy-theories-aside-there-something-fishy-about-great-reset/.

That raises another immediate effect of stakeholder capitalism: the degradation of law and order.

If today's stakeholder sees Black Lives Matter as the cause of crucial address, but tomorrow's stakeholder sees the plight of poor border-crossers—illegal as they may be—as the larger concern, then corporate interests go to the one with the biggest backing, to the group with the loudest spokespeople, to the gathering that wreaks the larger havoc. In other words, it's not legislation and law that guide America's society but rather mob rule and the whim of the culture and shift of political winds. Constitution? Schmonstitution. It's all about the voice that rises above the melee. It's all about what the 1-percenters at global levels of government think is most important.

Interestingly, openDemocracy isn't exactly a right-wing organization. Almost 80 percent of the group's funding for 2022 came by way of grants, notably from many groups that support LGBTQ rights and abortion access and fight climate change.[290] Among the listed donors are the following:

- Oak Foundation: to promote "journalism exposing the backlash against women's and LGBTIQ rights, influencing laws, policies and public opinion."[291]
- Open Society Foundations: "for exposing threats to sexual and reproductive health and rights and gender equality."[292]

[290] openDemocracy, "Who funded us in 2022," openDemocracy, accessed January 26, 2023, https://www.opendemocracy.net/en/supporters/.
[291] openDemocracy, "Who funded us in 2022," openDemocracy, accessed January 26, 2023, https://www.opendemocracy.net/en/supporters/.
[292] openDemocracy, "Who funded us in 2022," openDemocracy, accessed January 26, 2023, https://www.opendemocracy.net/en/supporters/.

- openTrust, supported by Ford Foundation: "to support our Latin American project, democraciaAbierta."[293]
- openTrust, supported by Partners for a New Economy and by the Rockefeller Brothers Fund: "to support our work on a fairer and more sustainable economy" and "to support our environmental journalism."[294]
- Journalismfund Europe: to "examine the role of London's influence industry in lobbying against climate-change action."[295]

If a group that takes money from the Open Society Foundations network founded by leftist billionaire George Soros, as well as from other famously globalist-minded and social justice warring organizations—Ford, Rockefeller—nonetheless finds cause for alarm over a globalization plan called the Great Reset, well then, pay attention. It's not just a tin-foil-hat warning. And based on the activities of corporations around the world, it's clear the Great Reset has moved from the pages of intellectualized study to real-life implementation.

United Airlines once again provides a great example, from Kirby:

> We're embracing a new goal to be 100% green by 2050 by reducing our greenhouse gas emissions 100%. And we'll get there not with flashy, empty gestures, but by taking the harder, better path of actually reducing the emissions from

[293] openDemocracy, "Who funded us in 2022," openDemocracy, accessed January 26, 2023, https://www.opendemocracy.net/en/supporters/.
[294] openDemocracy, "Who funded us in 2022," openDemocracy, accessed January 26, 2023, https://www.opendemocracy.net/en/supporters/.
[295] openDemocracy, "Who funded us in 2022," openDemocracy, accessed January 26, 2023, https://www.opendemocracy.net/en/supporters/.

flying. We (also) realize there's a limit to what a single company can do alone. That's why we are continuing to seek opportunities to collaborate with other industries. We must reach across industries to develop coordinated efforts to accomplish what must be our collective goal of carbon neutrality.[296]

United touted similar goals in 2018, stating on its website, "In 2018, we became the first U.S. airline to publicly commit to a carbon emissions reduction target. Since then, we've embraced the goal of becoming 100% green by reducing our greenhouse gas emissions 100% by 2050."[297] In part for that, United was recognized in *Newsweek*'s Green Rankings as the "top environmental airline globally."[298]

Whoopee.

There's that "multi-stakeholder model of global governance" the elites at the World Economic Forum seek.[299] There's that Great Reset radical environmentalism at work. Congress may not have passed zero emission laws for the citizens of the United States to follow, but Big Business—"Woke Business"—will

[296] United CEO Scott Kirby, "Our environmental commitment: From our CEO," United.com, accessed January 26, 2024, https://www.united.com/ual/en/us/fly/company/global-citizenship/environment.html.

[297] United Airlines, "Fuel efficiency and emissions reduction," United.com, accessed June 3, 2024, https://www.united.com/ual/en/us/fly/company/global-citizenship/environment/fuel-efficiency-and-emissions-reduction.html.

[298] Business Roundtable, "United Airlines: United Eco-Skies," BusinessRoundtable.org, accessed January 26, 2024, https://www.businessroundtable.org/policy-perspectives/energy-environment/sustainability/united-airlines.

[299] Ivan Wecke, "Conspiracy theories aside, there is something fishy about the Great Reset," openDemocracy, August 16, 2021, https://www.opendemocracy.net/en/oureconomy/conspiracy-theories-aside-there-something-fishy-about-great-reset/.

step in and press the policy, regardless. United has a diversity, equity, and inclusion (DEI) program aimed at advancing social justice and stakeholder capitalism over shareholder capitalism and profit-loss considerations. Among the corporation's touted achievements? Well, United's "achieved" "near-perfect pay equity for employees of all genders and races," "shared" corporate "diversity representation data with employees"—so as to hold themselves "accountable for change," and created an "Executive Council on DEI" with "monthly participation by our full executive team."[300] Let the brainwashing begin—and continue. United also created what's called a "Business Resource Group" (BRG) run by employees to "increase awareness and understanding, challenge inequities and create platforms for service, learning and leadership development."[301] These groups each get a "cross-cultural…sponsor to help lead their mission," and do things like hold "go purple for Spirit Day" events and plan for more "social responsibility" gatherings.[302]

"Our BRGs and the DEI team came together to stand side by side in support of each other's community with one clear message: Bullying, discrimination and hate do not fly with us," United reported on its "Diversity, Equity, and Inclusion in Action" webpage.[303]

---

[300] United Airlines, "Diversity, Equity and Inclusion (DEI) in action," United, accessed January 26, 2024, https://www.united.com/ual/en/us/fly/company/global-citizenship/DEI-in-action.html.

[301] United Airlines, "Diversity, Equity and Inclusion (DEI) in action," United, accessed January 26, 2024, https://www.united.com/ual/en/us/fly/company/global-citizenship/DEI-in-action.html.

[302] United Airlines, "Diversity, Equity and Inclusion (DEI) in action," United, accessed January 26, 2024, https://www.united.com/ual/en/us/fly/company/global-citizenship/DEI-in-action.html.

[303] United Airlines, "Diversity, Equity and Inclusion (DEI) in action," United, accessed January 26, 2024, https://www.united.com/ual/en/us/fly/company/global-citizenship/DEI-in-action.html.

Hurrah. Just what every frequent flier cares most about, right?

When companies stay in business for the cause of advancing social agendas rather than for the practical reason of making money, operations and missions cloud, boundaries become fuzzy, and services sometimes get compromised. How often are skilled pilots pushed to the side for those who check the desired demographic boxes? It happens.

"Our flight deck should reflect the diverse group of people on board our planes every day," United said in a social media post in April 2021. "That's why we plan for 50% of the 5,000 pilots we train in the next decade to be women or people of color."[304]

The Great Reset is here, and it is happening now.

Once enough corporate executives agree that social justice is more important than profit, the move from shareholder capitalism to stakeholder capitalism will be complete and no matter what citizens say, no matter how citizens vote, no matter how citizens demand their politicians act, legislate, and govern—it won't matter. The business tycoons will be in control of the means of production and consumption, the systems of travel and transport, and the sectors of finance and banking. The beauty is that these new bosses of society will be wholly unaccountable, unremovable—untouchable.

It's already happening. It's already here.

---

[304] @United, Twitter/X post by United Airlines, April 6, 2021, https://twitter.com/united/status/1379426304857141250?ref_src=twsrc%5Etfw%7Ctwcamp%5Etweetembed%7Ctwterm%5E1379426304857141250%7Ctwgr%5E5d6969311424d35de44fe1737e0e5a1817a79e38%7Ctwcon%5Es1_&ref_url=https%3A%2F%2Fwww.iwf.org%2F2021%2F04%2F08%2Funited-airlines-promises-to-train-pilots-based-on-their-sex-and-skin-color%2F.

In 1997, Business Roundtable wrote a "Statement on Corporate Governance" that "the principal objective of a business enterprise is to generate economic returns to its owners."[305] By 2019, that mission had shifted, and Business Roundtable instead emphasized the importance of companies sharing in a "fundamental commitment to all our stakeholders" while delivering "value to all of them."[306] Moneymaking—worded as "generating long-term value for shareholders"—didn't make it to the list of priorities until the end, at bullet point number five, after four other bullet points that spoke of support, ethics, respect, and more support.[307] Like that, the culture of corporations had changed.

"10 Companies Whose CEOs Care About All Stakeholders," InvestorPlace wrote in 2019. "It's no longer just about the shareholders."[308]

In 2019, Salesforce CEO Marc Benioff said "capitalism, as we know it, is dead,"[309] that it was time to stop thinking of

[305] Robert G. Eccles, "An Open Letter To The Business Roundtable 181," *Forbes*, August 19, 2020, https://www.forbes.com/sites/bobeccles/2020/08/19/an-open-letter-to-the-business-roundtable-181/?sh=739b76140010.

[306] Business Roundtable, "Business Roundtable Redefines the Purpose of a Corporation to Promote 'An Economy That Serves All Americans,'" Business Roundtable, August 19, 2019, https://www.businessroundtable.org/business-roundtable-redefines-the-purpose-of-a-corporation-to-promote-an-economy-that-serves-all-americans.

[307] Business Roundtable, "Business Roundtable Redefines the Purpose of a Corporation to Promote 'An Economy That Serves All Americans,'" Business Roundtable, August 19, 2019, https://www.businessroundtable.org/business-roundtable-redefines-the-purpose-of-a-corporation-to-promote-an-economy-that-serves-all-americans.

[308] Will Ashworth, "10 Companies Whose CEOs Care About All Stakeholders," Investor Place, October 31, 2019, https://investorplace.com/2019/10/10-companies-whose-ceos-care-about-all-stakeholders/.

[309] Paul R. La Monica, "Marc Benioff says capitalism, as we know it, is dead," CNN Business, October 4, 2019, https://www.cnn.com/2019/10/04/business/marc-benioff-capitalism-dead/index.html.

business as "just about making money,"[310] and that it was time to get more socially conscious in the workplace—that "business is the greatest platform for change."[311]

"Larry Fink Defends Stakeholder Capitalism," wrote the *New York Times* in a 2022 headline about the CEO of Black-Rock, the investment firm with an estimated $10 trillion in assets to manage. The *New York Times* went on to write:

> Stakeholder capitalism "is not woke," Fink wrote in [his most recent annual letter to CEOs]. "It is capitalism." It was a rebuke to those who say that BlackRock's new focus on environmental, social and corporate governance concerns, known as E.S.G., is either bowing to anti-business interests or merely marketing. Reducing a company's carbon footprint, for instance, ensures long-term viability, something investors and executives should care about, he wrote.[312]

Of course, his viewpoint changed a bit after Republican-run states started to get wise to his domineering ways and forced pension investments into far-left, radical environmental, ESG ventures. They filed a motion to a federal regulator to stop Fink from imposing his UN-like greenhouse gas emission controls

310 Ibid.
311 Will Ashworth, "10 Companies Whose CEOs Care About All Stakeholders," Investor Place, October 31, 2019, https://investorplace.com/2019/10/10-companies-whose-ceos-care-about-all-stakeholders/.
312 Andrew Ross Sorkin, et al., "Larry Fink Defends Stakeholder Capitalism," *New York Times*, January 18, 2022, https://www.nytimes.com/2022/01/18/business/dealbook/fink-blackrock-woke.html.

on utility companies.[313] When BlackRock signed the Climate Action 100+ promise and the Net Zero Asset Managers Initiative, both of which, The Hill reported, "call for fossil fuel use to be slashed by 25 percent in 2030 and as far down as 2 percent by 2050," Republicans fought back and went to court.[314] That was after Florida governor Ron DeSantis signed into law a bill that barred state and local businesses from considering ESG standards as part of their investment decisions—a direct flip-off to Fink's ESG pressures.[315] Texas, in another ding at Fink, similarly banned a handful of companies known for their boycotts of energy companies.[316] Fink, facing some financial losses and public relations dings from the backlash, then turned tail and announced the end of references to ESG. Notably, he didn't announce an end to BlackRock's push for ESG; rather, only an end to the use of that phrase.

> Americans who are tired of hearing BlackRock
> CEO Larry Fink advance the tenets of ESG
> investing are in luck. According to remarks he
> apparently gave...at the Aspen Ideas Festival,

---

[313] Stephen Neukam, "Republican states move to block giant asset manager's ESG push for utility companies," The Hill, May 10, 2023, https://thehill.com/policy/energy-environment/3998234-republican-states-move-to-block-giant-asset-managers-esg-push-for-utility-companies/#:~:text=The%20move%20from%20the%20GOP,as%202%20percent%20by%202050.

[314] Ibid.

[315] Gov. Ron DeSantis, "Governor Ron DeSantis Signs Legislation to Protect Floridians' Financial Future & Economic Liberty," Governor Ron DeSantis webpage, May 2, 2023, https://www.flgov.com/2023/05/02/governor-ron-desantis-signs-legislation-to-protect-floridians-financial-future-economic-liberty/#:~:text=%E2%80%94%20Today%2C%20Governor%20Ron%20DeSantis%20signed,duty%20to%20make%20the%20best.

[316] Andrew Freedman, "BlackRock, UBS and 348 ESG funds 'banned' in Texas," Axios, August 25, 2022, https://www.axios.com/2022/08/25/texas-bans-blackrock-ubs-esg-backlash.

the head of the world's largest asset management firm is finally acknowledging that he is not going to use the phrase 'ESG' anymore because it's become too 'weaponized' by both sides. He told the crowd, 'I'm ashamed of being part of this conversation,' according to an Axios reporter who was in attendance.[317]

It's not as if BlackRock had turned a leaf and turned back to capitalism—to the type of capitalism that puts revenues and profits as the purpose of business. Fink had just changed the narrative to disguise the fact he's using his company to press ESG and woke agendas because he found the backlash too uncomfortable for his wallet to bear. In other words: these elites can only stand so much of their own woke bull. When it starts to impact their personal finances, their principles are bendable.

"Apple Hires Ex-EPA Chief Lisa Jackson for a Green Sheen," Greentech Media wrote in 2013.[318] Jackson was a Barack Obama appointee; Apple CEO Tim Cook's hiring of her was seen by cynics as more a political move to get the environmentalists off the company's back and smooth bureaucratic bumps in Washington, DC. But it wasn't long before her role expanded to social justice. As *Harper's Bazaar* wrote in 2023:

> Apple's flagship Racial Equity and Justice Initiative (REJI) programme...[was launched] in

[317] Clint Rainey, "BlackRock CEO Larry Fink says he's officially retiring 'ESG' as an investing term," Fast Company, June 26, 2023, https://www.fastcompany.com/90915196/esg-investing-meaning-blackrock-ceo-larry-fink-definition.

[318] Pete Danko, "Apple Hires Ex-EPA Chief Lisa Jackson for a Green Sheen," Green Tech Media, May 31, 2013, https://www.greentechmedia.com/articles/read/apple-hires-ex-epa-chief-lisa-jackson-for-a-green-sheen.

June 2020 as part of a company-wide effort to address systemic racism in the wake of George Floyd's murder. [REJI] has grown from an initial commitment of $100 million to more than $200 million worth of investment in projects supporting its three key pillars: education, economic empowerment and criminal justice reform. "It's a very long-term initiative that will continue to see us work with communities that have borne the brunt of racism," [Jackson said].[319]

United. Salesforce. BlackRock. Apple. Those are but a tiny fraction of corporations who've bought into the Business Roundtable's new mission statement of stakeholder first, shareholder second—of social agenda first, profits second. This is the Great Reset in motion.

"What kind of capitalism do we want?" asked Klaus Schwab, founder and executive chairman of the World Economic Forum, in a December 2019 essay published in *TIME*.[320] His answer?

That may be the defining question of our era. If we want to sustain our economic system for future generations, we must answer it correctly. Generally speaking, we have three models to choose from. The first is "shareholder capitalism," embraced by most Western corporations,

---

[319] Frances Hedges, "Lisa Jackson, a VP at Apple, on the real value of tech," *Harper's Bazaar*, June 21, 2023, https://www.harpersbazaar.com/uk/people-parties/bazaar-at-work/a44251693/lisa-jackson-apple-interview/.

[320] Klaus Schwab, "What Kind of Capitalism Do We Want?" *Time*, December 2, 2019, https://time.com/5742066/klaus-schwab-stakeholder-capitalism-davos/.

which holds that a corporation's primary goal should be to maximize its profits. The second model is "state capitalism," which entrusts the government with setting the direction of the economy, and has risen to prominent in many emerging markets, not least China. But, compared to these two options, the third has the most to recommend it. "Stakeholder capitalism," a model I first proposed a half-century ago, positions private corporations as trustees of society, and is clearly the best response to today's social and environmental challenges.[321]

Why does he like it so much? For the same reason all the elites, bureaucrats, cowardly politicians, and partners-in-globalist-takeover like it: for them it's 100 percent power, 0 percent accountability. Companies aren't elected bodies. CEOs can't be removed by voters—but they can be bought, sold, and controlled by those with money and influence. But consider: the same people who long for corporations to manage societies are the same ones who fawn over communism and hate individual freedom.

This same Schwab in 2022 proclaimed this on Chinese state-run TV: "I think we should be very careful in imposing systems," at the Asia-Pacific Economic Cooperation (APEC) CEO Summit in Bangkok, Thailand. "But the Chinese model

---

[321] Klaus Schwab, "What Kind of Capitalism Do We Want?" *Time*, December 2, 2019, https://time.com/5742066/klaus-schwab-stakeholder-capitalism-davos/.

is certainly a very attractive model for quite a number of countries."[322]

The Chinese model, of course, is communism.

This is what Schwab's brainchild, the Great Reset, advances.

And it would be a mistake to think that it's not already taken root and spread its rot in America's free markets.

---

[322] Bradford Betz, "World Economic Forum chair Klaus Schwab declares on Chinese state TV: 'China is a model for many nations,'" Fox News, November 23, 2022, https://www.foxnews.com/world/world-economic-forum-chair-klaus-schwab-declares-chinese-state-tv-china-model-many-nations.

CHAPTER 9

MARXISTS IN THE MEDIA AND THE DEVILISH DESIGNS OF THE BRAINWASHERS

E phesians 5:11 (ESV) states, "Take no part in the unfruitful works of darkness, but instead expose them." That should be a journalist's creed. Too often, it is not. And my, what evil can come.

As Joseph Stalin was starving out the Soviet Union during his years of tyrannical rule in the late 1920s and early 1930s, a young *New York Times* reporter named Walter Duranty was busily reporting from Moscow that all was fine—that the five-year plan to reshape agriculture and industry, as well as the collectivization program that saw Communist Party activists stripping Ukrainian farmers and families of their food, were not, as rumor would have it, resulting in mass starvation, cannibalism, and death, particularly for the peasant class.[323] Rather, Duranty wrote, these reforms were great successes, and Stalin ought to be praised for the modernization of Soviet society.[324]

Stalin was grateful for the positive press. On Christmas of 1933, in an exclusive interview, Stalin reportedly told Duranty: "You have done a good job in your reporting [for] the USSR, though you are not a Marxist, because you try to tell the truth about our country and to understand it and explain it to your readers."[325]

Well, there was Duranty truth and then there was truthful truth. Rarely did the two meet. But Duranty's lies were so believed that he won a Pulitzer Prize in 1932 for his reporting.

Meanwhile, another journalist, Gareth Jones, whose newspaper career truly began when his foreign policy advising role with former British prime minister David Lloyd George ended, traveled to Moscow, traveled to Ukraine, and traveled by foot through feet of snow to talk to families and get their first-hand accounts of Stalin's rule. After facing great personal danger, both from harsh weather conditions and from the iron fist of Stalin and his circle of similarly iron-fisted defenders, he found

---

[323] David Folkenflik, "The New York Times can't shake the cloud over a 90-year-old Pulitzer Prize," NPR, May 8, 2022, https://www.npr.org/2022/05/08/1097097620/new-york-times-pulitzer-ukraine-walter-duranty.

[324] From official British documents, a series by Richard A. Pierce, edited by Marco Carynnyk, Lubomyr Y. Luciuk, and Bohdan S. Kordan, "The Foreign Office and the Famine: British Documents on Ukraine and the Great Famine of 1932-1933," The Limestone Press, printed 1988, accessed February 1, 2024, pp. 33–36, https://ia801001.us.archive.org/24/items/Britain-and-Holodomor-Docs/The%20Foreign%20Office%20and%20the%20Famine.%20British%20Documents%20on%20Ukraine%20and%20the%20Great%20Famine%20of%201932%E2%80%931933%20(1988)_text.pdf.

[325] Ron Radosh, "The mendacity of Walter Duranty," The New Criterion, June 2012, https://newcriterion.com/issues/2012/6/the-mendacity-of-walter-duranty.

something completely different. According to the Holodomor Museum website:

> By the early spring of 1933, the fact that famine was raging in Ukraine and the Kuban, two-thirds of the population of which happened to be Ukrainian, was common knowledge in Moscow among foreign diplomats, foreign correspondents and even the man in the street.... [A] ban had [been] imposed [on] foreign journalists traveling to [these] areas in question. Upon checking with his colleagues in Moscow [about] what they knew—on the understanding, of course, that their names would never be mentioned—Jones decided it was worth it to defy the prohibition and buy a ticket at the train station to the[se] places [disguised] as a private person, which was not forbidden. Once there, he employed his simple but logical method of getting off the train and walking for several hours until he was certain he was off the beaten track and start[ed] talking to the local[s]. He spent a couple of weeks, walked about forty miles, talked to people, slept in their huts, and was appalled at what he saw.[326]

Jones traveled back to Moscow and then left the Soviet Union. After arriving in Berlin, he issued a press release that

---

[326] Holodomor Museum, "A Tale of Two Journalists: Walter Duranty and Gareth Jones," HolodomorMuseum.org, March 29, 2022, https://holodomor-museum.org.ua/en/news/a-tale-of-two-journalists-walter-duranty-and-gareth-jones/.

was picked up and published in the *Manchester Guardian* and in the *New York Evening Post*. Among his first-hand witness statements, Jones reported this:

> I walked along through villages and twelve collective farms. Everywhere was the cry, "There is no bread. We are dying." This cry came from every part of Russia.... I stayed overnight in a village where there used to be two hundred oxen and where there now are six. The peasants were eating the cattle fodder and had only a month's supply left. They told me that many had already died of hunger. Two soldiers came to arrest a thief. They warned me against travel by night, as there were too many "starving" desperate men.[327]

The accounts told by Jones, based on information he gathered during a handful of trips to the region, so differed from what was reported by Duranty, the *New York Times* felt compelled to issue a clarification report. Duranty tried to discredit Jones, writing in a March 1933 piece that Jones had a "keen and active mind," but that his interviews of Ukraine residents represented "a rather inadequate cross-section of a big country."[328] He

[327] Jim Stovall, "Walter Duranty and Gareth Jones: one told the truth, the other did not," JPROF.com, May 21, 2022, https://www.jprof.com/2022/05/21/walter-duranty-and-gareth-jones-one-told-the-truth-the-other-did-not/.

[328] Walter Duranty, "Russians Hungry, But Not Starving," *New York Times*, March 31, 1933, via GarethJones.org, https://www.garethjones.org/soviet_articles/russians_hungry_not_starving.htm.

spoke of "malnutrition," rather than "famine."[329] He also wrote in glowing terms of Stalin's government seizure of agricultural lands and said the "excellent harvest about to be gathered shows that any report of a famine in Russia is today an exaggeration or malignant propaganda," and professed "there will be more than sufficient [food] to cover the nation's food supply for the coming year and to justify the Kremlin's policy of collectivization." This was all while privately telling a British diplomat in September 1933 that "as many as 10 million people may have died directly or indirectly from lack of food in the past year."[330]

It's not that Duranty didn't see the truth. It was that he didn't care about reporting the truth. He was obsessed with maintaining his own career and celebrity status, and he fought anyone who threatened his favor with Stalin. From Anne Applebaum, a journalist and the author of *Red Famine*, on the swell of negative press about Jones: "Duranty set out to tear him down and, of course, at the time, he succeeded because he was the famous Walter Duranty."[331] So what were the truths of Stalin's cruelty to the Soviet people? Famine was just one facet. Mass murder, secret police surveillance, and forced labor were other repercussions of Stalin's takeover of farming and industry. For the people of Ukraine in particular, Stalin's rule was a horror show.

Ukraine, with its history of resistance to the Soviet rule, was a threat to the Soviet regime.

[329] David Folkenflik, "'The New York Times can't shake the cloud over a 90-year-old Pulitzer Prize," NPR, May 8, 2022, https://www.npr.org/2022/05/08/1097097620/new-york-times-pulitzer-ukraine-walter-duranty.
[330] David Folkenflik, "'The New York Times can't shake the cloud over a 90-year-old Pulitzer Prize," NPR, May 8, 2022, https://www.npr.org/2022/05/08/1097097620/new-york-times-pulitzer-ukraine-walter-duranty. Brackets in original.
[331] Ibid.

Fearing that opposition to his policies in Ukraine could intensify and possibly lead to Ukraine's secession from the Soviet Union, Stalin set unrealistically high grain procurement quotas…accompanied by other Draconian measures intended to wipe out a significant part of the Ukrainian nation. In August of 1932, the decree of "Five Stalks of Grain" stated that anyone, even a child, caught taking any produce from a collective field, could be shot or imprisoned for stealing "socialist property." At the beginning of 1933, about 54,645 people were tried and sentenced; of those, 2,000 were executed.[332]

Farmers, in search of food, tried to leave, but Stalin sealed Ukraine's borders and set up a system of travel papers that prohibited Ukrainians from buying train tickets without state permission.[333] Meanwhile, government operatives continued to demand Ukrainians meet their grain quotas, and those who failed were put on blacklists and prevented from receiving any supplies, including food, from the state.[334] Under Stalin, small commissions of party supporters and secret police roamed the villages and searched out lawbreakers—those, for instance,

---

[332] University of Minnesota, College of Liberal Arts, Holocaust and Genocide Studies, "Holodomor," accessed February 1, 2024, https://cla.umn.edu/chgs/holocaust-genocide-education/resource-guides/holodomor.

[333] Gijs Kessler, "The passport system and state control over population flows in the Soviet Union, 1932–1940," Open Edition Journals, 2001, https://journals.openedition.org/monderusse/8464.

[334] Library of Congress, "Revelations from the Russian Archives, Internal Workings of the Soviet Union: Ukrainian Famine," LOC.gov, accessed February 1, 2024, https://www.loc.gov/exhibits/archives/intn.html.

hiding food from the government. Punishments included deportation and executions, even for children.[335] Ukrainian families were forced to eat anything they could find to survive, including cats, dogs, acorns, and grass.[336] At its most severe, the famine—the Holodomor, as it was called—saw twenty-eight thousand Ukrainians dying each day.[337] The death toll from the famine in Ukraine between 1932 and 1933 is estimated between six million and seven million.[338] However, an exact count is difficult to determine, as some deaths were unrecorded and unregistered—purposely, so as to disguise the atrocities from the world.[339]

> While Ukrainians were dying, the Soviet state extracted 4.27 million tons of grain from Ukraine in 1932, enough to feed at least 12 million people for an entire year. Soviet records show that in January of 1933, there were enough grain reserves in the USSR to feed well over 10 million people. The government could have organized famine relief and could have accepted help from outside of the USSR. Moscow

---

[335] Library of Congress, "Revelations from the Russian Archives, Internal Workings of the Soviet Union: Ukrainian Famine," LOC.gov, accessed February 1, 2024, https://www.loc.gov/exhibits/archives/intn.html.

[336] David Folkenflik, "'The New York Times can't shake the cloud over a 90-year-old Pulitzer Prize," NPR, May 8, 2022, https://www.npr.org/2022/05/08/1097097620/new-york-times-pulitzer-ukraine-walter-duranty.

[337] Holodomor National Awareness Tour, "Holodomor Timeline of Events," Holodomor Tour, accessed February 1, 2024, https://holodomortour.ca/educational-hub/timeline/.

[338] Library of Congress, "Revelations from the Russian Archives, Internal Workings of the Soviet Union: Ukrainian Famine," LOC.gov, accessed February 1, 2024, https://www.loc.gov/exhibits/archives/intn.html.

[339] University of Minnesota, College of Liberal Arts, Holocaust and Genocide Studies, "Holodomor," accessed February 1, 2024, https://cla.umn.edu/chgs/holocaust-genocide-education/resource-guides/holodomor.

rejected foreign aid and denounced those who offered it, instead exporting Ukraine's grain and other foodstuffs abroad for cash.[340]

All that—while Duranty was selling Stalin as a saint, at one point defending the tyrant while dismissing reports of a starving populace by writing, "Conditions are bad, but there is no famine," and this: "But—to put it brutally—you can't make an omelet without breaking eggs."[341]

All that—while Duranty and the *New York Times* were kicking to the curb Jones, as he tried to tell the world the truth of the Soviet horrors under Stalin.

All that—while the voices of victims were purposely silenced by a media that ultimately, to at least some degree, horrifically allowed the brutality to continue for years.

All that—while Duranty was living a lifestyle free of moral considerations. As an article from the site UnHerd states:

> Born in 1884, Duranty had become a disciple of Aleister Crowley in 1913, joining with the self-appointed Satanist messiah kin Paris in opium consumption and "sex magic." Crowley's motto was "Do as thou wilt shall be the whole of the law," and Duranty seemed to have

---

[340] University of Minnesota, College of Liberal Arts, Holocaust and Genocide Studies, "Holodomor," accessed February 1, 2024, https://cla.umn.edu/chgs/holocaust-genocide-education/resource-guides/holodomor.

[341] *New York Times*, "New York Times Statement About 1932 Pulitzer Prize Awarded to Walter Duranty," New York Times Co., full statement made in 1990, accessed February 1, 2024, https://www.nytco.com/company/prizes-awards/new-york-times-statement-about-1932-pulitzer-prize-awarded-to-walter-duranty/#:~:text=Even%20then%2C%20Duranty%20dismissed%20more,an%20omelet%20without%20breaking%20eggs.%E2%80%9D.

followed this immoralist maxim throughout all of his life.… Anything was permitted, truth was a fiction and a superior few were entitled to live "beyond good and evil." When Duranty described Bolshevism as a ruthless creed he may have been praising, not condemning it. Duranty's career was based on this philosophy. Freedom from ethical restraint, he believed, guaranteed success.[342]

Is it any wonder the lies Duranty so freely told while reporting from Moscow?

From 2 Peter 2:1–2 (RSV): "But false prophets also arose among the people, just as there will be false teachers among you, who will secretly bring in destructive heresies, even denying the Master who bought them, bringing upon themselves swift destruction. And many will follow their licentiousness, and because of them the way of truth will be reviled."

The media is powerful—and that means they can be powerfully evil. It can become an enabler of evil, to the point where it becomes evil in itself. A news organization that promotes lies it knows to be lies is one thing. A news organization that continues the lies even after all the world has called on it to repent of the lies is a special breed of chutzpah and an entirely new level of evil. The *New York Times* in the 1980s faced growing calls from the public and from within its own circle of journalists to acknowledge the epic failures of Duranty to report the truth, and these calls only grew louder after the 1990 publication of

---

[342] John Gray, "A cautionary tale for today's 'woke' movement," UnHerd, July 22, 2020, https://unherd.com/2020/07/what-the-woke-movement-shares-with-communism/.

Sally J. Taylor's book about Duranty, critically titled *Stalin's Apologist*.[343] Backlash from an outraged public continued to rise, and ultimately, the Pulitzer Prize Board was petitioned—twice—to revoke Duranty's 1932 Pulitzer. The newspaper ultimately distanced itself from Duranty.

- Then *New York Times* editorial board member Karl Meyer wrote, among other condemning bits of viewpoints, that Duranty's filings from Moscow showed as "some of the worst reporting to appear in this newspaper."[344]

- *New York Times* executives and editors put up a disclaimer alongside Duranty's photo in the building's Pulitzer hallway of fame that read: "Other writers in The Times and elsewhere have discredited this coverage."[345]

- Then *New York Times* executive editor Bill Keller told the *Washington Post* that Duranty's reporting on Stalin in the years leading to the 1937 Great Terror, or Great Purge, was "pretty dreadful" and moreover, "It was a parroting of propaganda."[346]

---

[343] Francine Du Plessix Gray, "The Journalist and the Dictator," *New York Times*, June 24, 1990, https://www.nytimes.com/1990/06/24/books/the-journalist-and-the-dictator.html.

[344] Karl Meyer, for editorial board, "The Editorial Notebook; Trenchcoats, Then and Now," *New York Times*, June 24, 1990, https://www.nytimes.com/1990/06/24/opinion/the-editorial-notebook-trenchcoats-then-and-now.html.

[345] Duncan M. Currie, "Revoking Stalin's Pulitzer," *The Harvard Crimson*, December 3, 2003, https://www.thecrimson.com/article/2003/12/3/revoking-stalins-pulitzer-in-the-annals/.

[346] Howard Kurtz, "N.Y. Times Agrees 1932 Pulitzer Prize Was Not Deserved," *Washington Post*, October 23, 2003, https://www.washingtonpost.com/archive/lifestyle/2003/10/23/ny-times-agrees-1932-pulitzer-prize-was-not-deserved/d7c1590e-07a6-4720-b4f0-4f0d245e7b48/.

But the Pulitzer Board refused to revoke Duranty's award.

In a statement published in 2003, the Pulitzer organization wrote in part:

> In its review of the 13 articles, the Board determined that Mr. Duranty's 1931 work, measured by today's standards for foreign reporting, falls seriously short.... However, the board concluded that there was not clear and convincing evidence of deliberate deception, the relevant standard in this case. Revoking a prize 71 years after it was awarded under different circumstances, when all principals are dead and unable to respond, would be a momentous step and therefore would have to rise to that threshold. The famine of 1932-1933 was horrific and has not received the international attention it deserves. By its decision, the board in no way wishes to diminish the gravity of that loss. The Board extends its sympathy to Ukrainians and others in the United States and throughout the world who still mourn the suffering and deaths brought on by Josef Stalin."[347]

This is what happens when men and women of weak principle, cowardly convictions, and immoral leanings control the means and modes of communication: the weak, cowardly, and

---

[347] The Pulitzer Prizes Board, "Statement on Walter Duranty's 1932 Prize," Pulitzer.org, November 21, 2003, https://www.pulitzer.org/news/statement-walter-duranty.

immoral are elevated while the dogged defenders and searchers of the truth are shunned, ignored, and attacked.

It's worth noting that Jones died at the age of twenty-nine, a victim of a mysterious murder—some say by Soviet secret police, the NKVD, exacting revenge on behalf of Stalin.[348] Others say it was by Japanese-hired bandits, who first captured and held him for ransom for sixteen days—and while trying to report on human atrocities from the grounds of Japanese-occupied Mongolia.[349] Among the statements about his life was this one, from the narrator of a BBC-reported documentary about the never-ending quest for truth: "Gareth Jones was almost an Icarus-type character, who knew how close to the sun he was flying, but couldn't seem to resist the temptation to expose tyrannical abuse of power."[350] Yet in life, and for many years after his death, Jones was not given the credit for taking on the powers and exposing the lies of the Soviet Union, the *New York Times*, and its famous foreign correspondent, as well as all the communist apologists of the political world.

In contrast, Duranty died in 1957 at the age of seventy-three in Orlando, Florida, a celebrity to the end, and his *New York Times* obituary blasted this headline in observance: "WALTER DURANTY, NEWSMAN, 73, DIES; Foreign Correspondent for The Times, 1913-41, Won Pulitzer Prize in 1932 WAS

---

[348] Neil Prior, "Journalist Gareth Jones' 1935 murder examined by BBC Four," BBC, July 5, 2012, https://www.bbc.com/news/uk-wales-south-east-wales-18691109.

[349] Dr. Margaret Siriol Colley and Nigel Linsan Colley, "Gareth Jones: Hero of Ukraine: An open letter to The Pulitzer Prize Committee," GarethJones.org, June 24, 2003, https://www.garethjones.org/overview/duranty.htm.

[350] Neil Prior, "Journalist Gareth Jones' 1935 murder examined by BBC Four," BBC, July 5, 2012, https://www.bbc.com/news/uk-wales-south-east-wales-18691109.

EXPERT ON SOVIET…"[351] It would take decades for Duranty's star to dim.

The now-deceased journalist Malcolm Muggeridge, speaking to producers from Ukraine and Canada who were making a documentary about Duranty, had this to say in 1990: "He was not only the greatest liar among the journalists in Moscow, but he was the greatest liar of any journalist that I ever met in 50 years in journalism."[352]

Liar. Drug user. Sympathizer of satanists. Sympathetic to Stalinists. Enabler of evil. Attacker of all that's truthful and good.

Oh. And Pulitzer recipient.

To those who think there could never be another Duranty—that modern media has self-corrected and has become so self-aware that such deceptive reports could never pass editorial muster to make it to the public arena again—wake up and smell, as Donald Trump might put it, today's "enemy of the people."[353] In media land, it's a virtual free fall of leftist infiltration.

"Study Exposes George Soros' Network of Media Ties," teleSUR reported in January 2023.[354] That story went on to describe how Soros spent upwards of $131 million between 2016 and

---

[351] *New York Times*/Associated Press, "WALTER DURANTY, NEWSMAN, 73, DIES…" *New York Times*, October 3, 1957, https://www.nytimes.com/1957/10/04/archives/walter-duranty-newsman-73-dies-foreign-correspondent-for-the-times.html.

[352] David Folkenflik, "'The New York Times can't shake the cloud over a 90-year-old Pulitzer Prize," NPR, May 8, 2022, https://www.npr.org/2022/05/08/1097097620/new-york-times-pulitzer-ukraine-walter-duranty.

[353] Brett Samuels, "Trump ramps up rhetoric on media, calls press 'the enemy of the people,'" The Hill, April 5, 2019, https://thehill.com/homenews/administration/437610-trump-calls-press-the-enemy-of-the-people/.

[354] TeleSur, "Study Exposes George Soros' Network of Media Ties," TeleSur English, January 26, 2023, https://www.telesurenglish.net/news/Study-Exposes-George-Soros-Network-of-Media-Ties-20230126-0002.html.

2020 to peddle influence through the likes of the Committee to Protect Journalists, the Aspen Institute, the Marshall Project, and ProPublica—all nonprofits dedicated, respectively, to upholding free speech, realizing an "equitable society," smoothing out unbalances in the justice system, and investigating and exposing abuses of power in government and business.[355] In other words—all nonprofits dedicated to swaying the tone of public debate and discourse, both in media and in government.

"George Soros tied to at least 54 influential media figures," Fox News wrote that same month.[356] That story went on to cite a study from MRC Business by analysts Joseph Vazquez and Daniel Schneider, who discovered money from the leftist billionaire had flowed into organizations served by various high-profile and celebrity journalists—from NBC's nightly anchor Lester Holt to *Washington Post*'s executive editor Sally Buzbee to Bloomberg News's cofounder Matthew Winkler.[357] For instance, Holt, Buzbee, and Winkler have all served at various times on the board of the Committee to Protect Journalists. Meanwhile, the Soros family's Open Society Institute has contributed generously to CPJ through the years, at one time giving a total of $2,775,000 in grants, according to its IRS Form 990 filings made for 2022.[358] Only the Knight Foundation and the Ford Foundation gave more that year, with $4.7 million and $4 million in grants,

---

[355] Ibid.

[356] Brian Flood, "George Soros tied to at least 54 influential media figures through groups funded by liberal billionaire: study," Fox News, January 17, 2023, https://www.foxnews.com/media/george-soros-tied-54-influential-media-figures-through-groups-funded-liberal-billionaire-study.

[357] Ibid.

[358] Form 990, "Return of Organization Exempt From Income Tax, Committee to Protect Journalists, Inc.," Public Disclosure Copy CPJ website, November 1, 2023, https://cpj.org/wp-content/uploads/2023/11/Form-990-2022.pdf.

respectively, to CPJ.[359] What other journalists serve on boards, foundations, or organizations that receive Soros funding? Dozens. As MRC found, fifty-four individuals in 253 various media groups received $131 million of Soros money between 2016 and 2020—but rather than running down the list, the more interesting note is this: Not one is a so-called conservative journalist. Not one is a so-called conservative media organization.[360] There are plenty of journalists and editors from CNN, the *New York Times*, the *Seattle Times*, the *Los Angeles Times*, the *Washington Post*, ABC News, CBS News, NPR, *USA Today*, PBS, the *New Yorker*—and more. There are zero from the likes of the *Washington Times*, Breitbart, the *New York Post*, Newsmax, One America News, Fox News—or others.[361]

This is how bias in the news frequently manifests. When journalists with the same worldviews, typically secular and liberal, band together and banter around ideas, it's easy for them to then determine that their ensuing agreement on issues is reflective of society at-large—because, after all, if there were dissenting views, then surely someone in their circle would have those views. Those outside the bubble are therefore easily painted as radicals, as the non-serious journalists, as the conspiracy theorists, and the like. Those within, meanwhile, stay comfortably within because that's where the accolades come from—that's where those with the keys to awarding media prizes, promotions, and career advancements live. The Pulitzer Prize Board

---

[359] Form 990, "Return of Organization Exempt From Income Tax, Committee to Protect Journalists, Inc.," Public Disclosure Copy CPJ website, November 1, 2023, https://cpj.org/wp-content/uploads/2023/11/Form-990-2022.pdf.

[360] MRC.org, "Top Journalists that Serve on Soros Boards of Directors or Advisers," MRC, accessed February 3, 2024, https://www.mrc.org/top-journalists-serve-soros-funded-boards-directors-or-advisers.

[361] Ibid.

picked Walter Duranty, not Gareth Jones. Soros's dollars are much more likely to continue funding the Center for Public Integrity if Christiane Amanpour of ABC and Arianna Huffington of the Huffington Post and AOL stay on its board and never, say, Tucker Carlson or Sean Hannity, giants as they are in more conservative media.[362] In that way, the bubble of bias remains afloat, and those within the bubble are able to deceive themselves into believing they're erudite and scholarly, defenders of the truth, rather than arrogant and elitist, the enablers of liars. It's a despicable situation.

Americans and the world of media would be much better served if all viewpoints were equally considered, welcomed, and tolerated, of course.

But Marxists cannot stand on principle, so they must stifle others' speech. Marxism cannot withstand the scrutiny of those who value freedom. And much of what goes forth in the media these days is taken right from Marxism 1.0 textbook training—that is to say, from the enemies of American exceptionalism.

"Tracing the fake news money trail: How Billionaire Globalists are paying to put far-left propaganda in Ohio's Mainstream Newsrooms," the Ohio Senate reported on its webpage in October 2023.[363] That story detailed the sneaky ways the Soros-globalist-leftist-Marxist ideologies weave into local and state coverage of various issues, all unbeknownst to viewers, readers, and consumers of news. Here's a rundown on the method, as reported on the Ohio Senate site:

---

[362] Ibid.

[363] Garth Kant, "Tracing the Fake News Money Trail: How Billionaire Globalists are paying to put far-left propaganda in Ohio's Mainstream Newsrooms," The Ohio Senate, October 18, 2023, https://ohiosenate.gov/news/on-the-record/tracing-the-fake-news-money-trail.

Point one: "Woke billionaires [George] Soros and [Bill] Gates, the Ford Foundation, and other far-left sugar daddies pour billions into an umbrella group called Arabella Advisors."[364] "Since 2006," the site went on, "far-left funders have donated $6.5 billion" to Arabella, including $36 million from Soros's Foundation to Promote Open Society into Arabella's New Venture Fund in 2021 and $490 million from the Bill & Melinda Gates Foundation to Arabella in the span between 2008 and 2022.[365]

Point two: "Arabella manages numerous organizations serving as its far-reaching tentacles, one of which is a nonprofit group called Hopewell," the Ohio Senate site reported.[366] The Hopewell Fund is a nonprofit with a mission to advance social change and a stated "commitment to race, equity, diversity, and inclusiveness," according to its website.[367]

Point three: "Hopewell funds a woke network they call States Newsrooms. Those 'newsrooms' are seeded around the country as a way to push woke propaganda as though it is real news.... The Newsroom Network became the States Newsroom in 2019 and obtained non-profit status. It still consists of a number of radical left media outlets. But now it is a tax-exempt 501(c)(3)

---

[364] Garth Kant, "Tracing the Fake News Money Trail: How Billionaire Globalists are paying to put far-left propaganda in Ohio's Mainstream Newsrooms," The Ohio Senate, October 18, 2023, https://ohiosenate.gov/news/on-the-record/tracing-the-fake-news-money-trail.

[365] Garth Kant, "Tracing the Fake News Money Trail: How Billionaire Globalists are paying to put far-left propaganda in Ohio's Mainstream Newsrooms," The Ohio Senate, October 18, 2023, https://ohiosenate.gov/news/on-the-record/tracing-the-fake-news-money-trail.

[366] Garth Kant, "Tracing the Fake News Money Trail: How Billionaire Globalists are paying to put far-left propaganda in Ohio's Mainstream Newsrooms," The Ohio Senate, October 18, 2023, https://ohiosenate.gov/news/on-the-record/tracing-the-fake-news-money-trail.

[367] Hopewell Fund, accessed February 3, 2024, https://www.hopewellfund.org/.

nonprofit, meaning it is not required to disclose the donors who keep it afloat," The Ohio Senate wrote.[368]

But States Newsroom maintained a budget of more than $21.6 million in 2021, with a mission of forming and partnering with "state-based news outlets," as well as with "a national bureau in Washington, D.C.," in order to provide news coverage for Congress, the Supreme Court and "administrative decisions that affect the states," InfluenceWatch reported.[369] The website also reported that more than thirty states were home to news organizations that were listed affiliates of States Newsroom—indicating the money was indeed being spread to influence coverage around the nation.

Then in March 2023, Pew Charitable Trusts announced it was folding its own nonprofit Stateline, a news service, into States Newsroom, as well as providing a $3 million grant for the new partnership.[370] Stateline executive director Scott Greenberger called the merger a "footprint [in news] that no one else can even come close to matching."[371] What this means in layman's terms is that local journalists covering the zoning board meeting may be taking a salary from a newspaper that somewhere along the chain of financing ties back to none other than

[368] Garth Kant, "Tracing the Fake News Money Trail: How Billionaire Globalists are paying to put far-left propaganda in Ohio's Mainstream Newsrooms," The Ohio Senate, October 18, 2023, https://ohiosenate.gov/news/on-the-record/tracing-the-fake-news-money-trail.

[369] Influence Watch, "States Newsroom (Newsroom Network)," InfluenceWatch.org, accessed February 3, 2024, https://www.influencewatch.org/non-profit/the-newsroom/.

[370] Sarah Scire, "Pew's Stateline finds a new home with nonprofit States Newsroom," Nieman Lab, March 8, 2023, https://www.niemanlab.org/2023/03/pews-stateline-finds-a-new-home-with-nonprofit-states-newsroom/.

[371] Influence Watch, "States Newsroom (Newsroom Network)," InfluenceWatch.org, accessed February 3, 2024, https://www.influencewatch.org/non-profit/the-newsroom/.

George Soros, or Bill Gates, or organizations like Hopewell and Arabella that have far-left visions—Marxist-like visions—for the America of the future. Maybe they're biased; maybe they're not. But for an industry that's supposed to be dedicated to peeling back the layers of bureaucracy and exposing the hidden agendas of others, such twists and turns and non-transparencies in newsroom financing is curious at best, nefarious at worst. It's curious-slash-nefarious enough that OpenSecrets, the organization dedicated to tracking money in politics, wrote this in a 2020 headline: "'Dark money' networks hide political agendas behind fake news sites."[372] How so?

> [P]olitical operations are pouring millions of "dark money" dollars into ads and digital content masquerading as news coverage to influence the 2020 election. One newer group heralding the new era of pseudo-news outlets is ACRONYM, a liberal dark money group with an affiliated super PAC called PACRONYM. The nonprofit also is an investor in a for-profit digital consulting firm that gained notoriety for its role in launching Shadow Inc., the secretive vendor behind a vote tabulation app at the center of the pandemonium at the Iowa Democratic caucuses.[373]

[372] Anna Massoglia, "'Dark money' networks hide political agendas behind fake news sites," OpenSecrets, May 22, 2020, https://www.opensecrets.org/news/2020/05/dark-money-networks-fake-news-sites/.

[373] Anna Massoglia, "'Dark money' networks hide political agendas behind fake news sites," OpenSecrets, May 22, 2020, https://www.opensecrets.org/news/2020/05/dark-money-networks-fake-news-sites/.

Just to refresh on the 2020 caucuses in Iowa: That's when
the Democrat Party required voters to download a new app that
would record their ballot, but due to technological difficulties,
the final tabulations were skewed. There were mysterious incon-
sistencies and errors with the counts, and for roughly twenty-two
hours after voting stopped, the caucus was in chaos.[374] It was
billed a "systemwide disaster," by one former Iowa Democrat
Party chairman.[375]

But back to the OpenSecrets story on dark money in news:
Shortly after the debacle at the 2020 Iowa caucuses, ACRO-
NYM announced it was divesting from Shadow Inc. But its
shadow work in news continued. OpenSecrets wrote:

> ACRONYM is behind Courier Newsroom,
> a network of websites emulating progressive
> local news outlets. Courier has faced scrutiny
> for exploiting the collapse of local journalism
> to spread "hyperlocal partisan propaganda." It
> claims to operate "independent from" ACRO-
> NYM and says ownership is shared with "other
> investors." But a new tax return obtained by
> OpenSecrets list[ed] ACRONYM as the full
> owner of Courier as of April 30, 2019.... An
> ACRONYM spokesperson told OpenSecrets

[374] Shane Goldmacher and Nick Corasaniti, "'A Systemwide Disaster': How the
Iowa Caucuses Melted Down," *New York Times*, February 4, 2020, updated
February 6, 2020, https://www.nytimes.com/2020/02/04/us/politics/what-
happened-iowa-caucuses.html.
[375] Shane Goldmacher and Nick Corasaniti, "'A Systemwide Disaster': How the
Iowa Caucuses Melted Down," *New York Times*, February 4, 2020, updated
February 6, 2020, https://www.nytimes.com/2020/02/04/us/politics/what-
happened-iowa-caucuses.html.

that Courier has attracted multiple private investors since [then].[376]

Readers probably aren't aware of the behind-scenes finagling, though, or of the deep connections of Courier Newsroom to far-left political hacks. OpenSecrets continued:

> Websites affiliated with Courier Newsroom that appear to be free-standing local news outlets are actually part of a coordinated effort with deep ties to Democratic political operatives…. Courier's newest appendage, Cardinal & Pine, spent more than $20,000 on digital advertising targeting North Carolina since launching its first Facebook ad campaigns in late March [2020]. The page's ads give the appearance of news but [were] mostly focused on the coronavirus pandemic or on criticizing President Donald Trump.[377]

Fake news, indeed.

That was 2020—and that was just one example of one news organization.

Now jump to 2023 when Pew partnered with States Newsroom with the intent to expand the footprint of these leftist investors into as many states and into as many news outlets as

---

[376] Anna Massoglia, "'Dark money' networks hide political agendas behind fake news sites," OpenSecrets, May 22, 2020, https://www.opensecrets.org/news/2020/05/dark-money-networks-fake-news-sites/.

[377] Anna Massoglia, "'Dark money' networks hide political agendas behind fake news sites," OpenSecrets, May 22, 2020, https://www.opensecrets.org/news/2020/05/dark-money-networks-fake-news-sites/.

possible—all while masquerading as unbiased, fair, and balanced journalism. It's Courier Newsroom on steroids.

But it gets worse. The dark money in news goes deeper. The Soros tentacles spread wider.

The Gareth Joneses of the world have a little bit of a harder time—perhaps—getting out their independently gathered reports and alternative truths and narratives that counter the elitist messaging.

"Open Society believes in the importance of a free and independent media to underpin democratic society and debate. Since 1995, the Soros Economic Development Fund has invested in critical media companies to foster their growth and safeguard their editorial independence," the Open Society Foundations reported on its Economic Development Fund webpage.[378]

Say what? News corporations with solid editorial staff, editors, executives, and publishers are constantly on guard to ensure advertising dollars don't cross into newsrooms, slant coverages, and tilt reports in favor of advertisers—and rightly so. How much more so, then, should the nonprofits and foundations that promise to "safeguard" the "editorial independence" of the news organizations they fund do the same—right? Soros isn't exactly a friend of American liberty, capitalism, Donald Trump and MAGA patriots, constitutional law and order, or of border protections. So, when his Open Society creates the Media Development Investment Fund (MDIF) as part of his vision to do just that—to "safeguard" the "editorial independence" of news organizations around the world—then it's not just that it's warranted to ask questions. It's worrisome.

---

[378] Open Society, "Soros Economic Development Fund: Independent Media," Open Society Foundations, accessed February 4, 2024, https://www. soroseconomicdevelopmentfund.org/how-we-work/independent-media.

"MDIF has invested in independent media outlets around the world for more than 25 years," Open Society wrote on its webpage. "The Fund provides affordable debt and equity financing, supported by tailored technical assistance and advisory services, to help independent media thrive and safeguard their editorial independence."[379]

It's the "advisory services" that are most concerning. That's sort of a nice way of saying, "Report what we want or lose funding." Of course, MDIF doesn't put it that way. Since 1996, MDIF has financed 150 or so media companies in forty-seven countries—and counting.[380] While the group says it doesn't "interfere in clients' editorial" but only assists them to "develop strong businesses so they can safeguard their independence,"[381] again, the skeptical query is one that goes like this: You think Soros would allow his money to be used for conservative outlets? Christian news sites? It's the bias of omission that gives the greatest cover. Soros's MDIF can talk about "independent media" all it wants, but when it comes to funding time, it's only those organizations who apply for the funds with proposals that are in line with MDIF's far-leftist ideals that get the money.

Meanwhile, once again, tracking the funding, tracking the influence, tracking the collaborations and partnerships and ties and binds of Soros dollars to these supposedly independent

---

[379] Open Society, "Soros Economic Development Fund: Media Development Investment Fund," Open Society Foundations, accessed February 4, 2024, https://www.soroseconomicdevelopmentfund.org/investments/media-development-investment-fund.

[380] Media Development Investment Fund, "MDIF: Investing in Diverse Media," MDIF.org, accessed February 4, 2024, https://www.mdif.org/our-work/media-we-finance/.

[381] Media Development Investment Fund, "MDIF: Investing in Diverse Media," MDIF.org, accessed February 4, 2024, https://www.mdif.org/our-work/media-we-finance/.

news organizations are like searches through haystacks for needles. Learning who and what funds news groups shouldn't be this difficult.

Among MDIF's listed fund recipients:

- Colab, a digital news enterprise in Brazil aimed at boosting "greater collaboration and information-sharing between local authorities and municipal citizens."
- El Faro, a digital news outlet in El Salvador that reports on "corruption, organized crime, migration, culture, inequality, impunity and human rights."
- Food for Mzansi, a digital news group covering agriculture in South Africa, with an emphasis on "stories about people of colour in farming."
- Liga.net, an online news source in Ukraine, "widely recognized as one of the country's most professional and successful digital news companies."
- *Mail & Guardian*, a weekly and digital investigative news site in South Africa, billed as "one of the most widely-read news sites on the continent."
- Melitopolskie Vedomosti, another online news site in Ukraine that briefly ceased operations in spring of 2022 during Russian army occupation but is now up and running again.
- OK Radio, "the most listened-to radio station in the region," located in Serbia.
- Petit Press, the second largest publisher in Slovakia, with a portfolio that publishes more than thirty-five printed and digital news products.

- Rappler, an online investigative journalism outlet in the Philippines whose founder, CEO Maria Ressa, won the 2021 Nobel Peace Prize.
- Suara, a political news group in Indonesia that targets |millennials.
- TV Vijesti, the most popular and trusted television station in Montenegro, supported by its closely connected daily newspaper, *Vijesti*.[382]

That's but a smattering.

But even in that smattering, it's easy to see that the Soros influence in news is massive, particularly in this day and age of digital media. What's reported by Ukraine's Liga.net doesn't stay in Ukraine but rather filters through the internet, airwaves, and broadcasts all across the world, impacting the coverage of other news organizations that don't take funding from Soros. What's opined in the pages of South Africa's *Mail & Guardian* doesn't stay within the boundaries of South Africa but rather has the potential to impact discussions among pundits and newscasters halfway across the world.

"With our headquarters in New York, operations center in Prague and regional presence in countries including Colombia, India, Indonesia, South Africa and Serbia, MDIF is truly a global organization," MDIF wrote on its webpage. "Each year, we respond to new opportunities and add countries to our portfolio.... Plus [we have] international projects with global reach based in The Netherlands and USA."[383]

---

[382] Media Development Investment Fund, "MDIF: Investing in Diverse Media," MDIF.org, accessed February 4, 2024, https://www.mdif.org/our-work/media-we-finance/.

[383] Media Development Investment Fund, "MDIF: Worldwide presence," MDIF, accessed February 4, 2024, https://www.mdif.org/our-work/where-we-work/.

That last line—about the Soros-funded media projects in the United States—isn't very prominently placed on MDIF's webpage. Once again, transparency isn't exactly order of the day. At the bottom of one of the MDIF webpages from June 3, 2024, describing "Where We Work" and under the headline of "Global organization with local expertise," is a listing of "programs and initiatives" containing names like "amplifyasia," "amplifyeurope," and "amplifysouthamerica," as well as a mention under the "Membership and recognition" section at the bottom of the page of what's called the "Global Forum for Media Development." It's that last one that showcases MDIF-tied organizations in North America—but you still have to dig deep to uncover the links.

The Global Forum for Media Development—listed, remember, as one of the "programs and initiatives" of MDIF[384]—bills itself as "the largest global community for media development, media freedom, and journalism support" with a membership at one time of 188 organizations and an open invitation for more to apply to join.[385] The webpage lists roughly a dozen groups from North America as members. They are:

- ACOS Alliance
- Border Center for Journalists and Bloggers
- Center for International Media Assistance (CIMA)
- Center for Journalism and Liberty
- Chicas Poderosas Inc.
- Global Investigative Journalism Network (GIJN)

---

[384] Media Development Investment Fund, "Where We Work: Global organization with local expertise," accessed June 3, 2024, https://www.mdif.org/our-work/where-we-work/.

[385] Global Forum for Media Development, "About," GFMD.info, accessed February 4, 2024, https://gfmd.info/about/.

- International Media Development Advisers (IMDA)
- Pilot Media Initiatives
- Stanley Center for Peace and Security
- The Coalition for Women in Journalism
- The Dart Center for Journalism & Trauma[386]

The rabbit hole gets deeper.

The ACOS Alliance, for instance, announces itself this way:

> ACOS…is a unique global coalition of news organizations, journalist associations and press freedom NGOs working together to champion safe and responsible journalism practices. The Alliance's mission is to embed a culture of safety within journalism so that independent media and journalists globally play their essential role in upholding democracy.… [ACOS is] a growing coalition of 150+ organizations.[387]

More than two thousand journalists are members.[388] With safety for journalists touted as a key feature of its mission, ACOS isn't perhaps as political as some of the other organizations tied to Soros funding—like the Stanley Center for Peace and Security.

Among the Stanley Center's listed areas of concerns are climate change, nuclear weapons, and mass violence and atrocities.

[386] Global Forum for Media Development, "Our Members," GFMD.info, accessed February 4, 2024, https://gfmd.info/members/.

[387] ACOS Alliance, "ACOS Alliance: Region North America," Global Forum for Media Development, accessed February 4, 2024, https://gfmd.info/members/acos-alliance-2/.

[388] ACOS Alliance, "Creating a Culture of Safety for Journalism," ACOS Alliance, accessed February 4, 2024, https://www.acosalliance.org/.

Its main concern: "Our strategic approach to creating policy change is the product of continuous, careful thought. At the core of all our work is an unending commitment to global cooperation and collective action."[389] Collective action? Its stated mission: "[We] catalyze just and sustainable solutions to critical issues of peace and security by driving policy progress, advancing effective global governance and advocating for collective action."

Collectivism. Global governance. Does it get more Marxist than that?

Everywhere you look, media has been infiltrated by the far left. And it shows no signs of slowing.

"Soros-backed investor completes 40% purchase of leading Polish media house," the media outlet Notes from Poland reported in early 2022.[390] The story opened this way: "An investment group backed by George Soros has finalized its purchase of a stake in a leading Polish publisher. It is the third recent media deal in Poland involving the Media Development Investment Fund (MDIF), which is supported by the Hungarian-American billionaire."[391]

And this, on the MDIF's own webpage, in early 2024: "Pluralis raises 50 million euros [$54 million] to invest in independent media in Europe."[392] Interestingly, Pluralis is a multi-mil-

[389] Stanley Center for Peace and Security, "Our Approach," Stanley Center, accessed February 4, 2024, https://stanleycenter.org/our-approach/.
[390] Notes from Poland, "Soros-backed investor completes 40% purchase of leading Polish media house," January 10, 2022, https://notesfrompoland.com/2022/01/10/soros-backed-investor-completes-40-purchase-of-leading-polish-media-house/.
[391] Ibid.
[392] Media Development Investment Fund, "Pluralis raises 50 million euros to invest in independent media in Europe," Pluralis, February 1, 2024, https://www.mdif.org/news/pluralis-raises-e50m-to-invest-in-independent-media-in-europe/.

lion-euro investor in Petit Press, Slovakia's second largest media group—listed above as a recipient of MDIF funds. It's one onion layer after another; one silent partner, secret partner, unknown partner, not-so-openly-talked-about partner after another.

News is supposed to expose the money, the corruption, the malfeasance—the Marxist. It shouldn't be this shadowy. It shouldn't be this hefty a push of propaganda. News shouldn't elevate and shield the Walter Durantys of the world, while tossing the Gareth Joneses and his type to the wolves.

And all this—all these Soros links, MDIF names, nonprofit listings, company connections, Open Society Foundation funds—all of that, well, it's all just one glimpse, one glance, one rabbit chase down one or two holes. Thousands more await.

"George Soros Hands Control to His 37-Year-Old Son: 'I'm More Political'"—said Alex Soros, in a mid-2023 interview with the *Wall Street Journal* about his future plans for his family's $25-billion philanthropic endeavors.[393] Well, there's a hint of what's to come. In order to sell those far-left politics and policies to the people, young Soros will need the media. Make way for more propaganda, more propaganda, more propaganda.

If you can't trust the ones whose jobs are supposed to be all about revealing and exposing truths, then it's obvious: that's all the more reason to turn to God. Our nation—our liberties—cannot be trusted to the Marxists masquerading as unbiased journalists.

---

[393] Gregory Zuckerman, "George Soros Hands Control to His 37-Year-Old Son: 'I'm More Political,'" *Wall Street Journal*, June 11, 2023, https://www.wsj.com/articles/george-soros-heir-son-alexander-soros-e3c4ca13.

CHAPTER 10

GOD-GIVEN OR BUST:
THE CLOCK IS TICKING, AMERICA

Listen up, churches: never, ever again close.

When Covid-19 came and government went amok and Democrats, drunk on power, began ordering businesses to close, children to stay home from school, Americans to stay off the streets, stay out of parks, stay off the beaches, and stick around the house, windows up, waiting for the stimulus check—all that was the clanging gong of disaster striking the Constitution. But when government ordered the churches to close, and the churches did—the churches actually closed!— that was the hushed moment the world saw that America was no longer a Christian nation. And yes, the moment was so painfully significant as to warrant a hush.

For a country like America—forged on a quest for religious freedom and built on a core principle of individual rights and liberties coming from God, with government only put in place to protect what's inherently granted to the individual at birth by God—the fact that churches closed on government order sent a clear message about who's really in charge. It said powerfully and severely, the days of God-given are nearing an end, and in its place is coming the era of government-granted.

Is this what we want?

It's what we're getting.

We're losing our love for liberty because we're losing our love for God. The two are inextricably tied.

In February 2024, Arizona Christian University's Cultural Research Center (CRC) released the findings of a survey showing children in America between the ages of eight and twelve years old were displaying "massive resistance to traditional biblical teachings," largely because their parents had failed to take them to church and teach them in the Bible-based and godly way to go.[394] Basically, Dr. George Barna, director of research for the CRC, found that fewer preteens saw the Bible as pertinent in today's times, fewer turned to the Bible as a life guide, fewer regarded the Bible as the word of God, fewer even believed in the concept of absolute moral truth, and fewer acknowledged Jesus Christ as the one and only way of salvation.

The weakening faith has ramifications for all of society.

By the numbers, the CRC survey revealed the following about preteens, ages eight to twelve:

---

[394] Tracy Munsil, "CRC Research Shows US Preteens on Track To Abandon Biblical Christianity in Record Numbers," Arizona Christian University, February 7, 2024, https://www.arizonachristian.edu/2024/02/07/us-preteens-on-track-to-abandon-biblical-christianity-in-record-numbers/.

- Only 60 percent have even read part of the Bible, and only half regard it as instructional in leading a "good life." Moreover, only 26 percent even turn to the Bible as a means of determining right from wrong. Only 21 percent see the Bible as the best teacher of rights versus wrongs.[395]
- Fully 97 percent believe there is a definite line separating right from wrong, yet only 21 percent recognize the existence of an absolute when it comes to moral truths.[396]
- Only 36 percent believe that eternal salvation rests with the cross—that the only way to heaven is by confessing sins and asking Jesus to save us from the consequences of sins.[397]
- While 90 percent believe their lives have purpose, only 27 percent identified their top purpose as loving and serving God with "all their heart, soul, mind, and strength." Rather, most named "making the world a better place" or "facilitating their own happiness" as their number one mission in life.[398]
- When it comes to success and the definition of success, only 17 percent named "consistent obedience to God" as the biggest determinant.[399]

---

[395] Tracy Munsil, "CRC Research Shows US Preteens on Track To Abandon Biblical Christianity in Record Numbers," Arizona Christian University, February 7, 2024, https://www.arizonachristian.edu/2024/02/07/us-preteens-on-track-to-abandon-biblical-christianity-in-record-numbers/.
[396] Ibid.
[397] Ibid.
[398] Ibid.
[399] Ibid.

Turning from the Bible as the basis for all opens the door for other factors, other influences, and other influencers to fill the void and take the lead. If children aren't turning to the Bible to forge their characters—something else forges their characters. If preteens aren't taking their moral instruction from biblical truths—something else teaches them morals. If the emerging generation of America's leaders aren't finding purpose and direction in their lives based on never-changing truths that carry unavoidable consequences for the afterlife—something else leads their walk in this life, and their steps become much more dogged in pursuit of material wins, selfish ambitions, power, and control.

So goes the youth—so goes the nation.

"Because of the strong correlation between biblical worldview and genuine Christian discipleship," Barna said, "we are on the precipice of Christian invisibility in this nation unless we get serious about this crisis and invest heavily in fixing what's broken."[400]

Don't expect the public schools to help.

The public schools, from kindergarten through twelfth grade, are busily teaching the coming generations in the way of Marxism. America's colleges and places of higher learning only solidify the rot; they have become little more than breeding grounds for atheistic, leftist propaganda parrots. The roots of the Ivy League—Harvard, Yale, Princeton, Columbia, Dartmouth, Cornell, Brown, the University of Pennsylvania—once steeped in Christianity, have been plucked and destroyed. Diversity,

---

[400] Tracy Munsil, "CRC Research Shows US Preteens on Track To Abandon Biblical Christianity in Record Numbers," Arizona Christian University, February 7, 2024, https://www.arizonachristian.edu/2024/02/07/us-preteens-on-track-to-abandon-biblical-christianity-in-record-numbers/.

equity, inclusion, wokeism, social justice—these are now the guiding principles of these once-great centers of enlightened, godly instruction.

The Christian History Institute wrote of the switch to secularism in these colleges that became complete in the 1960: "In faith's absence the Ivies struggled to find new foundational principles; most struck on some general concept of social good of which inclusion and diversity were a part. Today Yale aims for 'improving the world' through 'free exchange of ideas in an ethical, interdependent, and diverse community.' Cornell hopes to 'enhance...lives and livelihoods;' Brown prepares students 'to discharge the offices of life with usefulness and reputation.'"[401]

The preteens of Barna's study will fit in well with these places of higher learning. That's not a good thing.

The left-leaning intellectual class has sold its soul for self-serving and pride-filled ideology, claiming to have advanced beyond the need of God (such fairytales and nonsense, they say) because of the soundness and provable traits of science—so they think. "Claiming to be wise," as Romans 1:22 (ESV) teaches, "they became fools." The conservative intellectual, however, often gets it correct. From Sir Roger Scruton, a writer and philosopher who published more than fifty books before his death in 2020—an explanation of why intellectuals believe in Marxism:

> For Marx, the interests that are advanced by an ideology are those of a ruling class. We might similarly suggest that the interests advanced by

---

[401] Benjamin P. Leavitt, "Fruits of the ivy vine," Christian History Institute, Originally published in Christian History, Issue #139, 2021, https://christianhistoryinstitute.org/magazine/article/139-fruits-of-the-ivy-vine.

totalitarian ideology are those of an aspiring elite. And we might confront totalitarian ideology in Marxian spirit, by explaining it in terms of its social function, and thereby exploding its epistemological claims. It is not the truth of Marxism that explains the willingness of intellectuals to believe it, but the power it confers on intellectuals, in their attempts to control the world. And since, as [author and satirist Jonathan] Swift says [in 'A Letter to a Young Gentleman,' 1721],[402] it is futile to reason someone out of a thing that he was not reasoned into, we can conclude that Marxism owes its remarkable power to survive every criticism to the fact that it is not a truth-directed but a power-directed system of thought.[403]

All the divergences of the social and economic philosophy called Marxism are similarly "power-directed," rather than "truth-directed." Socialism, communism, progressivism, and today's Democrat Party all take the approach that government exists to control the people—to control the resources, to distribute and redistribute the resources, and to determine the fair and equitable flow of resources, all of which combine to control people. Who cares about minute differences in definitions when

---

[402] QuoteResearch, "You Cannot Reason People Out of Something They Were Not Reasoned Into," Quote Investigator, July 10, 2015, https://quoteinvestigator.com/2015/07/10/reason-out/.

[403] Rev. Ben Johnson, "10 quotes: Sir Roger Scruton," Acton Institute, January 13, 2020, https://rlo.acton.org/archives/114136-10-quotes-sir-roger-scruton.html.

the end game is the same? Conservativism, on the other hand, honors the rights of the individual, the very least of which are rooted in the recognition of God-given free will to all. It puts forth that government exists to protect the sovereignty of the nation, preserve the order of society, and administer law and order based on a model of blind justice—not so much to establish a political structure of collectivism but rather to maintain the concept of individualism, and not so much for the good of the state but more so for the good of the individual.

It's a fine line to keep conservativism from dabbling into the arenas of liberalism and progressivism because inevitably the question arises: At what point does one's individual freedom—individual desire and will—infringe upon another's? We saw this line obliterated during the Covid-19 years, when the justification for government's imposition of will on all became one of safety and health. Face masks became a must in order to protect the innocent, staying off the streets became a must as a means of saving the sickly, Covid-19 shots became a must as a way of keeping others from catching the virus, and staying out of church—not singing in church, as California governor Gavin Newsom pushed—became a must as a patriotic duty to save others from death. The lines between individualism and collectivism blurred; the boundaries separating an individual's right to choose and the state's interests to supposedly save and protect the people collided. America devolved into tyranny. Americans wondered why and what happened. The reason is simple.

God was pushed to the side.

So, it naturally follows that God-given rights and God-given liberties weren't given their proper due.

The only way to maintain the proper balance between the rights of opposing personalities is through God. In other words, when the rights of one individual butt up against the rights of another individual, and the two infringe upon each other, then it's law and order derived from moral and virtuous principles that ought to guide—not the person with the loudest voice or the person who's gained the most favor from those in power. The default position in a society governed by a Constitution is not to cede more control and decision-making power to the government, but rather to rely on established law and established order, both of which should be based on moral truths and absolutes. And those only come from God.

Remove God, remove moral absolutes. Remove God, remove truths. Remove God, let in Big Government, with all its wickedness and lusts and quests to control.

The entire war for America's freedom and America's future focuses on Americans' ability to regain and retain God-given individualism. And we don't have much time left to do it. It's now or never. The playbook is this: teach the coming generations to love God, and in so doing, they'll love liberty—and in so doing, they'll see the threats to liberty and be able to fight accordingly and effectively.

Those who understand who they are in God's eyes are those who cannot be pushed around by government, cannot be deceived by government, and cannot be easily moved by evil. Those raised to believe they are created in the image of God, endowed with gifts and talents of God, fashioned by God for special purposes in life, and set on Earth to worship and glorify God—in part, by using those gifts and talents to the highest level and to accomplish the greatest good—will grow to adulthood empowered with a calling from the heavens, not from the secular world. Those individuals will seek to accomplish what is in line with God's will by taking their

direction from the Bible and from godly guides and not looking solely to their neighbors, colleagues, teachers, and leaders
for direction. Those with a foundation of godly values will also
seek to utilize their spiritual gifts—the powers of discernment,
wisdom, knowledge, helping, administration, and the like—in
daily living and realize that with God in charge, little is left for
government to accomplish. Charity, for instance, in a godly
society, doesn't come from government but from churches
and individuals who follow the teachings of Jesus. That keeps
government in check; that keeps government from becoming
the go-to for what ails; that keeps government beholden to the
people, accountable to the people, and ultimately, restrained
in powers by the Constitution. Feed my sheep, said Jesus to
Peter in the Gospel of John. But if nobody's feeding the sheep,
where will the sheep go?

To the government, for handouts.

But in order to get the food, the government will take
from all.

Godly Americans do voluntarily what Jesus commands out
of their love for Jesus, but with the ensuing effect of keeping
the government irrelevant in areas where it shouldn't tread and
therefore limited in its powers.

Discernment: the ability to judge beyond the flesh and see
the spiritual truth—that's a key gift from God that comes in
large part from reading the Bible. It's also a key missing ingredient from today's society, where Americans are regularly led down
paths of evil, all the while thinking they're walking in good.

Transgenderism has been sold as love of children—masking
the horrors of medical mutilation and the mental anguish of
living a life of lies, masking the destruction of God's creations.

Abortion has been sold as love of women—masking the murder of the unborn and the destruction of God's creations.

Government handouts have been sold as love of the less fortunate—masking the depression of individual achievement and dependency on taxpayers for sustenance and the tearing down of dreams, hopes, aspirations, and ultimately, the destruction of God's creations.

Collectivism has been sold as love of humanity—masking its soul-sucking, soul-killing, secular-promoting and ugly, sinister ways, masking the destruction of God's creations.

The failure to discern good from evil and the refusal to then call out evil, even when it is discerned, are the two most dangerous forces affecting even self-professed Christians in America these days. Doors are being opened for Satan to enter with alarming frequency, and figuratively speaking, this silence of the lambs is a fast-track path toward slaughter of the lambs. Here's a personal example of how wickedness grows—of Marxism on the march—all under the guise of doing good.

In 2022, amid a Covid-19 fear that still gripped this nation, hotels slowly started opening doors back to guests, but with so-called precautions in place to supposedly "protect" guests. Among those precautions were requirements to social distance and face-mask—even as everyone knew by then of the unscientific nonsense of maintaining a six-foot buffer among humans and of the inability of a mask to protect against the spread of Covid-19. The forced face-masking that took place around the nation was especially egregious because common sense would tell us that pulling a face mask out of a glove box or from within a grubby coat pocket and slapping it on our face to walk into an establishment, but then lowering the face mask to eat or drink, and wearing the mask with gaps around the sides or beneath the nose, or using crochet masks—as they did in Hollywood and elsewhere—were unscientific, unsound, worthless actions insofar as protecting the health of self and others; they were more shows of compliance and obedience and fear. Truly, they were more shows of how much bullying the bureaucratic class could inflict on the free American citizens than anything else. They were indicators of the wearers' willingness to go along to get along, play into the lies and deceptions, and cast aside individualism and individual choice for the collective.

Face masks are for surgeons in sterile operating rooms. They're not for four-year-olds flying in airplanes with their parents. They're not for high school students running track in the open air. They're not for men and women of sound mind and body to wear under the conditions of entering a Walgreens or Walmart to buy shampoo and soap, stifling groans as they yank them out of purses and pockets to comply with signs that stick on store windows: "Face masks required: It's the law." No, face masks were not the law. They were dictates made by dictatorial dictators, who were fearful, ignorant, or readily compliant and who wanted you to behave in the same manner. The forced face-masking was almost as stupid as the plastic shields installed along countertops in grocery stores, dentist offices, pharmacies, and retail shops—the ones that rose about four feet in height and served no purpose except to make it impossible to pass bags of items from worker to customer unless they were shoved with difficulty through the small window cut in the bottom of the plastic, hoisted above, or passed awkwardly to the side of the plastic, which is coincidentally the very same route the virus could still travel.

But the face masks were signs of government domination.

The forced face-masking was an expression of citizen obedience.

In that regard, combined with the lie of their medical powers, they were the embodiment of evil.

So, in 2022, while walking into a five-star hotel in a very exclusive area of California and into the nearly empty foyer to check in at the entirely empty guest reception desk, a young man in what appeared to be his twenties skipped up to me to ask if I needed a face mask. I said no, and he pointed to the woman behind the desk and said she would be happy to give me one. I nodded and finished checking in and retrieving my key. I started to walk across the empty foyer toward the elevator when this same young man rushed from across the room to my side and said I needed to put on my face mask. I told him thanks and started to walk away, and he skirted closer and, with a more insistent tone, repeated his remark. I stopped and looked at him, and he pointed again to the woman behind the desk and said she would be happy to give me one. Instead of waiting for my reply, he walked over to her, reached around the counter, came back with a face mask, handed it to me, and recited hotel rules about face mask requirements and so on and so forth, all the while smiling broadly and nodding happily after I thanked him. As if he were helping me. As if he were being helpful.

This is a scene that repeated itself throughout America for years at hotels, restaurants, parks, libraries, college campuses, stores, groceries, bus stops—anywhere and everywhere there were people.

This was evil, playing in real time.

Whether or not the young man believed in the power of the face mask to prevent the spread of the virus is irrelevant. So, too, is whether or not the hotel owners and administrators thought they were doing the right thing and abiding local government orders by posting alerts on their website advising of the requirement to wear face masks in the lobby and public areas. We are not at war against young men working in hotels, hotel owners, or administrators.

"For we do not wrestle against flesh and blood, but against principalities, against powers, against the rulers of the darkness of this age, against spiritual *hosts* of wickedness in the heavenly *places*," Ephesians 6:12 (NKJV) tells us.

We are at war against a spirit of evil.

And regardless of whether that young man knew he was advancing a lie—an evil lie—or not does not change the fact that he was advancing an evil lie. It just means that for him, he may have not been committing a sin by advancing it.

"Therefore, to him who knows to do good and does not do it, to him it is sin," James 4:17 (NKJV) states.

There is a distinction made between sinning and doing evil. While all sin is evil, not all doers of sin are necessarily evil—that is to say, purposely doing evil. If that young man truly believed he was doing the right thing by running across an empty foyer and invading guests' personal—and socially distanced—space to order them to wear face masks, then the fact is he wasn't evil himself. But he was advancing evil.

Either wittingly or unwittingly, he was advancing a spirit of evil that had spread around the nation on wings of fear, on wings of ignorance, on wings of pride, on wings on quests for control. That so many Americans played along with this evil out of concern for creating a stir, or out of concern for making others feel uncomfortable, or out of concern of being ridiculed or mocked or derided or publicly shamed—that only underscores the need for God.

God doesn't govern by fear.

Your motives can be pure—that is, they can be pure in your own heart and mind—but still do the work of the evil one.

It's crucial, then, for those who value individual freedom to understand how God works, versus how Satan works, in order to choose wisely.

"But the fruit of the Spirit is love, joy, peace, patience, kindness, goodness, faithfulness, gentleness, self-control; against such things there is no law," Galatians 5:22–23 (ESV) tells us.

Stay in the spirit, and you don't have to worry about doing right versus wrong—you're covered.

We as a nation have become entirely too tolerant of people's motives and what we guess to be other people's motives—and in so doing, we've accommodated too much evil. Truthfully, that young man in the hotel demanding the wearing of face masks most likely knew he was acting out of a quest for control and power and not out of genuine love for his fellow man and woman and a genuine desire to protect them from sickness. How so? Well, had he honestly believed in the danger of the virus and the protective qualities of the face mask, he wouldn't have skirted up so closely to someone—myself—who wasn't wearing a face mask. He wouldn't have put himself in such Covid danger. Right?

If he had truly feared catching Covid or having it spread to others, he would not have rushed so closely to the side of someone who was so obviously, in his mind, such a high health risk. He would have shouted it from across the room to put on a face mask.

Discernment. The ability to judge motives and actions through a biblical worldview. The power to see past the façade and gauge truths that may not be so obvious and evident. The capacity to peer beyond the physical and see the spiritual elements at play—the good versus evil, the godly versus satanic. Discernment is one of the most important gifts, skills, and traits needed for today's times, because evil has been flipped for good, and all around are smiles masquerading as virtues and godly values.

All around are evil influences and forces pretending to be otherwise—and too many people are being fooled. If we can't see the evil, we can't fight the evil. If we can't see the evil, we can't flee the evil. If we can't see the evil, we very often participate in and spread the evil.

Under Covid, the lies, arrogance, and quests for control that were the face masks spread like a fast-moving cancer across the United States. Only God gives discernment. And as followers of Christ, we are encouraged and commanded to seek it. The world tells us not to judge; the world cries that judging is intolerant, hateful, discriminatory, and wrong. The Bible tells us to judge smartly, of the things of the spirit.

- 1 John 4:1: "Beloved, do not believe every spirit, but test the spirits to see whether they are from God, for many false prophets have gone out into the world."
- Romans 12:2: "Do not be conformed to this world, but be transformed by the renewal of your mind, that by testing you may discern what is the will of God, what is good and acceptable and perfect."
- 1 Kings 3:9: "Give your servant therefore an understanding mind to govern your people, that I may discern between good and evil, for who is able to govern this your great people?"
- 1 Corinthians 2:14: "The natural person does not accept the things of the Spirit of God, for they are folly

to him, and he is not able to understand them because they are spiritually discerned."

- Hebrews 5:14: "But solid food is for the mature, for those who have their powers of discernment trained by constant practice to distinguish good from evil."
- John 7:24: "Do not judge by appearances, but judge with right judgment." (ESV)

Judging the spirit that compels the human behavior is not wrong. Judging that someone is going to hell, however, is God's domain.

We have to judge, we have to be discerning, we have to be discriminating in choosing right from wrong—or else we face the wolves without a key tool of battle. How to have a godly nation if the people of the nation are either unable or unwilling to determine what's godly?

But it's not enough to just determine the spirit that's driving the action. Once discerned, we need to speak about it—with wisdom, of course. Truth left unstated is really an enabler of evil.

In July 2015, *TIME* wrote in a headline, "Hundreds Gather for Unveiling of Satanic Statue in Detroit."[404] In August 2018, the Associated Press wrote, "The Satanic Temple unveiled its statue...of a goat-headed, winged creature called Baphomet during a First Amendment rally at the Arkansas State Capitol to protest a Ten Commandments monument already on the

---

[404] Nash Jenkins, "Hundreds Gather for Unveiling of Satanic Statue in Detroit," *Time*, July 27, 2015, https://time.com/3972713/detroit-satanic-statue-baphomet/.

Capitol grounds."[405] In December 2018, NBC News wrote, "This holiday season, the Illinois State Capitol is celebrating both Santa and Satan. A statue designed and funded by the Satanic Temple of Chicago is on display in the statehouse in Springfield along with a Christmas tree, Nativity scene, and a menorah."[406] In December 2023, Fox News wrote, "A satanic altar has been set up at the Iowa State Capitol. The Satanic Temple erected the public display, depicting a ram's head with mirrors covering it, propped by a mannequin in red clothing.... Cofounder of The Satanic Temple, Lucien Greaves, [said] the display represents the group's right to religious freedom."[407]

Only it's not.

The Satanic Temple is not a religion. It's a group. In 2019, the IRS granted the group a 501(c)(3) tax exemption—in essence, recognizing it as a church. But that's a lie of the IRS, a lie of the Satanic Temple, a lie of the culture that has grown increasingly secular. By the Satanic Temple's own description, it's not a religion and therefore not a church. In the question-answer section on its website, the group answers the question, "Do you worship Satan?" this way:

No, nor do we believe in the existence of Satan or the supernatural. The Satanic Temple believes

[405] Hannah Grabenstein, "Satanic Temple unveils Baphomet statue at Arkansas Capitol," Associated Press, August 16, 2018, https://apnews.com/article/1dfef6715487416eadfd08f36c7dbb4b.

[406] Elisha Fieldstadt, "Satanic statue erected in Illinois State Capitol with other holiday decorations," NBC News, December 6, 2018, https://www.nbcnews.com/news/us-news/satanic-statue-erected-illinois-state-capitol-other-holiday-decorations-n944706.

[407] Adam Sabes, "The Satanic Temple sets up public display inside Iowa Capitol building: 'Very dark, evil force,'" Fox News, December 9, 2023, https://www.foxnews.com/us/satanic-temple-public-display-inside-iowa-capitol-building-very-dark-evil-force.

that religion can, and should, be divorced from superstition. As such, we do not promote a belief in a personal Satan. To embrace the name Satan is to embrace rational inquiry removed from supernaturalism and archaic tradition-based superstitions. Satanists should actively work to hone critical thinking and exercise reasonable agnosticism in all things. Our beliefs must be malleable to the best current scientific understandings of the material world—never the reverse.[408]

The Satanic Temple members neither worship a deity, nor believe in the existence of a deity.

Under the question, "Do you adhere to the satanic bible or have any books that you recommend?" the Satanic Temple answers this way: "The Satanic Temple does not have any sacred book or scripture and we do not adhere to The Satanic Bible. We do have a suggested reading list that provides some illumination on the philosophical origins of our beliefs."[409]

The Satanic Temple members do not read, learn, or worship from any particular book.

Under the question, "What are some of the rituals of TST?" the Satanic Temple answers this way: "The Satanic Temple does not have any required rituals, but some members choose to participate in rituals that they find personally meaningful. There is no absolute 'right' way to perform any of them. Typically, they are composed by members themselves, adhere to the TST tenets, and are tailored to meet their individual or local needs."

---

[408] The Satanic Temple, "Frequently Asked Questions," The Satanic Temple, accessed February 17, 2024, https://thesatanictemple.com/pages/faq.
[409] Ibid.

Among some of the rituals members have held: "Black mass," a "celebration of blasphemy," and "unbaptism," to "renounce superstitions that may have been imposed upon them…as a child."[410]

The Satanic Temple members do not have any established protocols, practices, routines, or formalities as part of their worship services.

Under the question, "If you do not believe in the supernatural, how is TST a religion?" the Satanic Temple answers this way: "The idea that religion belongs to supernaturalists is ignorant, backward, and offensive. The metaphorical Satanic construct is no more arbitrary to us than are the deeply held beliefs that we actively advocate. Are we supposed to believe that those who pledge submission to an ethereal supernatural deity hold to their values more deeply that we?… Satanism provides all that a religion should be without a compulsory attachment to untenable items of faith-based belief."[411]

What a joke.

So Satanic Temple members do not believe in a deity, do not have a Bible or its equivalent, do not have any particular manner of holding services, and moreover, outright mock the idea of a "faith-based belief"—meaning they have no faith in anything that's not of the tangible world—and yet they're a religion; they're a church; they're a recognized IRS religious organization. And Christians can't stop the spread of this rot in America?

This is an evil that's unstoppable?

Fact is, the Satanic Temple never should have been recognized as a church according to IRS standards. The criteria the

---

[410] Ibid.

[411] The Satanic Temple, "Frequently Asked Questions," The Satanic Temple, accessed February 17, 2024, https://thesatanictemple.com/pages/faq.

IRS uses to determine whether an organization is a bona fide church versus a group simply seeking to skirt taxes is generic enough that cause could easily have been found to reject the Satanic Temple's application for 501(c)(3) status[412]—had there only been will, had there been a will to fight. That there wasn't any only underscores how far America has strayed from God.

It is not God's will for His people to stay silent in the face of evil.

Elijah, prophet of the Lord, speaking in 1 Kings 18 to the 450 false prophets who worshipped Baal, and to a crowd gathered from Israel at Mount Carmel under the order of the wicked Ahab, said, "If the Lord is God, follow him; but if Ba'al, then follow him" (1 Kings 18:21, RSV). In other words: choose. Then Elijah lay down this challenge:

> "I, even I only, am left a prophet of the Lord; but Ba'al's prophets are four hundred and fifty men. Let two bulls be given to us; and let them choose one bull for themselves, and cut it in pieces and lay it on the wood, but put no fire to it; and I will prepare the other bull and lay it on the wood, and put no fire to it. And you call on the name of your god and I will call on the name of the Lord; and the God who answers by fire, he is God."
>
> (1 Kings 18:22–24, RSV)

---

[412] Richard R. Hammar, "Top Ten Tax Developments for Churches and Clergy in 2024," *Christianity Today*, January 31, 2024, https://www.churchlawandtax.com/understand-taxes/clergy/top-ten-tax-developments-for-churches-and-clergy-in-2024/.

So the prophets of Baal prepared their bull. Here's more from 1 Kings:

> And they...called on the name of Ba'al from morning until noon, saying, "O Ba'al, answer us!" But there was no voice, and no one answered. And they limped about the altar which they had made. And at noon Eli'jah mocked them, saying, "Cry aloud, for he is a god; either he is musing, or he has gone aside, or he is on a journey, or perhaps he is asleep and must be awakened." And they cried aloud, and cut themselves after their custom with swords and lances, until the blood gushed out upon them. And as midday passed, they raved on until the time of the offering of the oblation, but there was no voice; no one answered, no one heeded.
>
> (1 Kings 18:26–29, RSV)

Then Elijah built an altar of stones to God, surrounded it with a trench, cut and placed the pieces of his bull upon the altar, soaked the flesh as well as the wood for fire with water, filled the trench with water—and then called out to God.

"Then the fire of the Lord fell, and consumed the burnt offering, and the wood, and the stones, and the dust, and licked up the water that was in the trench. And when all the people saw it, they fell on their faces; and they said, 'The Lord, He is God,'" 1 Kings 38–40 states.

This is how evil is vanquished: by godly people standing strong for God.

In the 2015 *TIME* story about the unveiling of satanic statue in Detroit, the author wrote, "In a sense, the statue is a stress test of American plurality: at what point does religious freedom make the people uncomfortable?"[413] One answer should clearly be "at the point when satanic entities are given the same platform as godly entities." Elijah wouldn't have stood for this. So why is America—a nation supposedly built on a foundation of Bible commandments, biblical beliefs, and Judeo-Christian morals and virtues? We're losing our compass. Soon, it will be gone.

"The Satanic Temple is planning an 'After School Satan club' at a Memphis elementary school, marking the fifth active club in the country announced this year," WCSC Live 5 News announced in December 2023.[414] The story goes on to report:

> The Satanic Temple's mission states that it is a "non-theistic religion that views Satan as a literary figure who represents a metaphorical construct of rejecting tyranny and championing the human mind and spirit." A sign-up sheet... says that children will learn benevolence and empathy, critical thinking, problem solving, creative expression, personal sovereignty, and compassion.[415]

[413] Nash Jenkins, "Hundreds Gather for Unveiling of Satanic Statue in Detroit," *Time*, July 27, 2015, https://time.com/3972713/detroit-satanic-statue-baphomet/.

[414] Jacob Gallant, Bria Bolden, and Emily Van de Riet, "Satanic Temple plans 'After School Satan Club' at another elementary school," WCSC Live 5 News, December 13, 2023, https://www.live5news.com/2023/12/13/satanic-temple-plans-after-school-satan-club-another-elementary-school/.

[415] Ibid.

Sounds wonderful. But this is where discernment is needed. Satan, after all, was a most beautiful angel. The devil's best work is done when it's dressed in all that seems good.

Evil is coming for the children. And once the minds of the young are corrupted and trained to believe in self—which is to say, Satan—not God, and to think their own minds and hearts can best guide how they ought to live and behave, then evil wins. God becomes unnecessary. The Bible becomes just another book. Biblical truths and moral absolutes fade, then disappear. Society becomes comprised of individuals who base their decisions on feelings, passions, desires, and moral considerations that shift with the political and cultural winds.

That's when chaos comes.

Stealing anything in God's eyes is a sin. Stealing food in the eyes of a hungry person is justified. So goes the logic of immoral humanity to the point where circumstances can rationalize the breaking of all Ten Commandments—of yes, even murder. This is where America currently stands. Abortion rights activists, remember, say they feel what they feel and believe what they believe out of love—out of love for women, out of love for freedom and civil rights, out of love even for a baby to save him or her from the cruelty of an unwanted life.

The only hope for America is God.

God first, God always, God above all else.

Romans 8:31 (NKJV) states, "What then shall we say to these things? If God *is* for us, who *can be* against us?" Exactly. One individual—one individual under God—can make a massive difference.

Elijah did.

So did Noah—who built the ark and, because of obedience to God, saved humanity from total destruction. That, even though he drank too much and sinned with wine.

So did Moses—who led the Jews out of Egyptian slavery and served as God's most important prophet. That, even though he committed murder and was "slow" in speech—quite possibly, a stutterer.

So did Rahab—who helped God's spies escape so they could overtake Jericho and in so doing won favor with Joshua and God and saved her family from certain death. That, even though she was a prostitute.

So did Esther—who risked her own life while married to the king of Persia by persuading him to retract an order to kill all the Jews. That, even as she was an orphan, raised in her uncle's home.

So did Paul—who was one of the twelve disciples of Jesus, credited with spreading the word of Christ far and wide and converting untold numbers to the faith in the process. That, even as he had been a harsh defender of the Jewish religion, known for his violent persecution and imprisonment of Christians until God struck him blind on a road to Damascus, and for three days, he lived in darkness.

So can you.

God doesn't need a majority.

And the power of one with God is greater than the power of all without God.

The time to save America grows perilously short. Either we realize that and turn with speed to God and, in humility and obedience, repent—turn from our sins, both individually and as a society—and walk a new path, or we'll be crushed. China will overtake; Russia will dominate; Iran and Iraq's proxies will rise with terrorist abandon. Our Constitution will crumble. Individual liberty will be replaced by collectivism. Marxists will cheer on their communist rot. Technology will enslave, and surveillance society will stifle all freedom. Globalists will rule with top-down force. The coming generation will know only that America is racist; America is discriminatory; America is unfair, intolerant, and the cause of all that ails the world. The coming generation won't know God—only government. Their souls will weep over the blackness of human hearts, but they won't hear; they won't see. Their consciousness will no longer prick. They will be immune to all manners of evil.

That's the world according to Marxists.

Darkness and dullness, slavery and servitude, subsisting only to provide the master called "The State."

America without God equals collectivism. America plus God equals freedom. The choice is simple.

It starts with opening your Bible and seeing what He wants you to do. There's no time like the present. If not now—when? Psalm 33: 12–19 (RSV):

> Blessed is the nation whose God is the Lord, the people whom he has chosen as his heritage! The Lord looks down from heaven, he sees all the sons of men; from where he sits enthroned he looks forth on all the inhabitants of the earth, he who fashions the hearts of them all, and observes all their deeds. A king is not saved by his great army; a warrior is not delivered by his great strength. The war horse is a vain hope for victory, and by its great might it cannot save. Behold, the eye of the Lord is on those who fear

him, on those who hope in his steadfast love, that he may deliver their soul from death, and keep them alive in famine.

So God does for the individual.
So God does for a nation.
Therein lies America's only hope.

ACKNOWLEDGMENTS

A very special thank you...

      to Anthony Ziccardi, publisher of Post Hill Press, for interest and faith in publishing my book;

      to Madeline Sturgeon and the staff of Post Hill, for tremendous creativity, skill, and expertise;

      to AJ Rice, of Publius PR, for public relations and professionalism;

      to Craig Shirley, and his lovely wife, Zorine, for ongoing friendship;

      to Tom Dimitri, for cover design genius, and for other stuff;

      to Eden Gordon Hill, of Eden Gordon Media, for prayers and promotion and godly guidance;

to Chris Dolan, president and executive editor of the *Washington Times*, for career support above and beyond;

to Pastor Jack Hibbs, Cavalry Chapel Chino Hills, for fighting when others won't and for such wonderful endorsement of my work;

to Mike Pompeo, Bill O'Reilly, Troy Miller, Monica Crowley, and Shea Bradley Farrell, for your very kind and generous expressions of support;

and last, but certainly never least, to my Christian, conservative children—Savanna, Keith, Colvin, and Chloe: you hold the key to America's future in your faith.

ABOUT THE AUTHOR

Cheryl Chumley is the online opinion editor and host of the Bold & Blunt podcast at the Washington Times, a bestselling author, a public speaker, and a frequent media guest for national audiences. She is also a certified private investigator, an Army veteran, and the mother of four.